The Challenges of our time

Disarmament and Social Progress

Highlights, 27TH Congress, CPSU

The Challenges of our time

Disarmament and Social Progress

INTERNATIONAL PUBLISHERS, New York

Manufactured in the USA

Library of Congress Cataloging-in-Publication Data
The Challenges of our time.
   Translated from Russian.
   Includes the political report of the CPSU Central Committee, delivered
by Mikhail Gorbachev to the 27th Congress of the CPSU.
   1. Kommunisticheskaia partiia Sovetskogo Soiuza—
Congresses.   2. Soviet Union—Economic policy—
1981–   —Congresses. I. Gorbachev, M. S. (Mikahil
Sergeevich), 1931–   . II. Kommunisticheskaia
partiia Sovetskogo Soiuza. S"ezd (27th : 1986 :
Moscow, R.S.F.S.R.)
JN6598.K5   1986   324.247'075   86-10473
ISBN 0-7178-0642-1 (pbk.)

PUBLISHER'S NOTE

The Challenges of Our Time presents new thinking, new ideas from the 27th Congress of the Communist Party of the Soviet Union.

Observers across the political spectrum agree that the 27th was no ordinary Congress. The aims it projected for the next fifteen years are indeed breathtaking. Among them: a doubling of Soviet industrial capacity, a remolding of every aspect of its internal life, and a crusade to eliminate nuclear weapons by the year 2000.

Millions of Soviet people took part in the discussions leading up to the Congress and are currently involved in an ongoing struggle to realize its decisions. It is an undertaking of such dimensions that it can now be described as "a second revolution."

Here is something quite different from U.S. political discourse, but in no way threatening to the interests of the people of the United States. In fact, a better and updated understanding of Soviet reality can accelerate mutual steps toward disarmament and social progress in our time.

CONTENTS

COMMENTARY

The Program of the CPSU — A new edition   159

The Challenges of our time

Disarmament and Social Progress

Highlights, 27TH Congress, CPSU

1. Political Report of the CPSU Central Committee Delivered by General Secretary Mikhail Gorbachev to the 27th Congress, February 25, 1986

Comrade Delegates,
Esteemed Guests,
The 27th Congress of the CPSU has gathered at a crucial turning point in the life of the country and the contemporary world as a whole. We are beginning our work with a deep understanding of our responsibility to the Party and the Soviet people. It is our task to elaborate a broad conception, in the Leninist way, of the times we are living in, and to work out a realistic, well-thought-out program of action that would organically blend the grandeur of our aims with our real capabilities, and the Party's plans with the hopes and aspirations of every person. The resolutions of the 27th Congress will determine both the character and the rate of our movement towards a qualitatively new state of the Soviet socialist society for years and decades ahead.

The Congress is to discuss and adopt a new edition of the Program of the CPSU, amendments to the Party Rules, and Guidelines for Economic Development for the next five years and a longer term. I need hardly mention what enormous importance these documents have for our Party, our state, and our people. Not only do they contain an assessment of the past and a formulation of the urgent tasks, but also a glimpse into the future. They speak of what the Soviet Union will be like as it enters the 21st century, of the image of socialism and its positions in the international arena, of the future of humanity.

Soviet society has gone a long way in its development since the currently operative Party Program was adopted. In fact, we have built the whole country anew, have made tremendous headway in the economic, cultural, and social fields, and have raised generations of builders of the new society. We have blazed the trail into outer space for humanity. We have secured military strategic parity and have thereby substantially restricted imperialism's aggressive plans and capabilities to start a nuclear war. The positions of our Motherland and of world socialism in the international arena have grown considerably stronger.

The path travelled by the country, its economic, social and cultural achievements convincingly confirm the vitality of the Marxist-Leninist doctrine, and socialism's tremendous potential as embodied in the progress of Soviet society. We can be justly proud of everything that has been achieved in these years of intensive work and struggle.

While duly appraising our achievements, the leadership of the CPSU considers it its duty to tell the Party and the people honestly and frankly about the shortcomings in our political and practical activities, the unfavourable tendencies in the economy and the social and moral sphere, and about the reasons for them. For a number of years the deeds and actions of Party and Government bodies lagged behind the needs of the times and of life—not only because of objective factors, but also for reasons above all of a subjective nature. The problems in the country's development grew more rapidly than they were being solved. The inertness and rigidity of the forms and methods of management, the decline of dynamism in our work, and increased bureaucracy—all this was doing no small damage. Signs of stagnation had begun to surface in the life of society.

The situation called for change, but a peculiar psychology—how to improve things without changing anything—took the upper hand in the central bodies and, for that matter, at local level as well. But that cannot be done, comrades. Stop for an instant, as they say, and you fall behind a mile. We must not evade the problems that have arisen. That sort of attitude is much too costly for the country, the state and the Party. So let us say it loud and clear!

The top-priority task is to overcome the negative factors in society's socio-economic development as rapidly as possible, to accelerate it and impart to it an essential dynamism, to learn from the lessons of the past to a maximum extent, so that the decisions we adopt for the future should be absolutely clear and responsible, and the concrete actions purposeful and effective.

The situation has reached a turning point not only in internal but also in **external** affairs. The changes in current world developments are so deep-going and significant that they require a reassessment and a comprehensive analysis of all factors. The situation created by the nuclear confrontation calls for new approaches, methods, and forms of relations between the different social systems, states and regions.

Owing to the arms race started by imperialism, the 20th century, in the field of world politics, is coming to an end burdened with the question: will humanity be able to avert the nuclear danger, or will the policy of confrontation take the upper hand, thus increasing the probability of nuclear conflict. The capitalist world has not abandoned the ideology and policy of hegemonism, its rulers have not yet lost the hope of taking social revenge, and continue to indulge themselves with illusions of superior strength. A sober view of what is going on is hewing its way forward with great difficulty through a dense thicket of prejudices and preconceptions in the thinking of the ruling class. But the complexity and acuteness of this moment in history makes it increasingly vital to outlaw nuclear weapons, destroy them and other weapons of mass annihilation completely, and improve international relations.

The fact that the Party has deeply understood the fundamentally new situation inside the country and in the world arena, and that it appreciates its responsibility for the country's future, and has the will and resolve to carry out the requisite change, is borne out by the adoption at the April 1985 Plenary Meeting of the **decision to accelerate the socio-economic development of our society**.

Formulating the long-term and fundamental tasks, the Central Committee has been consistently guided by Marxism-Leninism, the truly scientific theory of social development. It expresses the vital interests of the working people, and the ideals of social justice. It derives its vitality from its everlasting youthfulness, its constant capacity for development and creative generalisation of the new facts and phenomena, and from its experience of revolutionary struggle and social reconstruction.

Any attempt to turn the theory by which we are guided into an assortment of rigid schemes and formulas which would be valid everywhere and in all contingencies is most definitely contrary to the essence and spirit of Marxism-Leninism. Lenin wrote back in 1917 that Marx and Engels rightly ridiculed the ''mere memorising and repetition of 'formulas,' that at best are capable only of marking out **general** tasks, which are necessarily modifiable by the **concrete** economic and political conditions of each particular **period** of the historical process.'' Those are the words, comrades, that everyone of us must ponder and act upon.

The **concrete** economic and political situation we are in, and the particular **period** of the historical process that Soviet society and the whole world are going through, require that the Party and its every member display their creativity, their capacity for innovation and ability to transcend the limits of accustomed but already outdated notions.

A large-scale, frank and constructive examination of all the crucial problems of our life and of Party policy has taken place during the discussion of the pre-Congress documents. We have come to the Congress enriched by the wisdom and experience of the whole Party, the whole people. We can now see more clearly what has to be done and in what order, and what levers we must set in motion so that our progress will be accelerated at a desired pace.

These days, many things, in fact everything, will depend on how effectively we will succeed in using the advantages and possibilities of the socialist system, its economic power and social potential, in updating the obsolescent social patterns and style and methods of work, in bringing them abreast of the changed conditions. That is the only way for us to increase the might of our country, to raise the material and spiritual life of the Soviet people to a qualitatively new level, and to enhance the positive influence of the example of socialism as a social system on world development.

We look to the future confidently, because we are clearly aware of our tasks and of the ways in which they should be carried out. We look to the future confidently, because we rely on the powerful support of the people. We look to the future confidently, because we are acting in the interests of the socialist Homeland, in the name of the great ideals to which the Communist Party has dedicated itself wholeheartedly.

I.
THE CONTEMPORARY WORLD:
ITS MAIN TENDENCIES
AND CONTRADICTIONS

Comrades, the draft new edition of the Program of the Party [pp. 00–00] contains a thorough analysis of the main trends and features of the development of the world today. It is not the purpose of the Program to anticipate the future with all its multiformity and concrete developments. That would be a futile exercise. But here is another, no less important point: if we want to follow a correct, science-based policy, we must clearly understand the key tendencies of the current reality. To penetrate deep into the dialectic of the events, into their objective logic, to draw the right conclusions that reflect the motion of the times, is no simple matter, but it is imperatively necessary.

In the days before the October Revolution, referring to the capitalist economy alone, Lenin noted that the sum-total of the changes in all their ramifications could not have been grasped even by seventy Marxes. But, Lenin continued, Marxism has discovered "the laws . . . and the objective logic of these changes and of their historical development . . . in its chief and basic features."

The modern world is complicated, diverse and dynamic, and shot through with contending tendencies and contradictions. It is a world of the most difficult alternatives, anxieties and hopes. Never before has our home on earth been exposed to such great political and physical stresses. Never before has man exacted so much tribute from nature, and never has he been so vulnerable to the forces he himself has created.

World developments confirm the fundamental Marxist-Leninist conclusion that the history of society is not a sum of fortuitous elements, that it is not a disorderly "Brownian motion," but a law-governed onward process. Not only are its contradictions a verdict on the old world, on everything that impedes the advance; they are also a source and motive force for social progress. This is progress which takes place in conditions of a struggle that is inevitable so long as exploitation and exploiting classes exist.

The liberation revolutions triggered by the Great October Revolution are determining the image of the 20th century. However considerable the achievements of science and technology, and however great the influence which rapid scientific and technological progress has on the life of society, nothing but the social and spiritual emancipation of man can make him truly free. And no matter what difficulties, objective and artificial, the old world may create, the course of history is irreversible.

The social changes of the century are altering the conditions for the further development of society. New economic, political, scientific, technical, internal and international factors are beginning to operate. The interconnection between states and between peoples is increasing. And all this is setting new, especially exacting demands upon every state, whether it is a matter of foreign policy, economic and social activity, or the spiritual image of society.

The progress of our time is rightly identified with socialism. **World socialism** is a powerful international entity with a highly developed economy, substantial scientific resources, and a reliable military and political potential. It accounts for more than one-third of the world's population; it includes dozens of countries and peoples advancing along a path that reveals in every way the intellectual and moral wealth of man and society. A new way of life has taken shape, based on the principles of socialist justice, in which there are neither oppressors nor the oppressed, neither exploiters nor the exploited, in which power belongs to the people. Its distinctive features are collectivism and comradely mutual assistance, triumph of the ideas of freedom, unbreakable unity between the rights and duties of every member of society, the dignity of the individual, and true humanism. Socialism is a realistic option open to all humanity, an example projected into the future.

Socialism sprang up and was built in countries which were far from being economically and socially advanced at that time and which differed greatly from one another in mode of life and their historical and national traditions. Each one of them advanced to the new social system along its own way, confirming Marx's prediction about the "infinite variations and gradations" of the same economic basis in its concrete manifestations.

The way was neither smooth nor simple. It was exceedingly difficult to rehabilitate a backward or ruined economy, to teach millions of people to read and write, to provide them with a roof over their heads, with food and free medical aid. The very novelty of the social tasks, the ceaseless military, economic, political, and psychological pressure of imperialism, the need for tremendous efforts to ensure defence—all this could not but influence the course of events, their character, and the rate at which the socio-economic programes and transformations were carried into effect. Nor were mistakes in politics and various subjectivist deviations avoided.

But such is life; it always manifests itself in diverse contradictions, sometimes quite unexpected ones. The other point is much more important: socialism has demonstrated its ability to resolve social problems on a fundamentally different basis than previously, namely a collectivist one; it has brought the countries to higher levels of development, and has given the working people a dignified and secure life.

Socialism is continuously improving social relations, multiplying its achievements purposefully, setting an example which is becoming more and more influential and attractive, and demonstrating the real humanism of the socialist way of life. By so doing, it is erecting an increasingly reliable barrier to the ideology and policy of war and militarism, reaction and force, to all forms of inhumanity, and is actively furthering social progress. It has grown into a powerful moral and material force, and has shown what opportunities are opening for modern civilisation.

The course of social progress is closely linked with **anti-colonial** revolutions, national liberation movements, the renascence of many countries, and the emergence of dozens of new ones. Having won political independence, they are working hard to overcome backwardness, poverty, and sometimes extreme privation—the entire painful legacy of their past enslavement. Formerly the victims of imperialist policy, deprived of all rights, they are now making history themselves.

Social progress is expressed in the development of the **international communist and working-class movement** and in the growth of the new massive democratic movement of our time, including the anti-war and anti-nuclear movement. It is apparent, too, in the polarisation of the political forces of the capitalist world, notably in the USA, the centre of imperialism. Here, progressive tendencies are forcing their way forward through a system of monopolistic totalitarianism, and are exposed to the continuous pressure of organised reactionary forces, including their enormous propaganda machine which floods the world with stupefying misinformation.

Marx compared progress in exploitative society to "that hideous pagan idol, who would not drink the nectar but from the skulls of the slain." He went on: "In our days everything seems pregnant with its contrary. Machinery, gifted with the wonderful power of shortening and fructifying human labour, we behold starving and overworking it. The new-fangled sources of wealth, by some strange weird spell, are turned into sources of want. The victories of art seem bought by the loss of character. At the same pace that mankind masters nature, man seems to become enslaved to other men or to his own infamy. Even the pure light of science seems unable to shine but on the dark background of ignorance. All our invention and progress seem to result in endowing material forces with intellectual life, and in stultifying human life into a material force."

Marx's analysis is striking in its historical sweep, accuracy, and depth. It has, indeed, become still more relevant with regard to bourgeois reality of the 20th century than it was in the 19th century. On the one hand, the swift advance of science and technology has opened up unprecedented possibilities for mastering the forces of nature and improving the conditions of the life of man. On the other, the "enlightened" 20th century is going down in history as a time marked by such outgrowths of imperialism as the most devastating wars, an orgy of militarism and fascism, genocide, and the destitution of millions of people. Ignorance and obscurantism go hand in hand in the capitalist world with outstanding achievements of science and culture. That is the society we are compelled to be neighbours of, and we must look for ways of cooperation and mutual understanding. Such is the command of history.

The progress of humanity is also directly connected with the **scientific and technological revolution**. It matured slowly and gradually, and then, in the final quarter of the century, gave the start to a gigantic increase of man's material and spiritual possibilities. These are of a twofold nature. There is a qualitative leap in humanity's productive forces. But there is also a qualitative leap in means of destruction, in the military sphere, "endowing" man for the first time in history with the physical capacity for destroying all life on earth.

The facets and consequences of the scientific and technological revolution differ in different socio-political systems, Capitalism of the 1980s, the capitalism of the age of electronics and information science, computers and robots, is throwing more millions of people, including young and educated people, out of jobs. Wealth and power are being increasingly concentrated in the hands of a few. Militarism is thriving greatly on the arms race, and also strives gradually to gain control over the political levers of power. It is becoming the ugliest and the most dangerous monster of the 20th century. Because of its efforts, the most advanced scientific and technical ideas are being converted into weapons of mass destruction.

The scientific and technological revolution is setting this most acute question before the developing countries: are they to enjoy the achievements of science and technology in full measure in order to gain strength for combatting neocolonialism and imperialist exploitation, or will they remain on the periphery of world development? The scientific and technological revolution shows in bold relief that many socio-economic problems impeding progress in that part of the world are unresolved.

Socialism has everything it needs to place modern science and technology at the service of the people. But it would be wrong to think that the scientific and technological revolution is creating no problems for socialist society. Experience shows that its advance involves improvement of social relations, a change of mentality, the forging of a new psychology, and the acceptance of dynamism as a way and a rule of life. It calls insistently for a continuous reassessment and streamlining of the prevailing patterns of management. In other words, the scientific and technological revolution not only opens up prospects, but also sets higher demands on the entire organisation of the internal life of countries and international relations. Certainly, scientific and technological progress cannot abolish the laws of social development or the social purpose and content of such development. But it exercises a tremendous influence on all the processes that are going on in the world, on its contradictions.

It is quite obvious that the two socio-economic systems differ substantially in their readiness and in their capacity to comprehend and resolve the problems that arise.

Such is the world we are living in on the threshold of the third millennium. It is a world full of hope, because people have never before been so amply equipped for the further development of civilisation. But it is also a world overburdened with dangers and contradictions, which prompts the thought that this is perhaps the most alarming period in history.

The first and most important group of contradictions in terms of humanity's future is connected with the **relations between countries of the two systems, the two formations**. These contradictions have a long history. Since the Great October Revolution in Russia and the split of the world on the social-class principle, fundamental differences have emerged both in the assessment of current affairs and in the views concerning the world's social perspective.

Capitalism regarded the birth of socialism as an "error" of history which must be "rectified." It was to be rectified at any cost, by any means, irrespective of law and morality: by armed intervention, economic blockade, subversive activity, sanctions and "punishments," or rejection of all cooperation. But nothing could interfere with the consolidation of the new system and its historical right to live.

The difficulty that the ruling classes of the capitalist world have in understanding the realities, the recurrence of attempts at resolving by force the whole group of contradictions dividing the two worlds are, of course, anything but accidental. The intrinsic mainsprings and socio-economic essence of imperialism prompt it to translate the competition of the two systems into the language of military confrontation. Owing to its social nature, imperialism ceaselessly gives rise to aggressive, adventurist policy.

Here we can speak of a whole complex of motives involved: the predatory appetites of the arms manufacturers and the influential military-bureaucratic groups, the selfish interest of the monopolies in sources of raw materials and markets for their goods, the bourgeoisie's fear of the ongoing changes, and, lastly, the attempts to resolve its own increasingly acute problems at socialism's expense.

Such attempts are especially typical of US imperialism. It was nothing but imperial ideology and policy, the wish to create the most unfavourable external conditions for socialism and for the USSR that prompted the launching of the race of nuclear and other arms after 1945, just when the crushing defeat of fascism and militarism was, it would seem, offering a realistic opportunity for building a world without wars, and a mechanism of international cooperation—the United Nations—had been created for this purpose. But imperialism's nature asserted itself that time again.

Today, too, the right wing of the US monopoly bourgeoisie regards the stoking up of international tensions as something that justifies military spending, claims to global supremacy, interference in the affairs of other states, and an offensive against the interests and the rights of the American working people. No small role seems to be played by the idea of using tensions to put pressure on the allies, to make them absolutely obedient, to subordinate them to Washington's dictation.

The policy of total contention, of military confrontation has no future. Flight into the past is no answer to the challenges of the future. It is rather an act of despair which, however, does not make this posture any less dangerous. By its deeds Washington will show when and to what extent it will understand this. We, for our part, are ready to do everything we can in order radically to improve the international situation. To achieve this, socialism need not renounce any of its principles or ideals. It has always stood for and continues to stand for the peaceful coexistence of states with different social systems.

As distinct from imperialism, which is trying to halt the course of history by force, to regain what it had in the past, socialism has never, of its own free will, related its future to any military solution of international problems. This was borne out at the very first big discussion that took place in our Party after the victory of the Great October Revolution. During that discussion, as we may recall, the views of the "Left Communists" and the Trotskyites, who championed the theory of "revolutionary war" which, they claimed, would carry socialism to other countries, were firmly rejected. This position, as Lenin emphasised in 1918, "would be completely at variance with Marxism, for Marxism has always been opposed to 'pushing' revolutions, which develop with the growing acuteness of the class antagonisms that engender revolutions." Today, too, we are firmly convinced that promoting revolutions from outside, and even more so by military means, is futile and inadmissible.

The problems and crises experienced by the capitalist world arise within its own system and are a natural result of the internal antagonistic contradictions of the old society. In this sense, capitalism negates itself as it develops. Unable to cope with the acute problems of the declining phase of capitalism's development, the ruling circles of the imperialist countries resort to means and methods that are obviously incapable of saving the society which history has doomed.

The myth of a Soviet or communist "threat" that is being circulated today is meant to justify the arms race and the imperialist countries' own aggressiveness. But it is becoming increasingly clear that the path of war can yield no sensible solutions, either international or domestic. The clash and struggle of the opposite approaches to the perspectives of world development have become especially complex in nature. Now that the world has huge nuclear stockpiles and the only thing experts argue about is how many times or dozens of times humanity can be destroyed, it is high time to begin an effective withdrawal from the brink of war, from the equilibrium of fear, to normal, civilised forms of relations between the states of the two systems.

In the years to come, the struggle will evidently centre on the actual content of the policy that can safeguard peace. It will be a hard and many-sided struggle, because we are dealing with a society whose ruling circles refuse to assess the realities of the world and its perspectives in sober terms, or to draw serious conclusions from their own experience and that of others. All this is an indication of the wear and tear suffered by its internal "systems of immunity," of its social senility, which reduces the probability of far-reaching changes in the policy of the dominant forces and augments its degree of recklessness.

That is why it is not easy at all, in the current circumstances, to predict the future of the relations between the socialist and the capitalist countries, the USSR and the USA. The decisive factors here will be the correlation of forces on the world scene, the growth and activity of the peace potential, and its capability of effectively repulsing the threat of nuclear war. Much will depend, too, on the degree of realism that Western ruling circles will show in assessing the situation. But it is unfortunate when not only the eyesight but also the soul of politicians is blind. With nuclear war being totally unacceptable, peaceful coexistence rather than confrontation of the systems should be the rule in inter-state relations.

The second group of contradictions consists of the **intrinsic contradictions of the capitalist world itself**. The past period has amply confirmed that the **general crisis of capitalism** is growing keener. The capitalism of today, whose exploitative nature has not changed, is in many ways different from what it was in the early and even the middle 20th century. Under the influence and against the background of the scientific and technological revolution, the conflict between the productive forces, which have grown to gigantic proportions, and the private-owner social relations, has become still more acute. Here there is growth of unemployment and deterioration of the entire set of social problems. Militarism, which has spread to all areas, is applied as the most promising means of enlivening the economy. The crisis of political institutions, of the entire spiritual sphere, is growing. Reaction is exerting fierce pressure all along the line—in domestic and foreign policy, economy and culture, and the use of the achievements of human genius. The traditional forms of conservatism are giving place to authoritarian tendencies.

Special mention should be made of such dangerous manifestation of the crisis of capitalism as anti-communism and anti-Sovietism. This concerns not only foreign policy. In the present-day system of imperialism it is also a very important aspect of domestic policy, a means of exerting pressure on all the advanced and progressive elements that live and fight in the capitalist countries, in the non-socialist part of the world.

True, the present stage of the general crisis does not lead to any absolute stagnation of capitalism and does not rule out the possibilities for economic growth, and the mastering of new scientific and technical fields. This stage "allows for" sustaining concrete economic, military, political and other positions, and in some areas even the possibility for social revenge, for regaining what had been lost before. Because capitalism lacks positive aims and orientations, capable of expressing the interests of the working masses, it now has to cope with the unprecedented interlacement and mutual exacerbation of all of its contradictions. It faces more social and other impasses than it has ever known before in all the centuries of its development.

The contradictions **between labour and capital** are among the first to grow more acute. In the 1960s and 1970s, with the onset of a favourable economic situation, the working class and working people managed to secure a certain improvement of their condition. But from the mid-1970s on, the proliferating economic crises and another technological modernisation of production changed the situation, and enabled capital to go on the counter offensive, depriving the working people of a considerable part of their social gains. For a number of standard of living indicators, the working people were flung back many years. Unemployment has reached a postwar high. The condition of peasants and farmers is deteriorating visibly: some farms are going bankrupt, with their former owners joining the ranks of hired workers, while others become abjectly dependent on large agricultural monopolies and banks. The social stratification is growing deeper and increasingly striking. In the United States, for example, one per cent of the wealthiest families own riches that exceed by nearly 50 per cent the aggregate wealth of 80 per cent of all American families who make up the lower part of the property pyramid.

Imperialism's ruling circles are doubtlessly aware that such a situation is fraught with social explosions and political destabilisation. But this is not making their policies more considered. On the contrary, the most irreconcilable reactionary groups of the ruling class have, by and large, taken the upper hand in recent years. This period is marked by an especially massive and brutal offensive by the monopolies on the rights of the working people.

The whole arsenal of means at capitalism's disposal is being put to use. The trade unions are persecuted and economically blackmailed. Anti-labour laws are being enacted. The left and all other progressives are being persecuted. Continuous control or, to be more precise, surveillance of people's state of mind and behaviour has become standard. The deliberate cultivation of individualism, of the principle that might makes right in the fight for survival, of immorality and hatred of all that is democratic—this is practised on an unprecedented scale.

The future, the working people's fight for their rights, for social progress, will show how that basic contradiction between labour and capital will develop and what conclusions will be drawn from the prevailing situation. But mention must be made of the serious danger to international relations of any further substantial shift of policy, of the entire internal situation in some capitalist countries, to the right. The consequences of such a development are hard to predict, and we must not underrate their danger.

The last decades of the century are marked by new outbreaks of **inter-imperialist contradictions** and the appearance of their new forms and tendencies. This group of capitalist contradictions has not been eliminated either by class affinity, the interest in uniting forces, by military, economic and political integration, or by the scientific and technological revolution. The latter has incontestably accelerated the internationalisation of capitalist production, has given added impetus to the evening up of levels as well as to the leap-like development of capitalist countries. The competition that has grown more acute under the impact of scientific and technological progress is affecting those who have dropped behind ever more mercilessly. The considerable complication of the conditions of capitalist reproduction, the diversity of crisis processes, and the intensification of international competition have made imperialist rivalry especially acute and bitter. The commercial and economic struggle on the world market is witnessing ever greater reliance on the power of national state-monopoly capitalisms, with the role of the bourgeois state becoming increasingly aggressive and egoistic.

The **transnational monopoly capital** has gained strength rapidly. It is seizing control of, and monopolising, whole branches or spheres of production both on the scale of individual countries and in the world economy as a whole. By the early 1980s, the transnational corporations accounted for more than one-third of industrial production, more than one half of foreign trade, and nearly 80 per cent of the patents for new machinery and technology in the capitalist world.

The core of the transnational corporations consists of American firms. Their enterprises abroad use an additional army of wage and salary workers, whose number is half of those employed in manufacturing in the USA. At present, they produce something like 1.5 trillion dollars worth of goods and services a year, or nearly 40 per cent of gross US output.

The size of the "second economy" of the United States is double or triple that of the economies of such leading West European powers as the FRG, France, and Britain, and second only to that of Japan. Today, the biggest US transnational monopolies are empires whose scale of economic activity is comparable to the gross national product of an entire country.

A new knot of contradictions has appeared and is being swiftly tightened **between the transnational corporations and the nation-state form of society's political organisation**. The transnational corporations are undermining the sovereignty both of developing and of developed capitalist countries. They make active use of state-monopoly regulation when it suits their interests, and come into sharp conflict with it when they see the slightest threat to their profits from the actions of bourgeois governments. But for all that, the US transnational supermonopolies are, as a rule, active conductors of state hegemonism and the imperial ambitions of the country's ruling circles.

The relations between the three main centres of present-day imperialism—the USA, Western Europe and Japan—abound in visible and concealed contradictions. The economic, financial, and technological superiority which the USA enjoyed over its closest competitors until the end of the 1960s has been put to a serious trial. Western Europe and Japan managed to outdo their American patron in some things, and are also challenging the United States in such a traditional sphere of US hegemony as that of the latest technology.

Washington is continuously calling on its allies not to waste their gunpowder on internecine strife. But how are the three centres of present-day imperialism to share one roof if the Americans themselves, manipulating the dollar and the interest rates, are not loath to fatten their economy at the expense of Western Europe and Japan? Wherever the three imperialist centres manage to coordinate their positions, this is more often than not the effect of American pressure or outright dictation, and works in the interests and aims above all of the United States. This, in turn, sharpens, rather than blunts, the contradictions.

It appears that people are beginning to wonder about this cause-and-effect relationship. For the first time, governments of some West European countries, the social democratic and liberal parties, and the public at large have begun to discuss openly whether present US policy coincides with Western Europe's notions about its own security and whether the United States is going too far in its claims to "leadership"? The partners of the United States have had more than one occasion to see that someone else's spectacles cannot substitute for one's own eyes.

The clash of centrifugal and centripetal tendencies will, no doubt, continue as a result of changes in the correlation of forces within the imperialist system. Still, the existing complex of economic, politico-military and other common interests of the three "centres of power" can hardly be expected to break up in the prevailing conditions of the present-day world. But within the framework of this complex, Washington should not expect unquestioning obedience to US dictation on the part of its allies and competitors, and especially when this is to the detriment of their own interests.

The specificity of the inter-imperialist contradictions in the current period also includes the possibility for changes in their configuration in the coming decades, with new capitalist "centres of power" coming on the scene. This will doubtless lead to a further growth of the bulk of contradictions, to their closer interlacement and aggravation.

A new, complex and changing set of contradictions has taken shape between imperialism, on the one hand, and the developing countries and peoples, on the other. The liberation of former colonies and semi-colonies was a strong political and ideological blow to the capitalist system. It has ceased to exist in the shape that it assumed in the 19th century and which extended into the first half of the 20th. A slow, arduous, but irreversible process of socio-economic transformations is under way in the life of nations comprising the majority of mankind. This process, which has brought about not a few fundamental changes, has also encountered considerable difficulties.

By political manoeuvring, blandishments and blackmail, military threats and intimidation, and all too often by direct interference in the internal affairs of the newly free countries, capitalism has in many ways managed to sustain the earlier relationships of economic dependence. On this basis, imperialism managed to create and run the most refined system of neocolonialist exploitation, and to tighten its hold on a considerable number of newly free states.

The consequences of this are tragic. The developing countries with a population of more than two billion, have, in effect, become a region of wholesale poverty. In the early 1980s, the per capita income in the newly free countries was, on the whole, less than 10 per cent that of the developed capitalist states. And in the past thirty years, far from shrinking, the gap has grown wider. Nor is it a question of just comparative poverty. There is illiteracy and ignorance, chronic undernourishment and hunger, appalling child mortality, and epidemics that afflict hundreds of millions of people.

This is a disgrace for civilised humanity! And its culprit is imperialism. Not only from the point of view of history, that is, of colonial plunder on entire continents which left behind a heritage of unbelievable backwardness, but equally in terms of present-day practices. In just the past ten years, the profits squeezed out of the developing countries by US corporations exceeded their inputs four-fold. And in Latin America and the Caribbean, in the same period, the profits of US monopolies were over eight times greater than their inputs.

It is no exaggeration to say that, to a large extent, the imperialist system still lives by plundering the developing countries, by mercilessly exploiting them. The forms and methods are changing, but the essence remains the same. In the United States, for example, a tangible portion of the national income comes from these very sources. The developing countries are being exploited by all the imperialist states, but, unquestionably, US imperialism is doing it with the greatest impudence. Non-equivalent exchange, unequal trade, manipulations and arbitrary actions regarding interest rates and the pump of the transnational corporations are being used to one and the same end. They are adding still more to the poverty and misery of some, and to the wealth of others, and increasing the polarisation in the capitalist world economy.

The distressing condition of the developing countries is a major worldwide problem. This and nothing else is the true source of many of the conflicts in Asia, Africa, and Latin America. Such is the truth, however hard the ruling circles of the imperialist powers may invoke the "hand of Moscow" in order to vindicate their neocolonialist policy and global ambitions.

Take the problem of debts. Together with the profits shipped out yearly from the developing countries, the accumulated debt means just one thing: the prospects for their development have shrunk, and a further aggravation of the already grave social, economic, and other problems is inevitable.

In the existing circumstances, these countries will not, of course, be able to repay their debts. And if no fair solution is devised, the situation will be fraught with grave socio-economic and political consequences on the international scene. It would be wrong to say that the imperialist ruling circles are blind to the underlying danger here. But all their concerns boil down to one thing—how to save the present system of enriching themselves through the exploitation and super-exploitation of the peoples of the developing countries.

This other thing is certain as well: there is an irrefutable causal connection between the trillion-sized debt of these countries and the more than trillion-sized growth of US military expenditures in the past ten years. The 200-odd billion dollars that are being annually pumped out of the developing countries and the practically equal size of the US military budget in recent years, are no coincidence. That is why militarism has a direct stake in maintaining and tightening the system of neocolonial super-exploitation.

It is also obvious that with capitalism's contradictions growing sharper and its sphere of predominance shrinking, neocolonialism is becoming an increasingly important source of means that provide monopoly capital with the possibility for social manoeuvring, reducing social tensions in the leading bourgeois states, and for bribing some sections of the working people. It is a truly extraordinary source, for a worker's hourly rate in the advanced capitalist states is higher, sometimes several times higher, than a day's earnings in the countries of Asia, Africa and Latin America.

All this cannot go on forever. But, of course, no miracle can be expected: the situation is not going to straighten itself out on its own. The military force that the USA is counting on to maintain the status quo, to safeguard the interests of the monopolies and the military-industrial complex, and to prevent any further progressive change in the newly free countries can only complicate the situation and precipitate new conflicts. The bags of money are liable to become kegs of gunpowder. Sooner or later, in this area too, capitalism will have to choose between the policy of force and shameless plunder, on the one hand, and the opportunity for cooperation on an equitable basis, on the other. The solutions must be radical—in the interests of the peoples of the developing states.

Analysis of yet another group of contradictions—those on a global scale, affecting the very foundations of the existence of civilisation—leads to serious conclusions. This refers first of all to pollution of the environment, the air and ocean, and to the depletion of natural resources. The problems are aggravated not just by the excessive loads on the natural systems as a consequence of the scientific and technological revolution and the increasing extent of man's activity. Engels, in his time, foresaw the ill effects of subordinating the use of natural resources to the blind play of market forces. The need for effective international procedures and mechanisms, which would make for the rational use of the world's resources as an asset belonging to all humanity, is becoming increasingly apparent.

The global problems, affecting all humanity, cannot be resolved by one state or a group of states. This calls for cooperation on a worldwide scale, for close and constructive joint action by the majority of countries. This cooperation must be based on completely equal rights and a respect for the sovereignty of each state. It must be based on conscientious compliance with accepted commitments and with the standards of international law. Such is the main demand of the times in which we live.

Capitalism also causes an impoverishment of culture, an erosion of the spiritual values created over the centuries. Nothing elevates man more than knowledge. But in probably no other period of history has mankind experienced any stronger pressure of falsehood and deceit than it does now. Bourgeois propaganda foists cleverly doctored information on people all over the world, imposing thoughts and feelings, and inculcating a civic and social attitude advantageous to the ruling forces. What knowledge, what values and moral standards are implicit in the information dispensed to the people and in the system of education is, first and foremost, a political problem.

Life itself brings up the question of safeguarding culture, of protecting it from bourgeois corruption and vandalisation. That is one of the most important worldwide tasks. We cannot afford to neglect the long-term psychological and moral consequences of imperialism's current practices in the sphere of culture. Its impoverishment under the onslaught of unbridled commercialism and the cult of force, the propaganda of racism, of lowly instincts, the ways of the criminal world and the "lower depths" of society, must be, and certainly will be, rejected by mankind.

The problems, as you see, comrades, are many, and they are large-scale and intricate. But it is clear that their comprehension is, on the whole, lagging behind the scope and depth of the current tasks. The imperative condition for success in resolving the pressing issues of international life is to reduce the time of search for political accords and to secure the swiftest possible constructive action.

We are perfectly well aware that not everything by far is within our power and that much will depend on the West, on its leaders' ability to see things in sober perspective at important crossroads of history. The US President said once that if our planet were threatened by a landing from another planet, the USSR and the USA would quickly find a common language. But isn't a nuclear disaster a more tangible danger than a landing by extra-terrestrials? Isn't the ecological threat big enough? Don't all countries have a common stake in finding a sensible and fair approach to the problems of the developing states and peoples?

Lastly, isn't all the experience accumulated by mankind enough to draw well-substantiated practical conclusions today rather than wait until some other crisis breaks out? What does the United States hope to win in the long term by producing doctrines that can no longer ensure US security within the modest dimensions of our planet?

Imperialism is resorting to all possible means to keep in the saddle of history, but such a policy is costing the world dearly. The nations are compelled to pay an ever higher price for it. To pay both directly and indirectly. To pay with millions of human lives, with a depletion of national resources, with the waste of gigantic sums on the arms race. With the failure to solve numerous, increasingly difficult problems. And in the long run, perhaps, with the highest possible price that can be imagined.

The US ruling circles are clearly losing their realistic bearings in this far from simple period of history. Aggressive international behaviour, increasing militarisation of politics and thinking, contempt for the interests of others—all this is leading to the inevitable moral and political isolation of US imperialism, widening the abyss between it and the rest of humanity. It is as though the opponents of peace in that country are unaware that when nuclear weapons are at the ready, for civilisation time and space lose their habitual contours, and mankind becomes the captive of an accident.

Will the ruling centres of the capitalist world manage to embark on the path of sober, constructive assessments of what is going on? The easiest thing is to say: maybe yes and maybe no. But history denies us the right to make such predictions. We cannot take "no" for an answer to the question: will mankind survive or not? We say: the progress of society, the life of civilisation, must and will continue.

We say this not only by dint of the optimism that is usual for Communists, by dint of our faith in people's intelligence and common sense. We are realists and are perfectly well aware that the two worlds are divided by very many things, and deeply divided, too. But we also see clearly that the need to resolve the most vital problems affecting all humanity must prompt them towards interaction, awaken humanity's heretofore unseen powers of self-preservation. And here is the stimulus for solutions commensurate with the realities of our time.

The course of history, of social progress, requires ever more insistently that there should be **constructive and creative interaction between states and peoples on the scale of the entire world**. Not only does it so require, but it also creates the requisite political, social and material premises for it.

Such interaction is essential in order to prevent nuclear catastrophe, in order that civilisation could survive. It is essential in order that other worldwide problems that are growing more acute should also be resolved jointly in the interests of all concerned. The prevailing dialectics of present-day development consists in a combination of competition and confrontation between the two systems and in a growing tendency towards interdependence of the countries of the world community. This is precisely the way, through the struggle of opposites, through arduous effort, groping in the dark to some extent, as it were, that the controversial but **interdependent and in many ways integral world** is taking shape.

The Communists have always been aware of the intrinsic complexity and contradictoriness of the paths of social progress. But at the centre of these processes—and this is the chief distinction of the communist world outlook—there unfailingly stands man, his interests and cares. Human life, the possibilities for its comprehensive development, as Lenin stressed, is of the greatest value; the interests of social development rank above all else. This is what guides the CPSU in its practical activity.

As we see it, the main trend of struggle in contemporary conditions consists in creating worthy, truly human material and spiritual conditions of life for all nations, ensuring that our planet should be habitable, and in cultivating a caring attitude towards its riches, especially to man himself—the greatest treasure, and all his potentials. And here we invite the capitalist system to compete with us under the conditions of a durable peace.

II.
THE STRATEGIC COURSE: ACCELERATION OF THE COUNTRY'S SOCIO-ECONOMIC DEVELOPMENT

Comrades, by advancing the strategy of accelerating the country's socio-economic development at the April Plenary Meeting, the Central Committee of the CPSU adopted a decision of historic significance. It won the wholehearted support of the Party, of the entire people, and is being submitted for discussion at the Congress.

What do we mean by acceleration? First of all, raising the rate of economic growth. But that is not all. In substance it means a new quality of growth: an all-out intensification of production on the basis of scientific and technological progress, a structural reconstruction of the economy, effective forms of management and of organising and stimulating labour.

The policy of acceleration is not confined to changes in the economic field. It envisages an active social policy, a consistent emphasis on the principle of socialist justice. The strategy of acceleration presupposes an improvement of social relations, a renovation of the forms and methods of work of political and ideological institutions, a deepening of socialist democracy, and resolute overcoming of inertness, stagnation and conservatism—of everything that is holding back social progress.

The main thing that will ensure us success is the living creativity of the masses, the maximum use of the tremendous potentials and advantages of the socialist system.

In short, comrades, acceleration of the country's socio-economic development is the key to all our problems: immediate and long-term, economic and social, political and ideological, domestic and foreign. That is the only way a new qualitative condition of Soviet society can and must be achieved.

A. The Results of Socio-Economic Development and the Need for Its Acceleration

Comrades, the program tasks of the Party raised and discussed at our Congress necessitate a broad approach to the assessment of the results of the country's development. In the quarter of a century since the adoption of the third CPSU Program, the Soviet Union has achieved impressive successes. The fixed production assets of our economy have increased seven times. Thousands of enterprises have been built, and new industries created. The national income has gone up by nearly 300 per cent, industrial production 400 per cent and agricultural production 70 per cent.

Before the war and in the early postwar years the level of the US economy appeared to us hard to attain, whereas already in the 1970s we had come substantially closer to it in terms of our scientific, technical and economic potential, and had even surpassed it in the output of certain key items.

These achievements are the result of tremendous effort by the people. They have enabled us to considerably enhance the wellbeing of Soviet citizens. In a quarter of a century real per capita incomes have gone up 160 per cent, and the social consumption funds more than 400 per cent. Fifty-four million flats have been built, which enabled us to improve the living conditions of the majority of families. The transition to universal secondary education has been completed. The number of people who finished higher educational establishments has increased fourfold. The successes of science, medicine, and culture are universally recognised. The panorama of achievements will not be complete if I say nothing about the deepgoing changes in social relations, the relations between nations, and the further development of democracy.

At the same time, difficulties began to build up in the economy in the 1970s, with the rates of economic growth declining visibly. As a result, the targets for eeonomic development set in the CPSU Program, and even the lower targets of the 9th and 10th five-year plans, were not attained. Neither did we manage to carry out fully the social program charted for this period. A lag ensued in the material base of science and education, health protection, culture, and everyday services.

Certainly, the state of affairs was affected, among other things, by certain factors beyond our control. But they were not decisive. The main thing was that we had failed to produce a timely political assessment of the changed economic situation, that we failed to apprehend the acute and urgent need for converting the economy to intensive methods of development, and for the active use of the achievements of scientific and technological progress in the national economy. There were many appeals and a lot of talk on this score, but practically no headway was made.

By inertia, the economy continued to develop largely on an extensive basis, being oriented towards drawing additional labour and material resources into production. As a result, the rate of growth of labour productivity and certain other efficiency indicators dropped substantially. The attempts to rectify matters by undertaking new projects affected the problem of balance. The economy, despite the enormous resources at its disposal, ran into shortage of them. A gap appeared between the needs of society and the attained level of production, between the effective demand and the supply of goods.

And though efforts have been made of late, we have not succeeded in wholly remedying the situation. The output of most types of industrial and agricultural goods fell short of the targets set by the 26th Congress of the CPSU for the 11th five-year-plan period. There are serious lags in engineering, the oil and coal industries, electrical engineering, in ferrous metals and chemical industries, and in capital construction. Neither have the targets been met for the main indicators of efficiency and the improvement of the people's standard of living.

And we, comrades, must draw the most serious lessons from all this.

The **first** of them may be described as the lesson of truth. A responsible analysis of the past clears the way to the future, whereas a half-truth which shamefully evades the sharp corners holds down the elaboration of realistic policy, and impedes our advance. "Our strength," Lenin said, "lies in stating the truth." That is precisely why the Central Committee deemed it essential to refer once more in the new edition of the Party Program to the negative processes that had surfaced in the 1970s and the early 1980s. That is why, too, we speak of them at the Congress today.

The **other lesson** concerns the sense of purpose and resolve in practical actions. The switchover to an intensive development of such an enormous economy as ours is no simple matter and calls for considerable effort, time, and the loftiest sense of responsibility. But once transformations are launched, we must not confine ourselves to half-hearted measures. We must act consistently and energetically, and must not hesitate to take the boldest of steps.

And **one more lesson**—the main one, I might say. The success of any undertaking depends to a decisive degree on how actively and consciously the masses take part in it. To convince broad sections of the working people that the chosen path is correct, to interest them **morally** and materially, and to restructure the psychology of the cadres—these are the crucial conditions for the acceleration of our growth. The advance will be all the more rapid, the tighter our discipline and organisation will be, and the higher the responsibility of each for his job and its results.

Today, the prime task of the Party and the entire people is to reverse resolutely the unfavourable tendencies in the development of the economy, to impart to it the due dynamism and to give scope to the initiative and creativity of the masses, to truly revolutionary change.

There is no other way. In the absence of accelerated economic growth our social programs will remain wishful thinking, even though, comrades, they cannot be put off. Soviet people must within a short time feel the results of the common effort to resolve cardinally the food problem, to meet the need for high-quality goods and services, to improve the medical services, housing, the conditions of life, and environmental protection.

The acceleration of socio-economic development will enable us to contribute considerably to the consolidation of world socialism, and will raise to a higher level our cooperation with fraternal countries. It will considerably expand our capacity for economic ties with the peoples of developing countries, and with countries of the capitalist world. In other words, implementation of the policy of acceleration will have far-reaching consequences for the destiny of our Motherland.

B. Economic Policy Guidelines

Comrades, the draft Program of the CPSU and the draft Guidelines define the main targets of our economic and social development. By the end of this century we intend to increase the national income nearly twofold while doubling the production potential and qualitatively transforming it. Labour productivity will go up by 2.3-2.5 times, energy consumption per rouble of national income will drop by 28.6 per cent and metal consumption by nearly 50 per cent. This will signify a sharp turn towards intensifying production, towards improving quality and effectiveness.

Subsequently, by intensifying these processes we intend to switch over to an economy having a higher level of organisation and effectiveness, with comprehensively developed productive forces, mature socialist relations of production, and a smoothly-functioning economic mechanism. That is our strategic line.

As was emphasised at the conference in the Central Committee of the CPSU in June 1985, the main factors behind this line are scientific and technological progress and a fundamental transformation of society's productive forces. It is impossible to effect cardinal changes with the previous material and technical foundation. The way out, as we see it, lies in thorough modernisation of the national economy on the basis of the latest scientific and technological advances, breakthroughs on the leading avenues of scientific and technological progress, and restructuring of the economic mechanism and management system.

1. Modernisation of the National Economy on the Basis of Scientific and Technological Progess

The CPSU has tremendous experience in carrying out major scientific-technological and socio-economic transformations. However significant they are, the scale and complexity of the work we carried out in the past cannot be compared with what has to be done in the period ahead to modernise the national economy.

What do we need for this?

First of all changing the structural and investment policy. The substance of the changes lies in shifting the centre of attention from quantitative indices to quality and efficiency, from intermediate results to end results, from building up production assets to renewing them, from expanding fuel and raw material resources to making better use of them, and also to speeding up the development of research-intensive industries and of the production and social infrastructures.

A big step forward is to be made in this direction in the current five-year period. It is intended to allocate upwards of 200 billion roubles of capital investments—more than during the past ten years—for modernising and technically reequipping production. Sizeable though these amounts are, the planning and economic bodies will have to continue the search for additional resources for these purposes.

Large-scale integrated programs in the strategic areas have been drawn up, and their implementation has begun. The industries that play the key role in scientific and technological progress, that assure a quick economic return and the solution of urgent social problems, will move ahead more dynamically. Substantial funds and material, scientific, and manpower resources are being concentrated to speed up their development.

It is clear that the effectiveness of modernisation and also the economic growth rates depend to a crucial degree on **machine-building**. This is where the fundamental scientific and technological ideas are materialised, where new implements of labour and machine systems that determine progress in the other branches of the national economy are developed. Here the foundations are laid down for a broad advance to basically new, resource-saving technologies, higher productivity of labour and better quality of output.

The Congress delegates know that the CPSU Central Committee and the USSR Council of Ministers recently adopted a decision on the further development of machine-building. In substance, it is a national program for modernising this essential sector of industry. A single management body has been set up in it. The machine-building complex has been set the goal of sharply raising the technical-economic level and quality of machines, equipment and instruments already by the end of the 12th five-year plan period [1990]. The capital investments allocated for modernising this industry will be 80 per cent greater than in the previous five years.

What, specifically, do we expect from the implementation of this program? The output of machinery and equipment is to increase by more than 40 per cent, and their quality standards will be improved.

The growing stream of new-generation machinery will pave the way for a fundamental retooling of the national economy and a growth in its effectiveness. The resultant annual savings will amount to the labour of about 12 million people, more than 100 million tons of fuel, and many billions of roubles. Calculations show that the use of the Don-1500 harvester alone, for example, will lead to a considerable reduction in the number of grain harvesting machines, will release about 400,000 machine-operators, and will reduce grain losses by millions of tons.

Large-scale introduction of computers and comprehensive automation of production will tremendously influence the rate of technical modernisation. Concrete targets in the development and large-scale application of modern computers and expansion of the manufacture of their components have been defined. The development of computer software and of management information systems is being put on an industrial footing. The Academy of Sciences of the USSR has set up an information science and computer technologies division to coordinate research and development.

Radical modernisation of the fuel and energy complex is the keynote of the Energy Program. The Program puts the emphasis on energy-saving technologies, on the replacement of liquid fuel by natural gas and coal, and on more sophisticated methods of oil refining. Advanced technologies are also to be employed in the extraction industry: open-cast coal mining, the use of hydromonitors in coal extraction, the development of improved and more reliable oil extraction equipment and the universal introduction of automated systems. In the course of the current five-year period two and a half times more nuclear power plant generating capacities will be started up than in the previous five years, and outmoded units at thermal power stations will be replaced on a large scale.

A great deal will have to be done in the metal-making and chemical industries, in introducing more highly productive equipment there. The production of fundamentally new and improved structural and other advanced materials will accelerate the development of electronics, machine-building, construction, and other branches of the economy.

The Party attaches enormous importance to technical reequipment of the production infrastructure, in the first place, in transport and communications. Top priority will be given to the development of light industry and other industries that directly meet consumer demand. Advanced equipment for them is to be manufactured not only by specialised industries but also by other industries.

We will not be able to carry out technical modernisation unless we radically improve capital construction. This calls for raising the entire building industry complex to a new industrial and organisational level, shortening the investment cycle by a minimum of 50 per cent both in modernising enterprises and in the construction of new facilities. We cannot reconcile ourselves any longer to slow construction rates that freeze enormous sums and retard scientific and technological progress in the national economy.

All these tasks, comrades, are gigantic in scale and significance. How they are carried out will, in the final analysis, determine the fulfilment of our plans and the rates of our growth. Each sector and each enterprise must have a clear-cut program for the continuous modernisation of production. The responsibility of the planning and economic bodies for the achievement of planned targets will increase accordingly. Party organisations should also direct their activities towards this.

It is especially important to prevent window dressing and the use of palliative instead of substantive measures. There are disquieting instances, and by no means solitary ones, of ministries and departments erecting new facilities under the guise of modernisation, of stuffing them with outdated equipment, and of drawing up costly projects that do not assure the rise of production to higher technical-economic levels.

Here is an illustration of that approach. The Bryansk Engineering Works, which puts out motors for diesel locomotives, is now in the middle of a 140-million rouble retooling program. What results will this modernisation of capacities yield? It turns out that the program does not provide for the introduction of advanced technologies, the number of workers has already been increased by nearly 1,000, and the return on the assets has dropped. The worst part of it is that they intend to use the new capacities to manufacture an outdated motor, although a more efficient model has been designed and tested.

What does the stance of the executives of the Ministry of the Heavy Machine-Building Industry and of the Ministry of Railways mean? Evidently some comrades have failed to grasp the profound importance of the tasks confronting them. Such facts deserve stern condemnation as undermining the Party's policy of modernisation and of accelerated scientific and technological progress. Such cases should be examined with all severity.

The need for modernisation poses new tasks for **scientific research**. The CPSU will consistently pursue a policy of strengthening the material and technical base of scientific research to the maximum, of providing scientists with the conditions for fruitful work. However, our country is entitled to expect discoveries and inventions from its scientists that will bring about genuinely revolutionary changes in the development of machinery and production methods.

Important measures to make the work of research establishments more effective have been outlined lately. They deal with incentives for scientists and new forms of interaction between science and production. A decision was recently adopted to set up inter-sectoral research-and-technological complexes, including the large institutes that are leaders in their respective fields, among them institutes under Academies of Sciences, design organisations and pilot plants.

Steps are also being taken to intensify the work of sectoral research institutes and to increase their contribution to speeding up scientific and technological progress. However, this process is going ahead at an impermissibly slow pace. Many institutes are still an appendage of ministry staffs; not infrequently they support departmental interests and are bogged down in red tape and paper-work. The question of bringing science closer to production, of including sectoral research institutes into production and research-and-production associations, was forcefully raised at the June conference. We must ascertain who is opposing this, what stand the ministries and their Party committees take on this issue, and how they are reacting to life's demands.

The research potential of higher educational establishments must also be used more effectively. Upwards of 35 per cent of our country's research and educational personnel, including about half of the holders of doctoral degrees, are concentrated there but they carry out no more than ten per cent of the research projects. The respective departments should draft and submit proposals for strengthening the links between university research and production. The proposals should also take into account the training of the next generation of researchers. Just as a forest cannot live on without undergrowth, a true scientist is inconceivable without students. This is a question of the future of science, and, therefore, of our country, too. Beginning with their freshman year, college and university students should be drawn into research work and into participation in applying research findings in production. This is the only way that real scientists and creatively-thinking specialists can be trained.

In sum, comrades, the orientation of science towards the needs of the national economy should be carried out more energetically. However, it is equally important to orient production towards science, to make it maximally receptive to scientific and technological advances. Regrettably, no few scientific discoveries and major inventions fail to find practical application for years, and sometimes for decades. I shall cite a few examples.

The non-wear and tear effect, which Soviet scientists discovered three decades ago, led to the development of fundamentally new lubricants that greatly increase the service life of machine parts subjected to friction and sharply reduce labour outlays. This discovery, which may yield a saving of many millions of roubles, has not yet been applied on a broad scale because of the inertness of some high-ranking executives of the USSR Ministry of Petrochemical Industry and of a number of other ministries and departments.

The Ministry of the Motor Vehicle Industry and planning bodies are to blame for the fact that for about ten years now a newly invented anti-friction bearing, which makes machines more reliable and failure-safe under the most rigorous operating conditions, has not been applied on a large scale. The Ministry of the Machine-Tool Industry has impermissibly held up the manufacture of unique hydraulic motors enabling extensive use of hydraulic techniques in mining and elsewhere, to increase labour productivity several-fold and to improve working conditions.

Unfortunately, this list could be continued. This kind of attitude to new inventions is not infrequently based on the ambitions of some groups of scientists, on departmental hostility towards inventions made "by others," and a lack of interest on the part of production managers in introducing them. It is no secret that even the examination of invention applications is sometimes an ordeal that drags on for years.

We cannot reach our targets in accelerating scientific and technological progress unless we find levers that will guarantee priority only to those research establishments and industrial enterprises whose work collectives actively introduce whatever is new and progressive and seek ways and means of manufacturing articles of high quality and effective yield.

We have already accumulated a definite amount of experience in improving the economic mechanism in the sphere of science and its interaction with production. It must be thoroughly analysed and then applied without delay, closely linking up material incentives for research collectives and individual researchers with their actual contribution to the resolving of scientific and technological problems.

At all levels of economic management there should be a new attitude to the introduction of new methods and technology. This also refers to the State Planning Committee of the USSR, which should go over more boldly to all-inclusive planning of scientific and technological progress, as well as to the USSR State Committee for Science and Technology, which is reorganising its work too slowly. The Academy of Sciences of the USSR, ministries and departments should pay more attention to basic research and to applying its findings in production. This is a sacred duty of every scientist, engineer, designer, and manager of an enterprise.

Our activity in the sphere of **foreign economic contacts** must be tied up more closely with the new tasks. There should be a large-scale, forward-looking approach to mutually advantageous economic relations. The member-countries of the Council for Mutual Economic Assistance have worked out a policy of this kind. It presupposes a switchover in economic relations among them from primarily trade relations to deeper specialisation and cooperation in production, above all, in machine-building, and to the establishment of joint associations and research-and-production complexes.

We have no few departments and organisations that are responsible for separate spheres of foreign economic relations but they do not always coordinate their work. In setting the aim of actively using foreign economic contacts to speed up our development we have in mind a step-by-step restructuring of foreign trade, of making our exports and imports more effective.

2. Solving the Food Problem: A Top-Priority Task

Comrades, a problem we will have to solve in the shortest time possible is that of fully supplying our country with food. This is the aim of the Party's present agrarian policy, formulated in the decisions taken by the CPSU Central Committee at its May 1982 Plenary Meeting and in the Food Program of the USSR. In the period since their adoption a good deal has been done to expand the material and technical base of agriculture and of the related industries. The economy of the collective farms, state farms, inter-farm enterprises and processing plants has become stronger; the productivity of crop farming and livestock farming has risen.

There is progress, but the lag in agriculture is being overcome slowly. A decisive turn is needed in the agrarian sector to improve the food supply noticeably during the 12th five-year plan period [1986–1990]. It is planned to more than double the growth rate of farm production and to ensure a substantial increase in the per capita consumption of meat, milk, vegetables, and fruit.

Can we do this? We can and we must. The Party has therefore worked out additional measures to raise the efficiency of all sectors of the agro-industrial complex. Their substance consists in changing the socio-economic situation in the rural areas, in creating the conditions for greater intensification and guaranteed farm produce. The emphasis is put on economic methods of management, broader autonomy of collective farms and state farms and their higher responsibility for the results of their work.

In carrying out this policy we will have to make more effective use of the production potential in the agro-industrial complex and concentrate efforts and resources on the most important sectors providing the highest returns. It is a question, first and foremost, of increasing soil fertility and creating the conditions for stable farming. As the experience of recent years has shown, the key to success lies in large-scale application of intensive technologies. They have a tremendous effect. Their application made it possible to obtain, last year alone, an additional 16 million tons of grain and a substantial amount of other produce.

Reducing losses of farm produce during harvesting, transportation, storage, and processing is the most immediate source of augmenting food stocks. We have no small potentialities in this respect; an increase in consumption resources could amount to as much as 20 per cent, and in the case of some products to as much as 30 per cent. Besides, eliminating the losses would cost two to three times less than supplying the same amount of produce.

The Central Committee and the Government have now defined major steps to reduce losses. Rapid expansion of agricultural machine-building will make it possible to equip the collective farms and state farms with highly productive machines capable of performing all the field jobs faster and better. We have also made additional outlays to increase the manufacture of machinery for the food industry and facilities for the processing and storage of food.

The Party and the state will persistently continue to strengthen the material and technical base of the agro-industrial complex. It is equally clear, however, that people will, as before, be the mainspring and inspiration of progress. Today, more than ever before, agriculture needs people who want to work actively, who have a high level of professional skill and a feeling for the new. Constant attention to the working and living conditions of the people in rural areas is the best guarantee of all our successes. All our plans are geared to this, and it is important that they should be carried out unswervingly.

All these are urgent measures, but the program of action is not confined to them. The switchover of the agrarian sector to new methods of administration and management has to be completed. The establishment, in the centre and in the localities, of unified management bodies of the agro-industrial complex, called upon to carry out genuine and effective integration of agriculture and of the related industries, is undoubtedly a step of fundamental significance.

The establishment of this organisational framework is backed up by an effective economic mechanism. Proposals on this score have already been drafted. The main idea is to give broad scope to economic methods of management, to substantially broaden the autonomy of collective farms and state farms, to increase their interest in and responsibility for the end results. In substance, it is a question of creatively applying, in the conditions of today, Lenin's idea of the food tax.

It is intended to establish fixed plans for the purchase of produce from the collective farms and state farms for each year of the five-year period; these plans will not be altered. Simultaneously, the farms will be given the opportunity to use all the produce harvested over and above the plan, and in the case of fruit and potatoes and other vegetables a considerable part of the planned produce, as they see fit. The farms can sell it, additionally, to the state, can sell it, either fresh or processed, on the collective-farm market or through cooperative trade outlets, or use it for other needs, including the needs of personal subsidiary holdings. Additional allocations of material resources for which there is a heightened demand, and also other incentives, will encourage farms to sell grain to the state over and above the plan.

In future, the republics, territories, and regions will be given fixed quotas for the delivery of produce to centralised stocks; everything produced over and above that will be kept for the local supply system.

There is to be a transition to improved planning methods based on advanced standards. The role of cost accounting will be substantially increased. Past experience shows that neglect of the principles of self-support, material interest and responsibility for performance led to a deterioration of the financial and economic position of collective farms and state farms and also to their considerable indebtedness. Genuine cost accounting, with the incomes of enterprises depending upon the end results, should become the rule for all links of the agro-industrial complex and, first and foremost, the collective farms and state farms. The contract and job-by-job systems of payment at the levels of teams, groups, and families to whom the means of production, including land, will be assigned for a period specified by contract, will become widespread.

There will be big opportunities for displaying initiative and resourcefulness. This also presupposes, however, a higher sense of responsibility for meeting the targets of the Food Program, for the results of the financial and economic activity of collective farms, state farms, inter-farm enterprises and organisations. A reliable barrier must be erected in the way of mismanagement and parasitism, and an end must be put to excuses such as "objective circumstances," which some collective farms and state farms have been using to cover up their inaptitude and sometimes a lack of desire to work better. The farms will have to use chiefly their own funds to develop production, increase profits and incomes and provide incentives. The practice of providing bank loans will have to be substantially altered to stimulate a higher level of activity of collective farms and state farms.

As you see, comrades, conditions for rural economic management are undergoing a cardinal change. This calls for major changes in the style and methods of guidance of the agro-industrial complex. An end must be put to incompetent interference in production activity in rural areas. We expect the State Agro-Industrial Committee of the USSR and its local bodies to do everything so that our country receives weighty returns from the measures that are being taken.

3. Economic Management Must Measure Up to the New Demands

Comrades, the new economic tasks cannot be solved without an in-depth readjustment of the economic mechanism, without creating an integral, effective and flexible system of management that will make it possible to take fuller advantage of the possibilities of socialism.

It is obvious that economic management requires constant improvement. However, the situation today is such that we cannot limit ourselves to partial improvements. A radical reform is needed. Its meaning consists in truly subordinating the whole of our production to the requirements of society, to the satisfaction of people's needs, in orienting management towards raising efficiency and quality, accelerating scientific and technological progress, promoting a greater interest of people in the results of their work, initiative and socialist enterprise in every link of the national economy, and, above all, in the work collectives.

The Central Committee of the CPSU and its Political Bureau have defined guidelines for reorganising the economic mechanism. We set ourselves the aims of:

—heightening the efficiency of centralised guidance of the economy, strengthening the role of the centre in implementing the main goals of the Party's economic strategy and in determining the rates and proportions of national economic growth, its balanced development. Simultaneously, the practice of interference by the centre in the daily activities of the lower economic links must be overcome;

—resolutely enlarging the framework of the autonomy of associations and enterprises, increasing their responsibility for attaining the highest ultimate results. Towards this end, to transfer them to genuine cost accounting, self-support and self-financing, and to make the income level of collectives directly dependent on the efficiency of their work;

—going over to economic methods of guidance at all levels of the national economy, for which purpose to reorganise the system of material and technical supply, improve the system of price formation, financing and crediting, and work out effective incentives to eliminate overexpenditure;

—introducing modern organisational management structures, taking into account the trends towards concentration, specialisation and cooperation of production. This is a question of setting up complexes of interconnected industries, research and technological inter-sectoral centres, various forms of economic associations and territorial-production associations;

—ensuring the best possible combination of sectoral and territorial economic management, integrated economic and social development of republics and regions, and the organisation of rational inter-sectoral contacts;

—carrying out all-round democratisation of management, heightening the part played in it by work collectives, strengthening control from below, and ensuring accountability and publicity in the work of economic bodies.

Comrades, we now unquestionably stand before the most thorough reorganisation of the socialist economic mechanism. The reorganisation has begun. The direction along which work is going ahead in the agro-industrial complex has been already spoken about. Management of the machine-building complex is being upgraded. Industrial enterprises are being transferred, in the main, to a two-level system of management. Beginning with the current year, new economic management methods which have gone through experimental testing have been introduced in enterprises and associations that turn out half of the total industrial output. Their introduction in the service sphere, in construction and in transport has begun. Collective forms of organising work and providing incentives, and economic contract systems are being applied on an ever wider scale.

We are only at the beginning of the road, however. Time and energetic efforts are needed to reorganise the economic mechanism in our country with its vast and complex economy. Difficulties may arise, and we are not guaranteed against miscalculations either, but still the main thing now is to move ahead purposefully, step by step, along the direction we have chosen, supplementing and perfecting the economic mechanism on the basis of the accumulated experience and eliminating everything that has outlived itself or has failed to justify itself.

Success will depend largely on the **reorganisation of the work of the central economic bodies, first and foremost, the State Planning Committee of the USSR**. It must indeed become our country's genuine scientific and economic headquarters, freed from current economic matters. We have begun this work. New management bodies of the inter-sectoral complexes are being set up, and the major part of the day-to-day management functions is being delegated directly to the enterprises and associations. The State Planning Committee and other economic agencies must concentrate their efforts on long-term planning, on ensuring proportional and balanced economic development, on carrying out the structural policy, and on creating the economic conditions and incentives for attaining the best end results in each unit of the national economy. Considerable improvements are needed in the sphere of statistics.

Lately there has been a weakening of the **financial-credit influence on the economy**. The financial system does not sufficiently stimulate higher economic efficiency. The defective practice of income redistribution, with the losses of lagging enterprises, ministries and regions covered at the expense of those that operate profitably, has reached a large scale. This undermines cost accounting, promotes parasitism and prompts endless demands for assistance from the centre. Crediting no longer serves its purpose.

"Any radical reforms," said Lenin, "will be doomed to failure unless our financial policy is successful." Accordingly, we must radically change the substance, organisation and methods of the work of the financial and credit bodies. Their chief aim is not to exercise petty control over the work of enterprises but to provide economic incentives and to consolidate money circulation and cost accounting, which is the best possible controller. Everything must be made dependent on the end result. The question of improving collection of the turnover tax, deductions from the profit and other budget revenues has obviously come on the agenda. Their size and the procedure for their payment should more effectively help reduce losses in production, raise quality of output and promote its sale.

Prices must become an active factor of economic and social policy. We shall have to carry out a planned readjustment of the price system as an integral whole in the interests of organising effective cost accounting and in conformity with the aims of increasing the real incomes of the population. Prices must be made more flexible; price levels must be linked up not only with the outlays but also with the consumer properties of the goods, their effectiveness and the degree to which products meet the needs of society and consumer demand. Ceiling prices and contract prices are to be employed more widely.

The system of **material and technical supply** also needs thorough improvement. It must be turned into a flexible economic mechanism which helps the national economy to function rhythmically and steadily. It is the direct duty of the State Committee for Material and Technical Supply to contribute actively to the establishment of direct long-term relations between producers and consumers on a contractual basis, and to improve the observance of the terms of delivery. Wholesale trade in the means of production should be developed.

In the final analysis, everything we are doing to improve management and planning and to readjust organisational structures is aimed at creating conditions for the **effective functioning of the basic link of the economic system: the association or enterprise**.

As shown by analysis, the results of the experiments that have been carried out could have been much better, if, on the one hand, there had been a corresponding reorganisation of the work of industrial ministries and central economic agencies, which continue their attempts to restrict the powers of enterprises, and, on the other hand, if the incentives for higher efficiency had been brought home to every section, work team and workplace. Special attention should be paid to this.

It is high time to put an end to the practice of ministries and departments exercising petty tutelage over enterprises. Ministries should concentrate their attention on technical policy, on intra-sectoral proportions, and on meeting the requirements of the national economy in high-quality products put out by their respective industries. Enterprises and organisations should be given the right independently to sell to one another what they produce over and above the plan, as well as raw and other materials, equipment, etc. which they do not use. They should also be given the legal right to make such sales to the population. What sense is there in destroying or dumping onto waste heaps articles that could come in useful in the household, in building homes, garages or cottages on garden and vegetable plots?

It would be difficult to overestimate the role of economic **standards**. When the work collectives of enterprises know, ahead of time, specifics of the planned period—delivery targets, prices, deductions from profits to the budget, standards for forming wage funds and cost-accounting incentives funds—they can draw up creatively plans which provide for higher production growth rates and much higher efficiency without being afraid to reveal their as yet untapped potentialities. Moreover, enterprises should be given the possibility—

following the example of the Volga Auto Works and the Sumy Engineering Works—themselves to earn the funds needed to expand and retool production.

It is especially important to give enterprises and organisations greater autonomy in the sphere of consumer goods manufacture and services. Their task is to react quickly to consumer demand. It is along these lines that we are reshaping the economic mechanism of light industry. The range of targets approved from above is being sharply limited for enterprises in this sphere; their plans will be drawn up chiefly on the basis of contracts with trade organisations, which, in turn, must see to it that their orders conform to the actual consumer demand. In other words, the quantity, range, and quality of goods, that is, just what people need, will be the main thing, and not gross output. Besides, it is planned to establish inter-sectoral production and industrial-commercial associations for the manufacture and sale of light industry goods and to open more retail outlets operated by them.

The time has also come to solve another problem. An enterprise's wage fund should be directly tied in with the returns from the sale of its products. This will help to exclude the manufacture and supply of low-grade goods for which there is no demand, or, as they say, production for the warehouse. Incidentally, that approach should be applied not only in light industry. We can no longer reconcile ourselves to a situation in which the personnel of enterprises producing worthless goods lead an untroubled life, drawing their full pay and receiving bonuses and other benefits. Indeed, why should we pay for work which produces goods nobody wants to buy. One way or another all this goes against us, comrades! We must not forget about this.

A well-thought-out approach must also be taken to the question of a rational combination of **large, medium and small enterprises**. As experience shows, small, well-equipped plants have their own advantages in many cases. They can be quicker and more flexible in taking into account technological innovations and changes in demand, can faster meet the demand for small-batch and separate items, and can make better use of available manpower, especially in small towns.

Another substantial aspect of readjustment is consolidation of the territorial approach to planning and management. This is especially important for our vast and multinational country with its diverse features. The actions of ministries and departments that neglect the conditions in and the requirements of regions, with resulting economic imbalances, were rightly criticised at Party conferences and at congresses of the communist parties of constituent republics.

Some suggestions are also being received on this score. It is evidently worthwhile giving thought to enlarging the powers of republican and local bodies—following the example of the agro-industrial complex—in the management of construction, inter-sectoral production units, the social and production infrastructures, and many consumer goods factories. The work of the State Planning Committee of the USSR and of the ministries should get a broader territorial orientation. The question of national-economic management on the basis of large economic areas deserves study.

Our short- and long-term plans are linked, to a considerable degree, with the tapping of the natural wealth of Siberia and the Soviet Far East. This is a very important matter that requires a statesmanlike approach ensuring integrated regional development. Special attention should be paid to providing people there with the conditions for fruitful work and a full-blooded life. That is the main question today, and fulfilment of the set targets depends on how it is solved.

Attention should be drawn at our Congress to the problems involved in the further socio-economic development of the Non-Black-Earth Zone of the Russian Federation. I will stress two points. The Central Committee of the CPSU and the Soviet Government have adopted special decisions for an upswing in the agriculture of the Non-Black-Earth Zone, and they must be carried out unswervingly and fully. That is in the first place. And in the second place, the local Party, government and economic bodies and work collectives must pay much more attention to making effective use of the potential accumulated there and of the allocated resources.

Consolidation of the territorial principle of management calls for a higher level of economic guidance in each republic, region, city, and district. Proposals that come from the localities are at times not thought out thoroughly, not dictated by the interests of the national economy but rather by a dependant's mentality and sometimes even by self-seeking interests, which draw the economy into capital-intensive and low-productive projects. Due attention is not paid everywhere to raising the efficiency of production. In Kazakhstan, for example, the share of national income per unit of fixed production assets is a third less than the average for the Soviet economy. In Turkmenia, the productivity of social labour has not grown at all in 15 years. Thought should be given to how to tie in the resources allocated for social needs more closely with the efficiency of the regional economy.

Comrades, every readjustment of the economic mechanism begins, as you know, with a readjustment of thinking, with a rejection of old stereotypes of thought and actions, with a clear understanding of the new tasks. This refers primarily to the activity of our economic personnel, to the functionaries of the central links of administration. Most of them have a clear idea of the Party's initiatives, actively support them, boldly tackle complicated assignments, and seek and find the best ways of carrying them out. This attitude deserves utmost support. It is hard, however, to understand those who adopt a wait-and-see policy or who, like the Gogol character that thought up all kinds of fanciful ideas, do not actually do anything or change anything. There will be no reconciliation with the stand taken by functionaries of that kind. We will simply have to part ways with them. All the more so do we have to part ways with those who hope that everything will settle down and return to the old lines. That will not happen, comrades!

In our work on restructuring the economy and the economic mechanism it is more important than ever to rely on science. Life prompts us to take a new look at some theoretical ideas and concepts. This applies to such major problems as the interaction of the productive forces and the production relations, socialist ownership and its economic forms, commodity-money relations, the coordination of centralism with the autonomy of economic organisations, and so on.

Practice has revealed the insolvency of the ideas that under the conditions of socialism **the conformity of production relations to the nature of the productive forces** is ensured automatically, as it were. In real life, everything is more complicated. Indeed, the socialist production relations open up broad vistas for development of the productive forces. However, they must be constantly improved. And that means outdated economic management methods must be noticed in good time and replaced by new ones.

The forms of production relations and the economic management and guidance system now in operation took shape, basically, in the conditions of extensive economic development. These gradually grew out of date, began to lose their stimulating effect and in some respects became a brake. We are now striving to change the thrust of the economic mechanism, to overcome its costliness and to orient it towards a higher level of quality and efficiency, acceleration of scientific and technological progress and enhancement of the human factor. This is the main thing that will, in practice, signify further improvement of the socialist production relations and will provide new scope for the growth of the productive forces.

In this work we must not be stopped by long-established ideas, let alone by prejudices. If, for example, it is necessary and justifiable to apply economic standards instead of targets that are sent down as directives, this does not mean a retreat from the principles of planned guidance but only a change in its methods. The same can be applied to the need to broaden the autonomy, initiative and responsibility of associations and enterprises, and to enhance their role as socialist commodity producers.

Unfortunately, there is a widespread view when any change in the economic mechanism is regarded as practically being a retreat from the principles of socialism. In this connection I should like to emphasise the following: socio-economic acceleration and the consolidation of socialism in practice should be the supreme criterion in the improvement of management and of the entire system of the socialist production relations.

The **aspects of socialist property** as the foundation of our social system acquire great relevance. Socialist property has a rich content; it includes a multi-faceted system of relations among people, collectives, industries and regions of the country in the use of the means of production and its results, and a whole range of economic interests. This complex of relations requires a definite combination and constant regulation, especially since it is in motion. Unless we gain a deep understanding of these changes in theoretical terms we cannot arrive at correct practical decisions and consequently take prompt steps to mould a genuine sense of responsibility to socialist property.

We must provide the working people with greater incentives for putting the national riches to the best possible use and multiplying them. How can this be done? It would be naive to imagine that the feeling of ownership can be inculcated by words. A person's attitude towards property is shaped, first and foremost, by the actual conditions in which he has been put, by his possibilities of influencing the organisation of production, and the distribution and use of the results of work. The problem is thus one of further intensifying socialist self-government in the economic sphere.

The role of work collectives in the use of social property must be raised decisively. It is important to carry out unswervingly the principle according to which enterprises and associations are wholly responsible for operating without losses, while the state does not bear any responsibility for their obligations. This is where the substance of cost accounting lies. You cannot be a master of your country if you are not a real master in your factory or collective farm, in your shop or livestock farm. It is the duty of the work collective to answer for everything, to multiply the social wealth. Multiplication of the social wealth, as well as losses, should affect the income level of every member of the collective.

And, of course, a reliable barrier is needed against all attempts to extract unearned income from the social property. There are still "snatchers," persons who do not consider it a crime to steal from their plant everything that comes their way, and there are also sundry bribe-takers and grabbers who do not stop at using their position for selfish purposes. The full force of the law and of public condemnation should be applied to all of them.

Attention should also be paid to such a topical problem of regulating socialist property relations as ensuring unquestionable priority of the interests of the whole people over the interests of industries and regions. Ministries, departments and territorial bodies are not the owners of means of production but merely institutions of state administration responsible to society for efficient use of the people's wealth. We cannot allow departmental and parochial interests to hinder realisation of the advantages of socialist property.

We also stand for full clarity on the question of cooperative property. It has far from exhausted its possibilities in socialist production, in providing better satisfaction of people's needs. Many collective farms and other cooperative organisations are managed effectively. And wherever the need exists, utmost support should be given to the establishment and growth of cooperative enterprises and organisations. They should become widespread in the manufacture and processing of products, in housing construction and in construction on garden and vegetable allotments, and in the sphere of services and trade.

It is also time to overcome prejudices regarding **commodity-**

money relations and underestimation of these relations in planned economic guidance. Refusal to recognise the importance of their active influence on people's interest in working better and on production efficiency leads to a weakening of the cost-accounting system and to other undesirable consequences. Conversely, sound commodity-money relations on a socialist basis can create a situation and economic conditions under which the results depend entirely on the standards of the work done by the collective and on the ability and initiative of the managers.

Thus, comrades, we are obliged to assess the situation again and again and to resolutely reorganise everything that has become out of date, that has outlived itself. A profound understanding of this task by Party activists and by all personnel, as well as its comprehension by the broad masses are indispensable for success, are the point of departure in the exceptionally important work of building up a new economic mechanism and management system.

4. Putting Reserves of Economic Growth into Action

Comrades, the Party has worked out a strategy of deep-going transformations in the national economy and has begun to effect them. They will undoubtedly enable us to speed up economic growth. As was noted, however, this will require a good deal of time, but we must increase the growth rates at once, today. The specific feature of the 12th five-year plan period consists in retooling the national economy on a new scientific and technological basis while simultaneously stepping up the rates of our advance.

Hence the need to utilise all of our reserves to the maximum. It is more sensible to start with those that do not require big outlays but yield quick and tangible returns. This is a matter of economic-organisational and socio-psychological factors, of making better use of the production capabilities that have been built up, of making the incentives more effective, of improving the level of organisation and tightening discipline, and of eliminating mismanagement. Our reserves are at hand, and with a dedicated approach plus good management they promise high returns.

Just look at the capacities in operation. The value of our country's fixed production assets exceeds 1.5 trillion roubles, but they are not all being used properly. This applies to a number of industries—to machine-building, heavy industry, the power industry and agriculture. What is especially alarming is the fact that the most active assets—machinery, equipment, and machine-tools—often stand idle or else are operated at half capacity. In the engineering industry, for example, metalcutting machine-tools are in use only slightly more than one shift a day. On the whole, our country annually loses billions of roubles' worth of industrial output because capacities are underloaded. Planning and economic bodies and work collectives at enterprises must do everything possible to ensure the operation of existing capacities at the designed level. In heavy industry alone, this would nearly double the output growth rates.

Failure to meet component delivery obligations is another hindrance. A violation of this kind in one place has a ripple effect throughout the national economy and lowers its efficiency. Jerky production also does tangible damage. It is no secret that at the beginning of the month many plants stand idle longer than they function. But at the end of the month they begin a headlong rush, as a result of which output quality is low. This chronic disease must be eradicated. Strict observance of component delivery obligations is the duty of work collectives and also of management at all levels. We will not be able to achieve our aims unless we bring order into planning and supply, create the necessary stocks, and impose higher financial liability at all levels for failure to meet obligations and for spoilage.

There are also great reserves in the use of manpower. Some economic managers complain of a manpower shortage. I think the complaints are groundless in most cases. If you look into the matter more closely you will see that there is no shortage of labour. But there is a low level of labour productivity, inadequate work organisation and ineffective incentive schemes. Add to this the creation of superfluous jobs by planning and economic bodies. It is a well-known fact that some of our enterprises, design offices and research institutes have considerably larger staffs than their counterparts abroad with the same work load.

Once people at enterprises get down in earnest to improving work organisation and incentives, to tightening discipline and setting higher demands, reserves that had never been thought to exist previously are brought to light. Application of the Shchokino method and the certification of work places convincingly confirm this. When Byelorussian railwaymen went over to a new pay system, with one person doing two or more different jobs, about 12,000 workers were soon freed for jobs in other sectors.

Of course, more attention must also be paid to production mechanisation and automation. In tackling this problem one does not have to wait for machines and devices to be designed and made somewhere else. A great deal can be accomplished by using one's own capabilities. For instance, efforts in this direction in Zaporozhye Region led, in three years, to a nine per cent reduction in the number of workers employed in manual jobs in industry and a fifteen per cent reduction in the number of those in similar jobs in the building trades. I think that other regions, territories, and republics have no fewer possibilities. The important thing is to put persistent and dedicated effort into this, showing consideration for the people who have to perform manual operations, and striving to reduce production outlays.

Generally speaking, comrades, there are enormous economic reserves. We have not yet really begun to use many of them. The mentality of a substantial section of the managerial personnel at various levels took shape against the background of an abundance of resources. Many were spoiled by these riches, and that led to wastefulness. However, the situation changed long ago. The former influx of manpower has dwindled, and we have begun to pay a heavy price for every ton of oil, ore, and coal we extract and deliver. We cannot close our eyes to these facts; we must reckon with them. We must economise everywhere and always: on the job and at home. We must not ignore mismanagement and wastefulness. Nearly the whole of this year's growth in the national income is to come from raising labour productivity and lowering materials and energy consumption.

That is not simple but wholly feasible. All the more so since our country has accumulated experience in making thrifty use of resources; but it is not being spread fast enough. Party, YCL, and trade union organisations should constantly promote thrift and encourage those who make economical and rational use of raw materials, electrical energy, and fuel. We must make it a firm rule that overexpenditure of resources is disadvantageous and savings are tangibly rewarded.

I would like to put special emphasis on the problem of **output quality standards**. This is more than our immediate and major reserve. Accelerated scientific and technological progress is impossible today without high quality standards. We are sustaining great material and moral losses because of flaws in design, deviations from technology, the use of low-grade materials and poor finishing. This affects the precision and reliability of machines and instruments and hinders satisfaction of consumer demand for goods and services. Last year millions of metres of fabrics, millions of pairs of leather footwear and many other consumer items were returned to factories or marked down as inferior-grade goods. The losses are significant: wasted raw materials and the wasted labour of hundreds of thousands of workers. Radical measures must be taken to rule out the manufacture of defective or low-grade goods. The full force of pecuniary and administrative influence and legislation must be applied for this purpose. There is also evidently a need to adopt a special law on the quality of output.

Recently the Central Committee of the CPSU called upon Party committees, government and economic bodies, trade union and YCL organisations and all working people to make maximum efforts to radically improve the quality of goods. This must be a matter of concern for every Communist, for every Soviet citizen, for all who respect their own work, for all who cherish the honour of their enterprise, their industry, and the honour of our country.

A great deal of important and intensive work lies ahead of us. The first year of the five-year plan period is a year of persistent work, a year of tests for every manager and work collective. We must pass this test, draw all the reserves of the economy into production, and consolidate the foundation for further transformations.

The industry and talent of Soviet citizens are the key to attaining the goal that has been set. It is now up to efficient organisation and precise direction of this great force. The part to be played by socialist emulation in this effort cannot be overestimated. It should be spearheaded at raising the standards of work, economising and thriftiness, and reaching the targets set before each collective and at each workplace. Enthusiasm and the growing skills have been and, we are confident, will continue to be our reliable support.

C. The Basic Guidelines of Social Policy

Comrades, questions of social policy, concern for man's welfare, have always stood at the centre of our Party's attention.

The social sphere encompasses the interests of classes and social groups, nations and nationalities, the relationship between society and individual, the conditions of work and life, health and leisure. **It is the sphere in which the results of economic activity affecting the vital interests of the working people are realised, and the loftiest aims of socialism are carried into effect. It is the sphere in which the humanism of the socialist system, its qualitative difference from capitalism, is seen most distinctly and graphically.**

Socialism has eliminated the main source of social injustice—the exploitation of man by man, and inequality in relation to the means of production. Social justice reigns in all areas of socialist social relations. It is embodied in the real power of the people and the equality of all citizens before the law, the actual equality of nations, respect for the individual, and conditions for the all-round development of the personality. It is also embodied in broad social guarantees—employment, access to education, culture, medical care and housing, concern for people in old age, and mother and child welfare. Strict observance in life of the principle of social justice is an important condition for the unity of the people, society's political stability, and dynamic development.

But life, as they say, does not stand still. So we must look at the further development of the social sphere with new eyes, and appreciate the full measure of its increasing significance. We are obliged to do so in keeping with the general course worked out by the Party for the acceleration of socio-economic development, and with the program aim of our Party, that of achieving the complete wellbeing and a free all-round development of all members of society.

Lessons of the past, too, require that we pay greater attention to social issues. The Party's Central Committee holds that central and local bodies had underestimated relevant problems concerning the material base of the country's social and cultural sphere. As a result, a residual principle had actually taken shape governing allocation of resources for its development. There was a certain overemphasis on technocratic approaches, blunting attention to the social aspect of production, to everyday life and leisure; this could not but reduce the interest of the working people in the results of their work, slacken discipline and lead to other negative developments.

We are not at all indifferent to what ways and means are used to improve the material and spiritual aspects of life and what social consequences this entails. If private-owner, parasitic sentiments, and levelling tendencies begin to surface, this means that something is wrong about the choice of ways and means in our work, and has got to be rectified. During the discussion of the pre-Congress documents, Party members and non-members spoke with concern of the slackening of control over the measure of labour and consumption, of infringements of socialist justice, and of the need for stepping up the fight against unearned incomes. The gravity and importance of these questions is more than obvious.

In short, the attained level of development and the magnitude of the new tasks call for a long-term, deeply considered, integral, and strong social policy that would extend to all aspects of the life of society. It is essential for the planning and management bodies, for central and local economic organisations to deal resolutely with the needs of the social sphere.

The objectives of social policy are thoroughly characterised in the drafts of the Party Program and the Guidelines. Allow me to dwell on some issues related to its implementation.

1. Steady Improvement of the People's Standard of Living, Consistent Application of Social Justice

The long-term plans for the country's social and economic development envisage **raising the people's wellbeing to a qualitatively new level**. In the coming fifteen years, the volume of resources allocated for the improvement of the conditions of life is to be doubled. Real per capita incomes are to go up 60 to 80 per cent. The rise in incomes in the 12th five-year period is to cover millions of people. Huge funds are being earmarked for increasing the construction of homes and social and cultural facilities. Those are the plans. But we must mention the main thing: these plans will become reality only if every Soviet person works hard and efficiently. This applies to every person wherever he may work and whatever post he may occupy. What we accomplish is what we are going to have, and how we are going to live.

Socialist transformations have radically changed both the purpose of work and the attitude to work of the mass of workers and peasants. This is vividly reflected in the massive growth of socialist emulation.

Relying on its wealth of experience, the Party intends to continue promoting these traditions, and to cultivate a conscious and creative attitude to work as the prime duty to society.

At election meetings and conferences, Communists have rightly raised the question of not only improving the forms of moral incentives, but also of greatly increasing material incentives and establishing due order in this important matter. It was rightly pointed out that the so-called "figure juggling," payment of unearned money and unmerited bonuses, and setting "guaranteed" pay rates unrelated to the worker's contributed work, are impermissible. It should be said quite emphatically on this score that when equal payments are fixed for the work of a good employee and that of a negligent one this is a gross violation of our principles. And first of all it is an intolerable distortion of socialism's basic principle: "From each according to his ability, to each according to his work," which expresses the substance of the social justice of the new social system.

It is essential that the government's wage policy should ensure that incomes strictly correspond to the quantity and quality of work done. Proceeding from this, the increase of wage rates and basic salaries of factory and office workers in productive fields envisaged in the 12th five-year period will be enacted for the first time essentially at the expense and within the limits of the sums earned by the enterprises themselves. This procedure will make a more active impact on the acceleration of technical progress and on heightening the efficiency of production.

Rates and salaries in the non-productive sphere will go up, drawing on centralised sources. A phased increase of the salaries of doctors and other medical workers was started last year. The increase of the rates and salaries of those employed in public education is to be completed in 1987, and a start is to be made that year in raising the salaries of cultural workers. Measures are being taken to extend the wage and salary advantages of factory and office workers in certain regions of Eastern Siberia and the Soviet Far East.

Many proposals made by working people refer to the role of social consumption funds in enforcing the principle of justice. These funds already account for nearly one-third of the consumed material goods and services. We hold that they are in no way charity. They play an important role in providing equal access for members of society to education and culture, equalising conditions for the raising of children, and easing the life of those who may, for one reason or another, need a grant or continuous assistance. At the same time, it is a means of encouraging and stimulating qualified, conscientious work. The Party intends to continue promoting the further growth and more effective use of these social funds. In the 12th five-year period they are to go up by 20 to 23 per cent.

Combatting unearned incomes is an important function of the socialist state. We must admit today that owing to a slackening of control and for a number of other reasons groups of people have appeared with a distinct proprietary mentality and a scornful attitude to the interests of society.

Working people have legitimately raised the question of rooting out such things. The Central Committee agrees completely with these demands. It is considered necessary, already in the immediate future, to carry out additional measures against parasites, plunderers of socialist property, bribe-takers, and all those who embarked on a path alien to the work-oriented nature of our system. We should also give thought to proposals about perfecting our tax policy, including the introduction of a progressive inheritance tax.

But while combatting unearned incomes, we must not permit any shadow to fall on those who do honest work to earn a supplementary income. What is more, the state will promote various forms of satisfying popular demand and providing services. We must attentively examine proposals for regulating individual labour. It stands to reason that such labour must be in full conformity with socialist economic principles, and rest on either cooperative principles or on contracts with socialist enterprises. Society, the population only stand to gain from this.

All the efforts to perfect the distributive relations will have little effect and the objective of enhancing the people's wellbeing will not be attained if we fail to **saturate the market with diverse goods and services**. That, indeed, is the purpose of the Comprehensive Program for the Development of the Production of Consumer Goods and the Services.

In the current five years it is planned to secure higher growth rates for output of consumer goods and retail trade, and to considerably improve the organisation of trade and public catering. Heavy industry has been instructed to involve all enterprises in the production of manufactured goods and to ensure output of high-quality materials and equipment for light industry and the food industry.

We must build up an up-to-date services industry as quickly as possible. That is the job of central organisations, but also—no less, and perhaps even more—of the Councils of Ministers of Union Republics, and all bodies of local government. Resolute measures must be taken to eliminate the glaring disproportions between the supply and demand of services. This applies first of all to services that lighten domestic work and those connected with the improvement and renovation of flats, with tourism, and the servicing of cars—the demand for which is increasing at an especially swift rate. Responding to the proposals of the working people, we are promoting broad expansion of collective gardening and vegetable growing. This has gotten off the ground, but the work must be continued, and all artificial obstacles must be removed.

The social importance and acuteness of the **housing problem** have predetermined our serious attitude to it. To provide every family with a separate flat or house by the year 2000 is, in itself, a tremendous but feasible undertaking. In the current five years, and especially in the five-year periods to follow, the scale of housebuilding and of modernising available housing will increase. The building of cooperative and individual housing should be encouraged in every way. There are great reserves here for expanding the building of homes. Those who are backing the construction of youth complexes are doing the right thing. The motivation and energy of young people can do a lot in this respect.

Much is being said about the need for seriously improving the practice of distributing housing. These questions must be settled on a broad democratic basis and put under continuous public control. Proposals for fair changes in the system of house rents by gearing them to the size and quality of all the occupied living space merit attention. There have been many complaints about the low quality of house-building. It is essential to work out measures that would stimulate a substantial improvement of quality, and also an improvement of the layout, the amenities, and architecture of our towns and villages.

Comrades, the qualitative changes in the social sphere are impossible without **deep-going changes in the content of labour**. The main role here is to be played by the technical reconstruction of the economy: mechanisation, automation, computerisation and robotisation which, as I want to stress specially, must have an explicitly clear social orientation. Already in the current five years it is planned to sharply reduce the share of manual labour, and by the year 2000 to bring it down in the productive sphere to 15-20 per cent, relieving millions of people of manual operations. The further change of labour in the context of the scientitic and technological revolution sets high demands on education and the professional training of people. In substance, the task of **establishing a single system of continuous education** is now on the agenda.

In recent years, the Central Committee has taken important steps in that direction. A reform has been launched of the **general and vocational school**. It should be said that the rate and extent of the measures taken under the reform are not satisfactory as yet. A more profound approach is required to the study of the scientific basis of contemporary production and of the leading trends of its intensification. And what is especially urgent is that all pupils should learn the use of computers. In sum, it is essential that the Leninist principle of combining education with productive labour should be implemented more fully, that the effectiveness of education should be considerably raised, and that radical improvements should be carried out in the training of young people for independent life and labour and in bringing up politically conscious builders of the new society.

The Party is setting thc task of **restructuring higher and specialised secondary education**. In recent years, the growing output of specialists was not accompanied by the requisite improvement in the quality of their training. The material base of the higher school is lagging behind gravely. The use of engineers and technicians must be considerably improved.

At present, proposals have been drawn up to alter the prevailing situation. It is in the interests of society to raise the prestige of the work of engineers. The structure of higher and specialised secondary education is to be revised, so that the training of specialists will be abreast of the times and they acquire substantial theoretical knowledge and practical skills. The relationship of higher educational institutions and specialised secondary schools with various branches of the economy should evidently follow new lines, and their mutual interest in raising the level of training and retraining of cadres, in cardinally improving their use in production, should be enhanced.

Nothing is more valuable to every person and, for that matter, to society than health. **The protection and improvement of the health of people** is a matter of cardinal importance. We must consider the problems of health from broad social positions. Health depends above all on the conditions of work and life, and on the standard of living. It stands to reason, of course, that the public health service is also of tremendous importance. We must meet the needs of the population in high-quality medical treatment, health protection and pharmaceuticals as quickly as possible, and, moreover, everywhere. All this puts the question of the material and technical base of the health service in a new way, calling for the solution of many urgent scientific, organisational, and personnel problems. Considerable funds will be needed, of course, and we must see to it that they are made available.

It has long since been noted, and most aptly, that health cannot be bought in a pharmacy. The main thing is a person's way of life and, among other things, how sensibly and wholesomely a person uses his or her spare time. The opportunities for this are at hand, but the organisational side of the matter is very poorly run. Much depends on the initiative of the public, on people's avocational activity. But in towns and villages, and within work collectives, they often wait for instructions and count on assistance from above. Why do we make poor use of what is already at our disposal—of palaces, clubs, stadiums, parks, and many other facilities? Why don't the Soviets, the trade unions, and the Komsomol tackle these questions properly? Why not start a movement for more active building of simple playgrounds and gymnasiums on the residential principle? And finally, why not organise sports, tourist and other clubs on a cooperative basis?

A fight has been mounted across the country against hard drinking and alcoholism. In the name of the health of society and of the individual we have taken resolute measures and started a battle against traditions that were shaped and cultivated over the centuries. While we should have no illusions about what has been accomplished, we can safely say that incidents of drunkenness on the job and in public places have become fewer. The situation within families is improving, the number of industrial injuries has gone down, and discipline has been tightened. But extensive, persevering and varied efforts are still needed to secure a final break with prevailing habits. There must be no indulgence here!

We face the acute task of ensuring the **protection of nature and rational use of its resources**. Socialism, with its plan-governed organisation of production and humane world outlook, is quite capable of creating a harmonious balance between society and nature.

A system of measures to that effect has already been implemented in our country, and quite considerable funds are being allocated for this purpose. There are also practical results.

Still, in a number of regions the state of the environment is alarming. And the public, notably our writers, are quite right in calling for a more careful treatment of land and its riches, of lakes, rivers, and the plant and animal world.

Scientific and technical achievements are being introduced much too slowly in nature protection. The projects of new and the reconstruction of operating enterprises are still being based on outdated notions, with wasteless and low-waste production techniques being introduced on too small a scale. During the processing of minerals, most of the extracted mass goes to waste, polluting the environment. More resolute economic, legal and educational measures are required here. All of us living today are accountable to our descendants and to history for the environment.

2. Improvement of Social-Class Relations and Relations Among the Peoples of the USSR

Comrades, analysing problems involved in **interrelationship of classes and social groups** is of vital importance for a Marxist-Leninist party. By carefully taking into account both the community and the specific nature of their interests in its policy, the Communist Party ensures society's strong unity and successful fulfilment of its most important and complex tasks.

The working class holds a vanguard place in Soviet society. Owing to its position in the socialist production system, its political experience, high political awareness, good organisation, labour and political activity, the working class unites our society and plays the leading role in improving socialism, in communist construction. Constant concern for the consolidation of the alliance of the working class, the peasantry and the intelligentsia is the cornerstone of the policy pursued by the Communist Party of the Soviet Union. It is precisely this which enables us to muster forces for the speedy solution of the economic and social tasks we have set ourselves.

The unity of socialist society by no means implies a levelling of public life. Socialism encourages diversity of people's interests, requirements and abilities, and vigorously supports the initiative of social organisations that express this diversity. Moreover, socialism needs this diversity, which it regards as an essential condition for the further promotion of people's creative activity and initiative, and the competition of minds and talents, without which the socialist way of life and the movement forward would be inconceivable.

Generally speaking, the problem is as follows: unless we elevate emulation to a new, incomparably higher level in production, in the economy, as well as in the fields of science and the arts, we shall not be able to cope with the task of accelerating the country's socio-economic progress. To improve the socialist way of life is to ensure the maximum opportunities for fostering collectivism, the cohesion of society, and the individual's activity.

The **problems of consolidating the family** are attracting public attention. Our achievements in cultivating the new, socialist type of family are indisputable. Socialism has emancipated women from economic and social oppression, securing for them the opportunity to work, obtain an education and participate in public life on an equal footing with men. The socialist family is based on the full equality of men and women and their equal responsibility for the family.

Yet, the formation of the new type of family is no simple matter. It is a complicated process that involves many problems. In particular, although the divorce rate has dropped in the past few years, it is still high. There is still a large number of unhappy families. All this has a negative effect, above all, on the upbringing of children, as well as on the morale of men and women, on their labour and public activity. It stands to reason that society cannot be indifferent to such phenomena. The strong family is one of its principal pillars.

Young families need special care. Young people must be well prepared for family life. More thought should be given to the system of material assistance to newlyweds, above all in solving their housing and everyday problems. It would apparently be a good thing to consider the proposals for improving relevant legislation with a view to heightening the citizens' responsibility for consolidating the family. But that is not all. It is necessary to organise the practical work of state and public organisations so that it will promote in every way a strengthening of the family and its moral foundations. This means the creation of conditions for family participation in public festivities and in cultural and sports events, and for family recreation. Families in which successive generations work in a same profession should be widely honoured; good family traditions should be given every support and young people should be brought up on the basis of the experience of older generations. Here a big contribution can be made by the mass information media, television, literature, cinema and the theatre.

Securing living and working conditions for women that would enable them to successfully combine their maternal duties with active involvement in labour and public activity is a prerequisite for solving many family problems. In the 12th five-year period we are planning to extend the practice of letting women work a shorter day or week, or to work at home. Mothers will have paid leaves until their babies are 18 months old. The number of paid days-off granted to mothers to care for sick children will be increased. Lower-income families with children of up to 12 years of age will receive child allowances. We intend to fully satisfy the people's need for pre-school children's institutions within the next few years.

Thought should also be given to appropriate organisational forms. Why not reinstitute women's councils within work collectives or residentially, integrating them in a single system with the Soviet Women's Committee at its head? Women's councils could help to resolve a wide range of social problems arising in the life of our society.

Concern for the older generation, for war and labour veterans, should rank as one of the top priorities. The Party and the Soviet Government will do everything possible for the pensioners' wellbeing to rise with the growth of society's prosperity. In the 12th five-year period it is planned to increase the minimum old-age, disability, and loss-of-breadwinner pensions paid to factory and office workers, and to raise the previously fixed pensions of collective farmers. But man lives not by bread alone, as the saying goes. According to the information reaching the Central Committee, many retired veterans feel left out of things. Apparently, additional measures should be taken by government and public organisations, centrally and locally, to assist the veterans in becoming more actively involved in production and socio-political life. After all, more than 50 million Soviet people are veterans.

The setting up of a national mass organisation of war and labour veterans could be a new step in this direction. It could be instrumental in involving highly experienced people in social and political affairs, and first of all in educating the rising generation. The pensioners' involvement, both on a cooperative and on an individual, family basis, in the services or trade, producing consumer goods or turning out farm produce could be highly useful. The new organisation could be helpful in improving everyday and medical services for pensioners and expanding their leisure opportunities. As we see it, it will certainly have a lot of work to do.

Comrades, of tremendous importance for the multinational Soviet state is **development of relations among the peoples of the USSR**. The foundation for solving the nationalities problem in our country was laid by the Great October Socialist Revolution. Relying on Lenin's doctrine and on the gains of socialism the Communist Party has done enormous transformative work in this area. Its results are an outstanding achievement of socialism which has enriched world civilisation. National oppression and inequality of all types and forms have been done away with once and for all. The indissoluble friendship among nations and respect for national cultures and for the dignity of all peoples have been established and have taken firm root in the minds of tens of millions of people. The Soviet people is a qualitatively new social and international community, cemented by the same economic interests, ideology and political goals.

However, our achievements must not create the impression that there are no problems in the national processes. Contradictions are inherent in any kind of development, and are unavoidable in this sphere as well. The main thing is to see their emergent aspects and facets, to search for and give prompt and correct answers to questions posed by life. This is all the more important because the tendency towards national isolation, localism, and parasitism still persist and make themselves felt quite painfully at times.

In elaborating guidelines for a long-term nationalities policy, it is especially important to see to it that the republics' contribution to the development of an integrated national economic complex should match their grown economic and spiritual potential. It is in the supreme interests of our multinational state, and each of the republics, to promote cooperation in production, collaboration and mutual assistance among the republics. It is the task of Party organisations and the Soviets to make the fullest possible use of available potentialities in the common interests and to persistently overcome all signs of localism.

We are legitimately proud of the achievements of the multinational Soviet socialist culture. By drawing on the wealth of national forms and characteristics, it is developing into a unique phenomenon in world culture. However, the healthy interest in all that is valuable in each national culture must by no means degenerate into attempts to isolate oneself from the objective process by which national cultures interact and come closer together. This applies, among other things, to certain works of literature and art and scholarly writings in which, under the guise of national originality, attempts are made to depict in idyllic tones reactionary nationalist and religious survivals contrary to our ideology, the socialist way of life, and our scientific world outlook.

Our Party's tradition traceable to Lenin of being particularly circumspect and tactful in all that concerns the nationalities policy and the interests of every nation or nationality, national feelings, calls at the same time for resolute struggle against national narrow-mindedness and arrogance, nationalism and chauvinism, no matter what their guise may be. We Communists must unswervingly follow Lenin's wise teachings, must creatively apply them to the new conditions, and be extremely heedful and principled as regards relations among peoples in the name of the further consolidation of fraternal friendship among all the peoples of the USSR.

The social policy elaborated by the Party has many aspects to it and is quite feasible. However, its success will largely hinge on the social orientation of the cadres, on persistence and initiative in carrying out our plans. Concern for people's needs and interests must be an object of unflagging attention on the part of the Party, government and economic organisations, of trade unions and of each executive. If we succeed in securing a decisive switch to the social sphere, many of the problems that face us today and will face us tomorrow will be solved far more quickly and much more effectively than has so far been the case.

III.
FURTHER DEMOCRATISATION
OF SOCIETY AND PROMOTION
OF THE PEOPLE'S SOCIALIST
SELF-GOVERNMENT

Comrades, Lenin regarded democracy, the creative initiative of working people, as the principal force behind the development of the new system. Unmatched in his faith in the people, he showed concern for raising the level of the political activity and culture of the masses, stressing that illiterate people were outside politics. Nearly seventy years have elapsed since then. The general educational and cultural level of Soviet people has risen immeasurably and their socio-political experience has grown richer. This means that the possibility and need of every citizen to participate in managing the affairs of the state and society have grown enormously.

Democracy is the wholesome and pure air without which a socialist public organism cannot live a full-blooded life. Hence, when we say that socialism's great potential is not being used to the full in our country, we also mean that the **acceleration of society's development is inconceivable and impossible without a further development of all the aspects and manifestations of socialist democracy**.

Bearing that in mind, the Party and its Central Committee are taking measures aimed at deepening the democratic character of the socialist system. Among them are steps to heighten the activities of the Soviets, the trade unions, the Komsomol, the work collectives and the people's control bodies, and to promote publicity. But all that has been and is being done should be assessed in terms of the scale and complexity of our new tasks, rather than by yesterday's standards. As stressed in the new edition of the Party Program, these tasks call for consistent and unswerving development of the **people's socialist self-government**.

In socialist society, particularly under the present circumstances, government should not be the privilege of a narrow circle of professionals. We know from theory and from our extensive experience that the socialist system can develop successfully only when the people really run their own affairs, when millions of people are involved in political life. This is what the working people's self-government amounts to, as Lenin saw it. It is the essence of Soviet power. The elements of self-government develop within rather than outside our statehood, increasingly penetrating all aspects of state and public life, enriching the content of democratic centralism and strengthening its socialist character.

The Party is the guiding force and the principal guarantor of the development of socialist self-government. Playing the leading role in society, the Party is itself the highest form of a self-governing socio-political organisation. By promoting inner-Party democracy and intensifying the activity of Communists at all levels of the political system, the CPSU sets the right direction for the process of furthering the people's socialist self-government and broadening the participation of the masses and of each person in the affairs of the country.

The result of the revolutionary creativity of the working people, the **Soviets of People's Deputies** have stood the test of time, displaying their viability and vast potentialities in securing full power for the people, in uniting and mobilising the masses. The very logic of the development of socialist democracy shows the urgent need for making the maximum use of these potentialities of Soviet representative bodies.

The fact that the Supreme Soviet of the USSR and the Supreme Soviets of the Union and Autonomous Republics are becoming increasingly businesslike and effective in their activity with each passing year is most welcome. It is their duty to consistently improve legislation, supervise law enforcement and check on the actual outcome of the work done by each state body and each executive. At their sessions, the Supreme Soviets should place greater emphasis on discussing proposals submitted by trade unions, the Komsomol, and other public organisations, the reports of administrative bodies, the situation in different branches of the economy, and the development of the various regions.

I should like to draw special attention of Congress delegates to the activity of **local Soviets**. Today they can and must serve as one of the most effective means of mobilising the masses for the effort to accelerate the country's socio-economic development. As they receive the electorate's mandate, local government bodies undertake responsibility for all aspects of life on their territory. If someone may be allowed to say, "This is none of my business," this approach is certainly unacceptable to the Soviets. Housing and education, public health and consumer goods, trade and services, public transport and the protection of nature are principal concerns of the Soviets. Whenever we hear complaints from working people on these subjects, which is still fairly often, it means that the Soviets lack efficiency and initiative, and that their control is slack. But while making legitimate demands on the Soviets, we should not be blind to the fact that for the time being their ability to tackle many of the local problems is limited; excessive centralisation exists in matters that are not always clearly visible from the centre and can be much better solved locally.

That is why we resolutely follow a course of promoting the autonomy and activity of local government bodies. Proposals to this effect are currently being worked out by the CPSU Central Committee, the Presidium of the Supreme Soviet and the USSR Council of Ministers. Their goal is to make each Soviet a complete and responsible master in all things concerning the satisfaction of people's everyday needs and requirements; in using the allocated funds, the local potentialities and reserves; in coordinating and supervising the work of all organisations involved in servicing the population. In this connection, we must make a thorough examination of the relationship between Soviets and the centrally-managed enterprises in their territories, and increase the local governing bodies' interest in the results of their work.

The sessions of Soviets should be conducted far more effectively, the analytical and supervisory activity of standing committees should be more thorough, and the practice of deputies' enquiries should be improved. The committees' recommendations and the deputies' proposals and observations should be carefully considered and taken into account by the executive bodies.

While mapping out further improvements of the work of the Soviets, we should remember that none of them will yield the desired results unless backed by the deputies' initiative. The Party will continue to see to it that deputies are elected from among the worthiest people who are capable of effectively running state affairs, and that the composition of the Soviets is systematically renewed. In this connection, it is apparently time to make necessary corrections in our election procedures as well. There is quite a number of outstanding problems here awaiting solution.

The Party has always deemed it its duty to heighten the authority of the people's representatives, and, at the same time, to enhance their responsibility to the electorate in every way possible. The title of a deputy is not just something that goes with one's office; it is not an honorary privilege; it means a lot of hard work at the Soviet and among the population. And we must do all we can for the strict observance of the law on the status of deputies, and see to it that each deputy should be afforded every opportunity to exercise his or her authority.

The development of the people's self-government calls for **a further strengthening of democratic principles in administration,** in the activity of the Soviets' executive committees, of their apparatus, and of all other government bodies. Most of the people working in them are competent and take what they do close to heart. However, one should always remember that, even if its executives are masterminds, no apparatus will ever get what it wants unless it relies on the working people's motivated support and participation in government. The times are making increasingly exacting demands on the work of the apparatus. And there are quite a few shortcomings here; one often encounters departmental approach and localism, irresponsibility, red tape and formal indifference to people. One of the main reasons for this is the slackening of control over the activity of the apparatus by the working people, the Soviets themselves, and public organisations.

Bearing all this in mind, the Party has set itself the task of putting to use all the instruments that actually enable every citizen to actively influence administrative decision-making, verify the fulfilment of decisions, and receive necessary information about the activity of the apparatus. This should be the purpose of a system of regular reports to work collectives and general meetings by all administrative bodies. Much can be done in this area by people's control committees, groups and teams, by voluntary trade union inspectors, and the mass media.

The elective bodies themselves should be more exacting and strict towards their own apparatus. One cannot overlook the fact that executives who remain in office for long periods tend to lose their feel for the new, to shut themselves off from the people by instructions they have concocted themselves, and sometimes even hold back the work of elective bodies. Apparently it is time to work out a procedure which would enable Soviets, as well as all public bodies, to evaluate and certify the work of the responsible executives of their apparatus after each election, making desirable personnel changes.

Our time demands ever more active involvement on the part of **public organisations** in governing the country. When the work of our public organisations is considered from this angle, however, it becomes clear that many of them are lacking in initiative. Some of them try to operate above all through their regular staff, in a bureaucratic way, and lean only a little on the masses. In other words, the popular, creative, independent nature of public organisations is far from being fully realised.

In our country, the trade unions are the largest mass organisation. On the whole, they do a lot to satisfy the requirements of factory and office workers and collective farmers, to promote emulation, tighten discipline and heighten labour productivity. Still, trade union committees are in many cases lacking in militancy and resolve when it comes to defending the working people's legitimate interests, ensuring labour protection and safety, and constructing and running health-building, sports and cultural facilities. Understandably, such passivity suits those managers for whom production sometimes obscures the people. The trade unions, however, should always give priority to social policy objectives, to promoting the working people's interests. Properly speaking, this is the basic purpose of their activity. The All-Union Central Council of Trade Unions and other trade union bodies enjoy extensive rights and control considerable funds. both the state's and their own. It is up to them, therefore, to make extensive and confident use of them, instead of waiting for somebody else to fulfil the tasks they are charged with.

Comrades, our future largely depends on the kind of young people we are bringing up today. That is the task of the whole Party, of all the people. It is the most important and fundamental task of the **Leninist Young Communist League**. Our young people are hardworking, ready for exploits and self-sacrifice, and devoted to socialism. Nonetheless, it is the duty of the older generations to do everything they can for those who will replace them to be still more intelligent, more capable and better educated, worthy of taking the baton and carrying into the future the ideals of justice and freedom bequeathed to us by the Great October Revolution.

As Lenin said, it is impossible to master communism through books alone, it is impossible to cultivate a sense of responsibility without charging people with responsible tasks. The young people of the 1980s are broad-minded, well-educated and vigorous. I should say, they are ready for action and look for a chance to show their worth in all areas of public life. So, the YCL must make every effort to support their drive in all areas—the national economy, science and engineering, in achieving high levels of knowledge and culture, in political life, and in defending the Motherland. This effort, more than any other, should be of a questing nature, interesting and appealing to young people, and closely linked to the needs of the young in production, study, home life, and leisure.

Together with the YCL, the Party, government and economic bodies should consistently seek to promote deserving young people to leadership positions in management, production, science and culture. We say: in our country, all roads are open to young people. That is true. But persistent efforts are needed for these words not to lose lustre and the road for young people to be really wide.

By and large, the CPSU Central Committee deems it advisable to take further steps to increase the role of the trade unions, the YCL, the unions of creative workers and voluntary societies in the system of the people's socialist self-government. In particular, it is planned to extend the range of questions which governmental bodies can settle only with the participation or prior agreement of trade union, YCL or women's organisations and to grant these organisations the right to suspend, in some cases, the implementation of administrative decisions.

Our Party Program aims at the most effective exercise of all forms of **direct democracy**, of direct participation by the popular masses in the elaboration, adoption and execution of governmental and other decisions. An enormous role is played here by the **work collectives** operating in all spheres of the life of society, and chiefly in the national economy. The granting of broader powers to enterprises, the introduction of cost accounting, and promotion of the spirit of socialist enterprise will become truly effective only if the working man himself displays greater activity. We cannot put up with instances which still exist, where workers do not know the programs of their own enterprises, where their suggestions do not receive due attention and are not taken into account. These instances show that in some places the force of inertia determines the state of affairs, hinders the involvement of factory and office workers in management and impedes the process of fostering among them the feeling that they are full-fledged masters of production.

The Law on Work Collectives adopted two years ago has indisputably stimulated initiatives by work collectives. But we cannot yet say this Law is producing the results we expected. This is evident from the CPSU Central Committee's examination of its application at the Minsk Motor Works and elsewhere. Our conclusion is unambiguous: it is necessary to radically improve the mechanism that enables us to make the democratic principles and norms of the Law operative in everyday practice. Step by step we must extend the range of issues on which the work collective's decisions are final, enhance the role of the general meetings of factory and office workers and raise responsibility for implementing their decisions. There has arisen an idea of having a council, say, of the work collective made up of representatives of the management, Party, trade union and YCL organisations, team councils, rank-and-file workers, and specialists, function, in the period between general meetings, both at the level of teams and the enterprise as a whole.

Today the advanced teams which apply the cost-accounting principle are already becoming primary self-government units with elected managers. Life shows the viability of this practice. It has confirmed that in developing democratic economic management principles it is advisable to extend the principle of electiveness to all team leaders and then gradually to some other categories of managerial personnel—foremen, shift, sector or shop superintendents, and state-farm department managers. Long years of experience testify that this is the direction in which we must look for modern forms of combining centralism and democracy, of combining one-man management and the principle of electiveness in running the national economy.

Undeviating observance of the democratic principles of guiding collective farms and other cooperative organisations, including observance of their rules, is a matter which receives our constant attention. In recent times our efforts in this sphere have somehow relaxed, and too many organisations have been interfering in the activities of cooperative societies. Party and government bodies must see to it that collective farm or cooperative self-government is exercised unfailingly, that any attempts to resort to pressure or to practise armchair management are thwarted.

Our Constitution provides for nation-wide discussions and referendums on major issues of our country's life and for discussions on decisions to be passed by local Soviets. We must expedite the drafting of a law on this highly important question. We must make better use of such reliable channels for the development of direct democracy as citizens' meetings, constituents' mandates, letters from people, the press, radio, TV and all other means of eliciting public opinion and of quickly and sensitively responding to the people's needs and mood.

Broader publicity is a matter of principle to us. It is a political issue. Without publicity there is not, nor can there be, democracy, political creativity of the citizens and participation by the citizens in administration and management. This is an earnest, if you like, of a responsible statesmanlike attitude to the common cause on the part of millions upon millions of factory workers, collective farmers and members of the intelligentsia, and a point of departure in the psychological reorientation of our cadres.

When the subject of publicity comes up, calls are sometimes made for exercising greater caution when speaking about the shortcomings, omissions, and difficulties that are inevitable in any ongoing effort. There can only be one answer to this, a Leninist answer: Communists want the truth, always and under all circumstances. The experience of the past year has shown how forcefully Soviet people support an uncompromising appraisal of everything that impedes our advance. But those who have grown used to doing slipshod work, to practising deception, indeed feel really awkward in the glare of publicity, when everything done in the state and in society is under the people's control and is in full public view. Therefore, we must make publicity an unfailingly operative system. It is needed in the centre and no less, perhaps much more, in the localities, wherever people live and work. The citizen wants to know, and should know, not only decisions taken on a nation-wide scale but also decisions taken locally by Party and government bodies, factory managements and trade unions.

The whole range of the **Soviet citizen's socio-political and personal rights and freedoms** should promote the broadening and further development of socialist democracy. The Party and the state regard the deepening of these rights and freedoms and the strengthening of their guarantees as their primary duty. But the gist of socialism is that the rights of citizens do not, and cannot, exist outside their duties, just as there cannot be duties without corresponding rights.

It is essential to stimulate the activity of our citizens, of one and all, in constructive work, in eliminating shortcomings, abuses and all other unhealthy phenomena, all departures from our legal and moral standards. Democracy was and remains a major lever for **strengthening socialist legality**, and stable legality was and remains an inseparable part of our democracy.

A good deal of work has been done lately to strengthen law and order in all spheres of the life of society. But the efforts in this direction must not be slackened in any way. We must continue to improve Soviet legislation. Our legislation—the civil, labour, financial, administrative, economic and criminal laws—must help more vigorously in introducing economically viable management methods, in exercising effective control over the measure of labour and consumption and in translating the principles of social justice into reality.

We must persistently increase the responsibility of the law-enforcement and other bodies, and strengthen the legal service in the Soviets and in the national economy, and state arbitration, and also improve the legal education of the population. As before, full use must be made of Soviet legislation in combatting crime and other breaches of the law, so that the people in towns and villages know that the state is concerned about their peace and personal inviolability, and that not a single wrongdoer evades the punishment he deserves.

We must very strictly observe the democratic principles of justice, the equality of citizens before the law and other guarantees that protect the interests of the state and of every citizen. In this context it is necessary to take vigorous steps to enhance the role of the procurators' supervision, to improve the functioning of courts of law and the bar, and to complete, in the very near future, the drafting of a law, as provided for by the Constitution, on the procedure of filing appeals in court against unlawful actions by officials that infringe upon the rights of citizens. Naturally, the more vigorously Party and government bodies, trade unions, the YCL, work collectives, and volunteer public order squads, and the public at large, are involved in such effort, the more fully legality and law and order will be ensured.

In the context of the growing subversive activity by imperialist special services against the Soviet Union and other socialist countries, greater responsibility devolves upon the **state security bodies**. Under the Party's leadership and scrupulously observing Soviet laws, these bodies are conducting extensive work to expose enemy intrigues, to frustrate all kinds of subversion and to protect our country's sacred frontiers. We are convinced that Soviet security forces and border guards will always meet the demands made of them, will always display vigilance, self-control and tenacity in the struggle against any encroachment on our political and social system.

Taking into account the complicated international situation and the growing aggressiveness of the reactionary imperialist quarters, the CPSU Central Committee and its Political Bureau pay unflagging attention **to our country's defence capability, to the combat might of the Armed Forces of the USSR,** to the tightening of military discipline. The Soviet Army and Navy have modern arms and equipment, well-trained servicemen and skilled officers and political cadres who are completely dedicated to the people. They acquit themselves with honour in the most complicated, and at times rigorous, situations. Today we can declare with all responsibility that the defence capability of the USSR is maintained on a level that makes it possible to protect reliably the peaceful life and labour of the Soviet people.

The Party and the Government have always been striving to ensure that the Soviet soldier and officer are constantly aware of our society's care and attention while performing their arduous duties, and that our Armed Forces are a school of civic responsibility, fortitude and patriotism.

It is clear, comrades, that here, at this Congress, we are merely charting the general framework and the main outlines for perfecting our democracy, statehood, and the entire Soviet political system. Implementation of the Congress decisions undoubtedly will bring about fresh manifestations of the people's initiative and new forms of mass social and political creative activity.

IV.
BASIC AIMS AND DIRECTIONS
OF THE PARTY'S FOREIGN POLICY
STRATEGY

Comrades,

The tasks underlying the country's economic and social development also determine the CPSU's strategy in the world arena. Its main aim is crystal clear—to provide the Soviet people with the possibility of working under conditions of lasting peace and freedom. Such, in essence, is the Party's primary program requirement of our foreign policy. To fulfil it in the present situation means, above all, to terminate the material preparations for nuclear war.

After having weighed all the aspects of the situation that has taken shape, the CPSU has put forward a coherent program for the total abolition of weapons of mass destruction before the end of this century, a program that is historic in terms of its dimensions and significance. Its realisation would open for mankind a fundamentally new period of development and provide an opportunity to concentrate entirely on constructive labour.

As you know, we have addressed our proposals not only through the traditional diplomatic channels but also directly to world public opinion, to the peoples. The time has come to realise thoroughly the harsh realities of our day: nuclear weapons harbour a hurricane which is capable of sweeping the human race from the face of the earth. Our address further underscores the open, honest, Leninist character of the CPSU's foreign policy strategy.

Socialism unconditionally rejects war as a means of settling political and economic contradictions and ideological disputes among states. Our ideal is a world without weapons and violence, a world in which each people freely chooses its path of development, its way of life. This is an expression of the humanism of communist ideology, of its moral values. That is why for the future as well the **struggle against the nuclear threat, against the arms race, for the preservation and strengthening of universal peace** remains the fundamental direction of the Party's activities in the international arena.

There is no alternative to this policy. This is all the more true in periods of tension in international affairs. It seems that never in the decades since the war has the situation in the world been so explosive, and consequently complex and uncongenial as in the first half of the 1980s. The right-wing group that came to power in the USA and its main NATO fellow-travellers made a steep turn from detente to a policy of military strength. They have adopted doctrines that reject good-neighbourly relations and cooperation as principles of world development, as a political philosophy of international relations. The Washington administration remained deaf to our calls for an end to the arms race and an improvement of the situation.

Perhaps it may not be worth churning up the past? Especially today when in Soviet-US relations there seem to be signs of a change for the better, and realistic trends can now be detected in the actions and attitudes of the leadership of some NATO nations. We feel that it is worthwhile, for the drastic frosting of the international climate in the first half of the 1980s was a further reminder that nothing comes of itself: peace has to be fought for, and this has to be a persevering and purposeful fight. We have to look for, find, and use even the smallest opportunity in order—while this is still possible—to reverse the trend towards an escalation of the threat of war. Realising this, the Central Committee of the CPSU at its April Plenary Meeting once again analysed the character and dimensions of the nuclear threat and defined the practical steps that could lead to an improvement of the situation. We were guided by the following considerations of principle.

First. The character of present-day weapons leaves any country no hope of safeguarding itself solely with military and technical means, for example, by building up a defence system, even the most powerful one. The task of ensuring security is increasingly seen as a political problem, and it can only be resolved by political means. In order to progress along the road of disarmament what is needed is, above all, the will. Security cannot be built endlessly on fear of retaliation, in other words, on the doctrines of "containment" or "deterrence." Apart from the absurdity and amorality of a situation in which the whole world becomes a nuclear hostage, these doctrines encourage an arms race that may sooner or later go out of control.

Second. In the context of the relations between the USSR and the USA, security can only be mutual, and if we take international relations as a whole it can only be universal. The highest wisdom is not in caring exclusively for oneself, especially to the detriment of the other side. It is vital that all should feel equally secure, for the fears and anxieties of the nuclear age generate unpredictability in politics and concrete actions. It is becoming extremely important to take the critical significance of the time factor into account. The appearance of new systems of weapons of mass destruction steadily shortens time and narrows down the possibilities for adopting political decisions on questions of war and peace in crisis situations.

Third. The USA, its military-industrial machine remains the locomotive of militarism, for so far it has no intention of slowing down. This has to be taken into consideration, of course. But we are well aware that the interests and aims of the military-industrial complex are not at all the same as the interests and aims of the American people, as the actual national interests of that great country.

Naturally, the world is much larger than the USA and its occupation bases on foreign soil. And in world politics one cannot confine oneself to relations with only one, even a very important, country. As we know from experience, this only promotes the arrogance of strength. Needless to say, we attach considerable significance to the state and character of the relations between the Soviet Union and the USA. Our countries coincide on quite a few points, and there is the objective need to live in peace with each other, to cooperate on a basis of equality and mutual benefit, and on this basis alone.

Fourth. The world is in a process of swift changes, and it is not within anybody's power to maintain a perpetual status quo in it. It consists of many dozens of countries, each having perfectly legitimate interests. All without exception face a task of fundamental significance: without neglecting social, political, and ideological differences all have to master the science and art of restraint and circumspection on the international scene, to live in a civilised manner, in other words, under conditions of civil international intercourse and cooperation. But to give this cooperation wide scope there has to be an all-embracing system of international economic security that would in equal measure protect every nation against discrimination, sanctions, and other attributes of imperialist, neo-colonialist policy. Alongside disarmament such a system can become a dependable pillar of international security in general.

In short, the modern world has become much too small and fragile for wars and a policy of strength. It cannot be saved and preserved if the way of thinking and actions built up over the centuries on the acceptability and permissibility of wars and armed conflicts are not shed once and for all, resolutely and irrevocably.

This means the realisation that it is no longer possible to win an arms race, or nuclear war for that matter. The continuation of this race on earth, let alone its spread to outer space, will accelerate the already critically high rate of stock-piling and perfecting nuclear weapons. The situation in the world may assume such a character that it will no longer depend upon the intelligence or will of political leaders. It may become captive to technology, to technocratic military logic. Consequently, not only nuclear war itself but also the preparations for it, in other words, the arms race, **the aspiration to win military superiority can, speaking in objective terms, bring no political gain to anybody**.

Further, this means understanding that the present level of the balance of the nuclear potentials of the opposite sides is much too high. For the time being it ensures **equal danger** to each of them. But only for the time being. Continuation of the nuclear arms race will inevitably heighten this equal threat and may bring it to a point where even parity will cease to be a factor of military-political deterrence. Consequently, it is vital, in the first place, greatly to reduce the level of military confrontation. In our age, genuine equal security is guaranteed not by the highest possible, but by the lowest possible level of strategic parity, from which nuclear and other types of weapons of mass destruction must be totally excluded.

Lastly, this means realising that in the present situation there is no alternative to cooperation and interaction between all countries. Thus, the objective—I emphasise, objective—conditions have taken shape in which confrontation between capitalism and socialism can proceed **only and exclusively in forms of peaceful competition and peaceful contest**.

For us peaceful coexistence is a political course which the USSR intends to go on following unswervingly, ensuring the continuity of its foreign policy strategy. The CPSU will pursue a vigorous international policy stemming from the realities of the world we live in. Of course, the problem of international security cannot be resolved by one or two, even very intensive, peace campaigns. Success can only be achieved by consistent, methodical, and persevering effort.

Continuity in foreign policy has nothing in common with a simple repetition of what has been done, especially in tackling the problems that have piled up. What is needed is a high degree of accuracy in assessing one's own possibilities, restraint, and an exceptionally high sense of responsibility when decisions are made. What is wanted is firmness in upholding principles and stands, tactical flexibility, a readiness for mutually acceptable compromises, and an orientation on dialogue and mutual understanding rather than on confrontation.

As you know, we have made a series of unilateral steps—we put a moratorium on the deployment of intermediate-range missiles in Europe, cut back the number of these missiles, and stopped all nuclear explosions. In Moscow and abroad there have been talks with leaders and members of the governments of many countries. The Soviet-Indian, Soviet-French, and Soviet-US summits were necessary and useful steps.

The Soviet Union has made energetic efforts to give a fresh impetus to the negotiations in Geneva, Stockholm, and Vienna, the purpose of which is to curb the arms race and strengthen confidence between states. Negotiations are always a delicate and complex matter. Of cardinal importance here is to make an effort to achieve a mutually acceptable balance of interests. To turn weapons of mass destruction into an object of political scheming is, to say the least, immoral, while in political terms this is irresponsible.

Lastly, concerning our Statement of January 15 of this year: taken as a whole, our program is essentially an alloy of the philosophy of shaping a safe world in the nuclear-space age with a platform of concrete actions. The Soviet Union offers approaching the problems of disarmament in their totality, for in terms of security they are linked with one another. I am not speaking of rigid linkages or attempts at "giving way" in one direction in order to erect barricades in another. What I have in mind is a plan of concrete actions strictly measured out in terms of time. The USSR intends to work perseveringly for its realisation, regarding it as the **central direction of its foreign policy for the coming years**.

The Soviet military doctrine is also entirely in keeping with the letter and spirit of the initiatives we have put forward. Its orientation is unequivocally defensive. In the military sphere we intend to act in such a way as to give nobody grounds for fears, even imagined ones, about their security. But to an equal extent we and our allies want to be rid of the feeling that we are threatened. The USSR undertook the obligation not to be the first to use nuclear weapons and it will abide strictly by that obligation. But it is no secret that scenarios for a nuclear strike against us do exist. We have no right to overlook this. The Soviet Union is a staunch adversary of nuclear war in any variant. Our country stands for removing weapons of mass destruction from use, for limiting the military potential to reasonable adequacy. But the character and level of this ceiling continue to be restricted by the attitudes and actions of the USA and its partners in the blocs. Under these conditions we repeat again and again: **the Soviet Union lays no claim to more security, but it will not settle for less.**

I should like to draw attention to the problem of verification, to which we attach special significance. We have declared on several occasions that the USSR is open to verification, that we are interested in it as much as anybody else. All-embracing, strictest verification is perhaps the key element of the disarmament process. The essence of the matter, in our opinion, is that **there can be no disarmament without verification and that verification without disarmament makes no sense.**

There is yet another matter of principle. We have stated our attitude to Star Wars quite substantively. The USA has already drawn many of its allies into this program. There is the danger that this state of things may become irreversible. Before it is too late, it is imperative to find a realistic solution **guaranteeing that the arms race does not spread to outer space.** The Star Wars program cannot be permitted to be used as a stimulus for a further arms race or as a road-block to radical disarmament. Tangible progress in what concerns a drastic reduction of nuclear potentials can be of much help in surmounting this obstacle. For that reason the Soviet Union is ready to make a substantial step in that direction, to resolve the question of intermediate-range missiles in the European zone separately—without linking it to problems of strategic armaments and outer space.

The Soviet program has touched the hearts of millions of people, and among political leaders and public personalities interest in it continues to grow. The times today are such that it is hard to brush it off. The attempts to sow doubt in the Soviet Union's constructive commitment to accelerate the solution of the pressing problem of our day—the destruction of nuclear weapons—and to tackle it in practical terms are becoming less and less convincing. Nuclear disarmament should not be the exclusive domain of political leaders. The whole world is now pondering over this, for it is a question of life itself.

But, also, it is necessary to take into account the reaction of the centres of power that hold in their hands the keys to the success or failure of disarmament negotiations. Of course, the US ruling class, to be more exact its most egoistical groups linked to the military-industrial complex, have other aims that are clearly opposite to ours. For them disarmament spells out a loss of profits and a political risk; for us it is a blessing in all respects—economically, politically, and morally.

We know our principal opponents and have accumulated a complex and extensive experience in our relations and talks with them. The day before yesterday, we received President Reagan's reply to our Statement of January 15. The US side began to set forth its considerations in greater detail at the talks in Geneva. To be sure, we shall closely examine everything the US side has to say on these matters. However, since the reply was received literally on the eve of the Congress, the US administration apparently expects, as we understand it, that our attitude to the US stand will be made known to the world from this rostrum.

What I can say right away is that the President's letter does not give ground for amending in any way the assessment of the international situation as had been set forth in the report before the reply was received. The report says that the elimination of nuclear arms is the goal all the nuclear powers should strive for. In his letter the President agrees in general with some or other Soviet proposals and intentions as regards the issues of disarmament and security. In other words, the reply seems to contain some reassuring opinions and statements.

However, these positive pronouncements are drowning in various reservations, "linkages" and "conditions" which in fact block the solution of radical problems of disarmament. Reduction in the strategic nuclear arsenals is made conditional on our consent to the Star Wars program and reductions—unilateral, by the way—in the Soviet conventional arms. Linked to this are also problems of regional conflicts and bilateral relations. The elimination of nuclear arms in Europe is blocked by the references to the stand taken by Great Britain and France and the demand to weaken our defences in the eastern part of the country, while the US military forces in that region remain as they are. The refusal to stop nuclear tests is justified by arguments to the effect that nuclear weapons serve as a factor of "containment." This is in direct contradiction with the purpose reaffirmed in the letter—the need to do away with nuclear weapons. The reluctance of the USA and its ruling circles to embark on the path of nuclear disarmament manifests itself most clearly in their attitude to nuclear explosions, the termination of which is the demand of the whole world.

To put it in a nutshell, it is hard to detect in the letter we have just received any serious readiness by the US administration to get down to solving the cardinal problems involved in eliminating the nuclear threat. It looks as if some people in Washington and elsewhere, for that matter, have got used to living side by side with nuclear weapons linking with them their plans in the international arena. However, whether they want it or not, the Western politicians will have to answer the question: are they prepared to part with nuclear weapons at all?

In accordance with an understanding reached in Geneva there will be another meeting with the US President. The significance that we attach to it is that it ought to produce practical results in key areas of limiting and reducing armaments. There are at least two matters on which an understanding could be reached: the cessation of nuclear tests and the abolition of US and Soviet intermediate-range missiles in the European zone. And then, as a matter of fact, if there is readiness to seek agreement, the question of the date of the meeting would be resolved of itself: we will accept any suggestion on this count. But there is no sense in empty talks. And we shall not remain indifferent if the Soviet-US dialogue that has started and inspired some not unfounded hopes of a possibility for changes for the better is used to continue the arms race and the material preparations for war. It is the firm intention of the Soviet Union to justify the hopes of the peoples of our two countries and of the whole world who are expecting from the leaders of the USSR and the USA concrete steps, practical actions, and tangible agreements on how to curb the arms race. We are prepared for this.

Naturally, like any other country, we attach considerable importance to the security of our frontiers, on land and at sea. We have many neighbours, and they are different. We have no territorial claims on any of them. We threaten none of them. But as experience has shown time and again, there are quite a few persons who, in disregard of the national interests of either our country or those of countries neighbouring upon us, are endeavouring to aggravate the situation on the frontiers of the Soviet Union.

For instance, counter-revolution and imperialism have turned Afghanistan into a bleeding wound. The USSR supports that country's efforts to defend its sovereignty. We should like, in the nearest future, to withdraw the Soviet troops stationed in Afghanistan at the request of its government. Moreover, we have agreed with the Afghan side on the schedule for their phased withdrawal as soon as a political settlement is reached that will ensure an actual cessation and dependably guarantee the non-resumption of foreign armed interference in the internal affairs of the Democratic Republic of Afghanistan. It is in our vital, national interest that the USSR should always have good and peaceful relations with all its neighbours. This is a vitally important objective of our foreign policy.

The CPSU regards the **European direction** as one of the main directions of its international activity. Europe's historic opportunity and its future lie in peaceful cooperation among the nations of that continent. And it is important, while preserving the assets that have already been accumulated, to move further: from the initial to a more lasting phase of detente, to mature detente, and then to the building of dependable security on the basis of the Helsinki process and a radical reduction of nuclear and conventional weapons.

The significance of the **Asian and Pacific direction** is growing. In that vast region there are many tangled knots of contradictions and, besides, the political situation in some places is unstable. Here it is necessary, without postponement, to search for the relevant solutions and paths. Evidently, it is expedient to begin with the coordination and then the pooling of efforts in the interests of a political settlement of painful problems so as, in parallel, on that basis to at least take the edge off the military confrontation in various parts of Asia and stabilise the situation there.

This is made all the more urgent by the fact that in Asia and other continents the **flashpoints of military danger** are not being extinguished. We are in favour of vitalising collective quests for ways of defusing conflict situations in the Middle East, Central America, Southern Africa, in all of the planet's turbulent points. This is imperatively demanded by the interests of general security.

Crises and conflicts are fertile soil also for international terrorism. Undeclared wars, the export of counter-revolution in all forms, political assassinations, the taking of hostages, the highjacking of aircraft, and bomb explosions in streets, airports, and railway stations—such is the hideous face of terrorism, which its instigators try to mask with all sorts of cynical inventions. The USSR rejects terrorism in principle and is prepared to cooperate actively with other states in order to uproot it. The Soviet Union will resolutely safeguard its citizens against acts of violence and do everything to defend their lives, honour, and dignity.

Looking back over the past year one will see that, by all the evidence, the prerequisites for improving the international situation are beginning to form. But prerequisites for a turn are not the turn itself. The arms race continues and the threat of nuclear war remains. However, international reactionary forces are by no means omnipotent. The development of the world revolutionary process and the growth of mass democratic and anti-war movements have significantly enlarged and strengthened the **huge potential of peace, reason, and good will**. This is a powerful counter-balance to imperialism's aggressive policy.

The destinies of peace and social progress are now linked more closely than ever before with the dynamic character of the **socialist world system's economic and political development**. The need for this dynamism is dictated by concern for the welfare of the peoples. But for the socialist world it is necessary also from the standpoint of counteraction to the military threat. Lastly, it helps demonstrate the potentialities of the socialist way of life. We are watched by both friends and foes. We are watched by the huge and heterogeneous world of developing nations. It is looking for its choice, for its road, and what this choice will be depends to a large extent on socialism's successes, on the credibility of its answers to the challenges of time.

We are convinced that socialism can resolve the most difficult problems confronting it. Of vital significance for this is the increasingly vigorous interaction whose effect is not merely the adding up but the multiplication of our potentials and which serves as a stimulus for common advancement. This is reflected also in joint documents of countries of the socialist community.

Interaction between governing communist parties remains the heart and soul of the **political cooperation** among these countries. During the past year there has been practically no fraternal country with whose leaders we have not had meetings and detailed talks. The forms of such cooperation are themselves being updated. A new and perhaps key element, the multilateral working meetings of leaders of fraternal countries, is being established. These meetings allow for prompt and friendly consultations on the entire spectrum of problems of socialist construction, on its internal and external aspects.

In the difficult international situation the prolongation of the **Warsaw Treaty** by a unanimous decision of its signatories was of great significance. This Treaty saw its second birth, so to speak, and today it is hard to picture world politics as a whole without it. Take the Sofia Conference of the Treaty's Political Consultative Committee. It was a kind of threshold of the Geneva dialogue.

In the **economic sphere** there is now the Comprehensive Program of Scientific and Technological Progress. Its importance lies in the transition of the CMEA countries to a coordinated policy in science and technology. In our view, changes are also required in the work of the very headquarters of socialist integration—the Council for Mutual Economic Assistance. But the main thing is that in carrying out this program there is less armchair administration and fewer committees and commissions of all sorts, that more attention is given to economic levers, initiative, and socialist enterprise, and that work collectives are drawn into this process. This would indeed be a Party approach to such an extraordinary undertaking.

Vitality, efficiency, and initiative—all these qualities meet the requirements of the times, and we shall strive to have them spread throughout the system of relations between fraternal parties. The CPSU attaches growing significance to live and broad communication between citizens of socialist countries, between people of different professions and different generations. This is a source of mutual intellectual enrichment, a channel for exchanges of views, ideas, and the **experience of socialist construction**. Today it is especially important to analyse the character of the socialist way of life and understand the processes of perfecting democracy, management methods and personnel policy on the basis of the development of several countries rather than of one country. A considerate and respectful attitude to each other's experience and the employment of this experience in practice are a huge potential of the socialist world.

Generally speaking, one of socialism's advantages is its ability to learn: to learn to resolve the problems posed by life; to learn to forestall the crisis situations that our class adversary tries to create and utilise; to learn to counter the attempts to divide the socialist world and play off some countries against others; to learn to prevent collisions of the interests of different socialist countries, harmonise them by mutual effort, and find mutually acceptable solutions even to the most intricate problems.

It seems to us that it is worth taking a close look also at the relations in the socialist world as a whole. We do not see the community as being separated by some barrier from other socialist countries. The CPSU stands for honest, aboveboard relations with all communist parties and all countries of the world socialist system, for comradely exchanges of opinion between them. Above all, we endeavour to see what unites the socialist world. For that reason the Soviet Communists are gladdened by every step towards closer relations among all socialist states, by every positive advance in these relations.

One can say with gratification that there has been a measure of improvement of the Soviet Union's relations with its great neighbour—**socialist China**. The distinctions in attitudes, in particular to a number of international problems, remain. But we also note something else—that in many cases we can work jointly, cooperate on an equal and principled basis, without prejudice to third countries.

There is no need to explain the significance of this. The Chinese Communists called the victory of the USSR and the forces of progress in the Second World War a prologue to the triumph of the people's revolution in China. In turn, the formation of People's China helped to reinforce socialism's positions in the world and disrupt many of imperialism's designs and actions in the difficult postwar years. In thinking of the future, it may be said that the potentialities for cooperation between the USSR and China are enormous. They are great because such cooperation is in accordance with the interests of both countries; because what is dearest to our peoples—socialism and peace—is indivisible.

The CPSU is an inalienable component of the international communist movement. We the Soviet Communists are well aware that every advance we make in building socialism is an advance of the entire movement. For that reason the CPSU sees its primary internationalist duty in ensuring our country's successful progress along the road opened and blazed by the October Revolution.

The communist movement in the non-socialist part of the world remains the principal target of political pressure and persecution by reactionary circles of the bourgeoisie. All the fraternal parties are constantly under fire from anti-communist propaganda, which does not scruple to use the most despicable means and methods. Many parties operate underground, in a situation of unmitigated persecution and repressions. Every step the Communists take calls for struggle and personal courage. Permit me, comrades, on behalf of the 27th Congress, on behalf of the Soviet Communists to express sincere admiration for the dedicated struggle of our comrades, and profound fraternal solidarity with them.

In recent years the communist movement has come face to face with many new realities, tasks, and problems. There are all indications that it has entered upon a qualitatively new phase of development. The international conditions of the work of Communists are changing rapidly and profoundly. A substantial restructuring is taking place in the social pattern of bourgeois society, including the composition of the working class. The problems facing our friends in the newly independent states are not simple. The scientific and technological revolution is exercising a contradictory influence on the material condition and consciousness of working people in the non-socialist world. All this requires the ability to do a lot of reappraising and demands a bold and creative approach to the new realities on the basis of the immortal theory of Marx, Engels, and Lenin. The CPSU knows this well from its own experience.

The communist movement's immense diversity and the tasks that it encounters are likewise a reality. In some cases this leads to disagreements and divergences. The CPSU is not dramatising the fact that complete unanimity among communist parties exists not always and not in everything. Evidently, there generally cannot be an identity of views on all issues without exception. The communist movement came into being when the working class entered the international scene as an independent and powerful political force. The parties that comprise it have grown on national soil and pursue common end objectives—peace and socialism. This is the main, determining thing that unites them.

We do not see the diversity of our movement as a synonym for disunity, much as unity has nothing in common with uniformity, hierarchy, interference by some parties in the affairs of others, or the striving of any party to have a monopoly over what is right. The communist movement can and should be strong by virtue of its class solidarity, of equal cooperation among all the fraternal parties in the struggle for common aims. This is how the CPSU understands unity and it intends to do everything to foster it.

The trend towards strengthening the potential of peace, reason, and good will is enduring and in principle irreversible. At the back of it is the desire of people, of all nations to live in concord and to cooperate. However, one should look at things realistically: the balance of strength in the struggle against war is shaping in the course of an acute and dynamic confrontation between progress and reaction. An immutable factor is the CPSU's solidarity with the forces of national liberation and social emancipation, and our course towards close interaction with socialist-oriented countries, with revolutionary-democratic parties, and with the Non-Aligned Movement. The Soviet public is prepared to go on promoting links with non-communist movements and organisations, including religious organisations that are against war.

This is also the angle from which the CPSU regards its relations with the **social democratic movement**. It is a fact that the ideological differences between the Communists and the Social Democrats are deep, and that their achievements and experience are dissimilar and non-equivalent. However, an unbiased look at the standpoints and views of each other is unquestionably useful to both the Communists and the Social Democrats, useful in the first place for furthering the struggle for peace and international security.

We are living in a world of realities and are building our international policy in keeping with the specific features of the present phase of international development. A creative analysis of this phase and vision of prospects have led us to a conclusion that is highly significant. Now, as never before, it is important to find ways for closer and more productive cooperation with governments, parties, and mass organisations and movements that are genuinely concerned about the destinies of peace on earth, with all peoples in order to **build an all-embracing system of international security**.

We see the Fundamental Principles of this system in the following:

1. In the military sphere
— renunciation by the nuclear powers of war—both nuclear and conventional—against each other or against third countries;

— prevention of an arms race in outer space, cessation of all nuclear weapons tests and the total destruction of such weapons, a ban on and the destruction of chemical weapons, and renunciation of the development of other means of mass annihilation;

— a strictly controlled lowering of the levels of military capabilities of countries to limits of reasonable adequacy;

— disbandment of military alliances, and as a stage towards this—renunciation of their enlargement and of the formation of new ones;

— balanced and proportionate reduction of military budgets.

2. In the political sphere
— strict respect in international practice for the right of each people to choose the ways and forms of its development independently;

— a just political settlement of international crises and regional conflicts;

— elaboration of a set of measures aimed at building confidence between states and the creation of effective guarantees against attack from without and of the inviolability of their frontiers;

— elaboration of effective methods of preventing international terrorism, including those ensuring the safety of international land, air, and sea communications.

3. In the economic sphere
— exclusion of all forms of discrimination from international practice; renunciation of the policy of economic blockades and sanctions if this is not directly envisaged in the recommendations of the world community;

— joint quest for ways for a just settlement of the problem of debts;

— establishment of a new world economic order guaranteeing equal economic security to all countries;

— elaboration of principles for utilising part of the funds released as a result of a reduction of military budgets for the good of the world community, of developing nations in the first place;

— the pooling of efforts in exploring and making peaceful use of outer space and in resolving global problems on which the destinies of civilisation depend.

4. **In the humanitarian sphere**

— cooperation in the dissemination of the ideas of peace, disarmament, and international security; greater flow of general objective information and broader contact between peoples for the purpose of learning about one another; reinforcement of the spirit of mutual understanding and concord in relations between them;

— extirpation of genocide, apartheid, advocacy of fascism and every other form of racial, national or religious exclusiveness, and also of discrimination against people on this basis;

— extension—while respecting the laws of each country—of international cooperation in the implementation of the political, social, and personal rights of people;

— decision in a humane and positive spirit of questions related to the reuniting of families, marriage, and the promotion of contacts between people and between organisations;

— strengthening of and quests for new forms of cooperation in culture, art, science, education, and medicine.

These Principles stem logically from the provisions of the Program of the CPSU. They are entirely in keeping with our concrete foreign policy initiatives. Guided by them it would be possible to make peaceful coexistence the highest universal principle of relations between states. In our view, these Principles could become the point of departure and a sort of guideline for a direct and systematic dialogue—both bilateral and multilateral—among leaders of countries of the world community.

And since this concerns the destinies of peace, such a dialogue is particularly important among the permanent members of the Security Council—the five nuclear powers. They bear the main burden of responsibility for the destinies of humankind. I emphasise—not a privilege, not a foundation for claims to "leadership" in world affairs, but responsibility, about which nobody has the right to forget. Why then should their leaders not gather at a **round table** and discuss what could and should be done to strengthen peace?

As we see it, the entire existing mechanism of arms limitation negotiations should also start to function most effectively. We must not "grow accustomed" to the fact that for years these talks have been proceeding on a parallel course, so to speak, with a simultaneous build-up of armaments.

The USSR is giving considerable attention to a joint examination, at international forums as well as within the framework of the Helsinki process, of the world economy's problems and prospects, the interdependence between disarmament and development, and the expansion of trade and scientific and technological cooperation. We feel that in the future it would be important to convene a **World Congress on Problems of Economic Security** at which it would be possible to discuss as a package everything that encumbers world economic relations.

We are prepared to consider seriously any other proposal aimed in the same direction.

Under all circumstances success must be achieved in the battle to prevent war. This would be an epoch-making victory of the whole of humanity, of every person on earth. The CPSU sees active participation in this battle as the essence of its foreign policy strategy.

V.
THE PARTY

Comrades,

The magnitude and novelty of what we have to do make exceptionally high demands on the character of the political, ideological, and organisational work conducted by the CPSU, which today has more than 19 million members welded together by unity of purpose, will, and discipline.

The Party's strength is that it has a feel for the time, that it feels the pulse of life, and always works among the people. Whenever the country faces new problems the Party finds ways of resolving them, restructures and remoulds leadership methods, demonstrating its ability to measure up to its historic responsibility for the country's destiny, for the cause of socialism and communism.

Life constantly verifies our potentialities. Last year was special in this respect. As never before there was a need for unity in the Party ranks and unity in the Central Committee. We saw clearly that it was no longer possible to evade pressing issues of society's development, to remain reconciled to irresponsibility, laxity, and inertness. Under these conditions the Political Bureau, the CC Secretariat, and the Central Committee itself decided that the cardinal issues dictated by the times had to be resolved. An important landmark on this road was the April Plenary Meeting of the Central Committee. We told the people frankly about the difficulties and omissions in our work and about the plans for the immediate future and the long term. Today, at this Congress, we can state with confidence that the course set by the April Plenary Meeting received the active support of the Conmunists, of millions of working people.

The present stage, which is one of society's qualitative transformation, requires the Party and each of its organisations to make new efforts, to be principled in assessing their own work, and to show efficiency and dedication. The draft new edition of the Party Program and the draft amendments in the Party Rules presented to the Congress proceed from the premise that the task of mobilising all the factors of acceleration can only be carried out by a Party that has the interests of the people at heart, a Party having a scientifically substantiated perspective, asserting by its labour the confidence that the set targets would be attained.

The Party can resolve new problems successfully if it is itself in uninterrupted development, free of the "infallibility" complex, critically assesses the results that have been attained, and clearly sees what has to be done. The new requirements being made of cadres, of the entire style, methods, and character of work are dictated by the magnitude and complexity of the problems and the need to draw lessons from the past without compromise or reservations.

At present, comrades, we have to focus on the practical organisation of our work and the placing and education of cadres, of the body of Party activists, and to take a fresh look at our entire work from the Party's point of view—at all levels, in all echelons. In this context, I should like to remind you of Lenin's words: "When the situation has changed and different problems have to be solved, we cannot look back and attempt to solve them by yesterday's methods. Don't try—you won't succeed!"

1. To Work in a New Way, to Enhance the Role and Responsibility of Party Organisations

The purpose of restructuring Party work is that each Party organisation—from republican to primary—should vigorously implement the course set by the April Plenary Meeting and live in an atmosphere of quest, of renewal of the forms and methods of its activity. This can only be done through the efforts of all the Communists, the utmost promotion of democracy within the Party itself, the application of the principle of collective leadership at all levels, the promotion of criticism and self-criticism, control, and a responsible attitude to the work at hand. It is only then that the spirit of novelty is generated, that inertness and stagnation become intolerable.

We feel just indignation about all sorts of shortcomings and those responsible for them—people who neglect their duties and are indifferent to society's interests: hack worker and idler, grabber and writer of anonymous letters, petty bureaucrat and bribe-taker. But they live and work in a concrete collective, town, or village, in a given organisation and not some place away from us. Then who but the collective and the Communists should openly declare that in our working society each person is obliged to work conscientiously and abide strictly by the norms of socialist human association, which are the same for everybody? What and who prevents this?

This is where the task of enhancing the role of the Party organisation rises to its full stature. It does not become us, the Communists, to put the blame on somebody else. If a Party organisation lives a full-blooded life founded on relations of principle, if Communists are engaged in concrete matters and not in a chit-chat on general subjects, success is assured. It is not enough to see shortcomings and defects, to stigmatise them. It is necessary to do everything so that they should not exist. **There is no such thing as Communists' vanguard role in general: it is expressed in practical deeds.**

Party life that is healthy, businesslike, multiform in its concrete manifestations and concerns, characterised by openness and publicity of plans and decisions, by the humaneness and modesty of Communists—that is what we need today. We, the Communists, are looked upon as a model in everything—in work and behaviour. We have to live and work in such a way that the working person could say: "Yes, this is a real Communist." And the brighter and cleaner life is within the Party, the sooner we shall cope with the complex problems which are typical of the present time of change.

Guided by the decisions of the April and subsequent Plenary Meetings of the Central Committee and working boldly and perseveringly, many Party organisations have achieved good results. In defining the ways for advancement, the CPSU Central Committee relies chiefly on that experience, striving to make it common property. For example, the decisions on accelerating scientific and technological progress are based to a large extent on the innovatory approach to these matters in the Leningrad Party organisation, and its experience underlies the drafting of the programs for the intensification and integration of science and production, and socio-economic planning. Party organisations in the Ukraine should be commended for creating scientific and technological complexes and engineering centres and for their productive work in effectively utilising recycled resources. The measures to form a unified agro-industrial complex in the country underwent a preliminary trial in Georgia and Estonia.

Many examples could be given of a modern approach to work. A feel for the new, and active restructuring in accordance with the changing conditions are a characteristic of the Byelorussian, Latvian, Sverdlovsk, Chelyabinsk, Krasnodar, Omsk, Ulyanovsk, and other Party organisations. Evidence of this is also provided by many election meetings, conferences, and republican congresses. They were notable for their businesslike formulation of issues, the commitment of Communists to seeking untapped resources and ways of speeding up our progress, and exactingness in assessing the work of elective bodies.

But not everybody can see the need for restructuring, and not everywhere. There still are many organisations, as is also confirmed by the election campaign, in which one does not feel the proper frame of mind for a serious, self-critical analysis, for drawing practical conclusions. This is the effect of adherence to the old, the absence of a feel for the time, a propensity for excessive organisation, the habit of speaking vaguely, and the fear of revealing the real state of affairs.

We shall not be able to move a single step forward if we do not learn to work in a new way, do not put an end to inertness and conservatism in any of their forms, if we lose the courage to assess the situation realistically and see it as it actually is. To make irresponsibility recede into the past, we have to make a rule of calling things by their names, of judging everything openly. It is about time to stop exercises in misplaced tact where there should be exactingness and honesty, a Party conscience. Nobody has the right to forget Lenin's stern warning: "False rhetoric and false boastfulness spell moral ruin and lead unfailingly to political extinction."

The consistent implementation of the **principle of collectivism** is a key condition for a healthy life in every Party organisation. But in some organisations the role of plenary meetings and of the bureaus as collegiate bodies was downgraded, and the joint drafting of decisions was replaced by instructions issued by one individual, and this often led to gross errors. Such side-tracking from the norms of

Party life was tolerated in the Central Committee of the Communist Party of Kirghizia. A principled assessment was given at the Congress of the Republic's Communist Party of the activities not only of the former First Secretary but also of those who connived at unscrupulousness and servility.

It is only strict compliance with and the utmost strengthening of the principle of collective leadership that can be a barrier to subjectivist excesses and create the conditions for the adoption of considered and substantiated decisions. A leader who understands this clearly has the right to count on long and productive work.

More urgently than before there is now the **need to promote criticism and self-criticism and step up the efforts to combat window-dressing**. From the recent past we know that where criticism and self-criticism are smothered, where talk about successes is substituted for a Party analysis of the actual situation, all Party activity is deformed and a situation of complacency, permissiveness, and impunity arises that leads to the most serious consequences. In the localities and even in the centre there appeared quite a few officials who are oversensitive to critical remarks levelled at them and who go so far as to harass people who come up with criticism.

The labour achievements of the people of Moscow are widely known. But one can say confidently that these accomplishments would have been much greater had the city Party organisation not lost since some time ago the spirit of self-criticism and a healthy dissatisfaction with what had been achieved, had complacency not surfaced. As was noted at a city Party conference, the leadership of the City Committee had evaded decisions on complex problems while parading its successes. This is what generated complacency and was an impediment to making a principled evaluation of serious shortcomings.

Perhaps in their most glaring form negative processes stemming from an absence of criticism and self-criticism manifested themselves in Uzbekistan. Having lost touch with life the republic's former top leadership made it a rule to speak only of successes, paper over shortcomings, and respond irritably to any criticism. In the republican Party organisation discipline slackened, and persons for whom the sole principle was lack of principles, their own well-being, and careerist considerations were in favour. Toadyism and unbridled laudation of those "senior in rank" became widespread. All this could not but affect the state of affairs. The situation in the economy and in the social sphere deteriorated markedly, machinations, embezzlement, and bribery thrived, and socialist legality was grossly transgressed.

It required intervention by the CPSU Central Committee to normalise the situation. The republic was given all-sided assistance. Many sectors of Party, governmental, and economic work were reinforced with cadres. These measures won the approval and active support of the Communists and the working people of Uzbekistan.

There is something else that causes concern. The shortcomings in the republic did not appear overnight, they piled up over the years, growing from small to big. Officials from all-Union bodies, including the Central Committee, went to Uzbekistan on many occasions and they must have noticed what was happening. Working people of the Republic wrote indignant letters to the central bodies about the malpractices. But these signals were not duly investigated.

The reason for this is that at some stage some republics, territories, regions, and cities were placed out of bounds to criticism. As a result, in the localities there began to appear districts, collective farms, state farms, industrial facilities, and so on that enjoyed a kind of immunity. From this we have to draw the firm conclusion that **in the Party there neither are nor should be organisations outside the pale of control and closed to criticism, there neither are nor should be leaders fenced off from Party responsibility**.

This applies equally to ministries, departments, and any enterprises and organisations. The CPSU Central Committee considers that the role of Party committees of ministries and departments must be enhanced significantly, that their role in restructuring the work of the management apparatus and of industries as a whole must be raised. An examination of the reports of the Party committees of some ministries in the Central Committee shows that they are still using their right of control very timidly and warily, that they are not catalysts of the new, of the struggle against departmentalism, paper-work, and red tape.

The Party provides political leadership and defines the general prospect for development. It formulates the main tasks in socioeconomic and intellectual life, selects and places cadres, and exercises general control. As regards the ways and means of resolving specific economic and socio-cultural problems, wide freedom of choice is given to each management body and work collective, and managerial personnel.

In improving the forms and methods of leadership, the Party is emphatically against confusing the functions of Party committees with those of governmental and public bodies. This is not a simple question. In life it is sometimes hard to see the boundary beyond which Party control and the organisation of the fulfilment of practical tasks become petty tutelage or even substitution for governmental and economic bodies. Needless to say, each situation requires a specific approach, and here much is determined by the political culture and maturity of leaders. The Party will endeavour to organise work so that everyone on his job will act professionally and energetically, unafraid to shoulder responsibility. Such is the principled Leninist decision on this question and we should abide strictly by it at all levels of Party activity.

2. For the Purity and Integrity of the Image of Party Member, for a Principled Personnel Policy

Comrades,

The more consistently we draw the Party's huge creative potential into the efforts to accelerate the development of Soviet society, the more tangible becomes the profound substantiation of the conclusion drawn by the April Plenary Meeting **about the necessity of enhancing the initiative and responsibility of cadres and about the importance of an untiring struggle for the purity and integrity of the image of Party member**.

The Communist Party is the political and moral vanguard. During the past five years it has admitted nearly 1,600,000 new members. Its roots in the working class, in all strata of society are growing increasingly stronger. In terms of per hundred new members there are 59 workers and 26 trained specialists working in various branches of the economy, while four-fifths of all those admitted are young people.

By and large, the Party's composition is formed and its ranks grow in accordance with the Rules, but as in any matter the process of admittance to the Party requires further improvement. Some organisations hasten the growth of the Party ranks to the detriment of their quality, and do not set high standards for new members. Our task is to show tireless concern for the purity of the Party ranks and dependably close the Party to uncommitted people, to those who join it out of careerist or other mercenary considerations.

We have to go on improving the ideological education of Communists and insist upon stricter compliance with Party discipline and unqualified fulfilment of the requirements set by the Rules. In each Party organisation the Communists should themselves create an atmosphere of mutual exactingness that would rule out all possibility of anyone disregarding Party norms. In this context, we should support and disseminate the experience of many Party organisations in which Communists report regularly to their comrades, and where character references to Party members are discussed and endorsed at Party meetings. This helps to give all Party members without exception a higher sense of responsibility to their organisation.

We suffer quite a lot of damage because some Communists behave unworthily or commit acts that discredit them. Of late a number of senior officials have been discharged from their posts and expelled from the Party for various abuses. Some of them have been indicted. There have been such cases, for example, in the Alma-Ata, Chimkent, and some other regions as well as in some republics, and also in ministries and departments. Phenomena of this kind are, as a rule, generated by violations of Party principles in selecting and educating cadres, and in controlling their work. The Party will resolutely go on getting rid of all who discredit the name of Communist.

At this Congress I should like to say a few more words about **efficiency**. This is a question of principle. Any disparity between what is said and done hurts the main thing—the prestige of Party policy—and cannot be tolerated in any form. The Communist Party is a Party whose words are matched by deeds. This should be remembered by every leader, by every Communist. It is by the unity of words and deeds that the Soviet people will judge our work.

Important resolutions have been adopted and interesting ideas and recommendations have been put forward both in the centre and in the localities since the April Plenary Meeting. But if we were to analyse what of this has been introduced into life and been mirrored in work, it will be found that alongside unquestionable changes much has still got stuck on the way to practical utilisation. No restructuring, no change can take place unless every Communist, especially a leader, appreciates the immense significance of practical actions, which are the only vehicles that can move life forward and make labour more productive. Organisational work cannot be squandered on bombast and empty rhetoric at countless meetings and conferences.

And another thing. The Party must declare a determined and relentless war on bureaucratic practices. Vladimir Ilyich Lenin held that it was especially important to fight them at moments of change, during a transition from one system of management to another, where there is a need for maximum efficiency, speed, and energy. Bureaucracy is today a serious obstacle to the solution of our principal problem—the acceleration of the country's socio-economic development and the fundamental restructuring of the mechanism of economic management linked to that development. This is a troubling question and appropriate conclusions are required. Here it is important to bear in mind that bureaucratic distortions manifest theselves all the stronger where there is no efficiency, publicity, and control from below, where people are held less accountable for what they do.

Comrades, of late many new, energetic people who think in modern terms have been appointed to high positions. The Party will continue the practice of including experienced and young cadres in the leadership. More women are being promoted to leadership positions. There are now more of them in Party and local government bodies. The criteria for all promotions and changes are the same: political qualities, efficiency, ability, and actual achievements of the person concerned and the attitude to people. I feel it is necessary to emphasise this also because some people have dropped the Party tradition of maintaining constant contact with rank-and-file Communists, with working people. This is what undermines the very essence of Party work.

The person needed today to head each Party organisation is one who has close ties to the masses and is ideologically committed, thinks in an innovative way, and is energetic. It is hardly necessary to remind you that with the personality of a leader, of a Party leader in the first place, people link all the advantages and shortcomings of the concrete, actual life they live. The secretary of a district committee, a city committee or a regional committee of the Party is the criterion by which the rank-and-file worker forms an opinion of the Party committee and of the Party as a whole.

Cadres devoted to the Party cause and heading the efforts to implement its political line are our main and most precious asset.

Party activists, all Communists should master the great traditions of Bolshevism and be brought up in the spirit of these traditions. In the Party, at each level, a principled stand and Party comradeship should become immutable norms. This is the only attitude that can ensure the Party's moral health, which is the earnest of society's health.

3. To Reinforce Ideology's Link to Life and Enrich People's Intellectual World

Comrades,

"You cannot be an ideological leader without . . . theoretical work, just as you cannot be one without directing this work to meet the needs of the cause, and without spreading the results of this theory . . ." That is what Lenin taught us.

Marxism-Leninism is the greatest revolutionary world view. It substantiated the most humane objective that humankind has ever set itself—the creation of a just social system on earth. It indicates the way to a scientific study of society's development as an integral process that is law-governed in all its huge diversity and contradictoriness, teaches to see the character and interaction of economic and political forces, to select correct orientations, forms, and methods of struggle, and to feel confident at all steep turns in history.

In all its work the CPSU proceeds from the premise that fidelity to the Marxist-Leninist doctrine lies in creatively developing it on the basis of the experience that has been accumulated. The intricate range of problems stemming from the present landmark character of the development of our society and of the world as a whole is in the focus of the Party's theoretical thinking. The many-sided tasks of acceleration and its interrelated aspects—political, economic, scientific, technological, social, cultural-intellectual, and psychological—require further in-depth and all-embracing analysis. We feel a pressing need for serious philosophical generalisations, well-founded economic and social forecasts, and profound historical researches.

We cannot escape the fact that our philosophy and economics, as indeed our social sciences as a whole, are, I would say, in a state that is some distance away from the imperatives of life. Besides, our economic planning bodies and other departments do not display the proper interest in carrying rational recommendations of social scientists into practice.

Time sets the question of the social sciences broadly tackling the concrete requirements of practice and demands that social scientists should be sensitive to the ongoing changes in life, keep new phenomena in sight, and draw conclusions that would correctly orient practice. Viability can only be claimed by those scientific schools that come from practice and return to it enriched with meaningful generalisations and constructive recommendations. Scholasticism, doctrinairism, and dogmatism have always been shackles for a genuine addition to knowledge. They lead to stagnation of thought, put a solid wall around science, keeping it away from life and inhibiting its development. Truth is acquired not by declarations and instructions, it is born in scientific discussion and debate and is verified in action. The Central Committee favours this way of developing our social sciences, a way that makes it possible to obtain significant results in theory and practice.

The atmosphere of creativity, which the Party is asserting in all areas of life, is particularly productive for the social sciences. We hope that it will be used actively by our economists and philosophers, lawyers and sociologists, historians and literary critics for a bold and innovative formulation of new problems and for their creative theoretical elaboration.

But in themselves ideas, however attractive, do not give shape automatically to a coherent and active world view if they are not coupled to the socio-political experience of the masses. **Socialist ideology draws its energy and effectiveness from the interaction of advanced ideas with the practice of building the new society.**

The Party defines the basic directions of ideological work in the new edition of the CPSU Program. They have been discussed at Plenary Meetings of the CPSU Central Committee and at the USSR Practical-Scientific Conference held in December 1984. I shall mention only a few of them.

The most essential thing on which the entire weight of Party influence must be focused is that every person should understand the urgency and landmark character of the moment we are living in. Any of our plans would hang in the air if people are left indifferent, if we fail to awaken the labour and social vigour of the masses, their energy and initiative. **The prime condition for accelerating the country's socio-economic development is to turn**

**society towards new tasks and draw upon the creative potential
of the people, of every work collective for carrying them out.**

It is an indisputable fact that intelligent and truthful words exercise a tremendous influence. But their significance is multiplied
a hundred-fold if they are coupled to political, economic, and social
steps. This is the only way to get rid of tiresome edification and to
fill calls and slogans with the breath of real life.

Divergence of words from reality dramatically devalues ideological efforts. No matter how many lectures we deliver on tact and
how much we censure callousness and bureaucracy, this evaporates
if a person encounters rudeness in offices, in the street, in a shop.
No matter how many talks we may have on the culture of behaviour,
they will be useless if they are not reinforced by efforts to achieve
a high level of culture in production, association between people
and human relations. No matter how many articles we may write
about social justice, order, and discipline, they will remain unpro-
ductive if they are not accompanied by vigorous actions on the part
of the work collective and by consistent enforcement of the law.

People should constantly see and feel the great truth of our ideology and the principled character of our policy. Work and the
distribution of benefits should be so organised and the laws and
principles of socialist human relationships so scrupulously observed
that every Soviet citizen should have firm faith in our ideals and
values. Dwellings, food supplies, the quality of consumer goods,
and the level of health care—all this most directly affects the consciousness and sentiment of people. It is exactly from these positions
that we should approach the entire spectrum of problems linked to
the educational work of Party and government bodies, and mass
organisations.

Exceedingly favourable social conditions are created for boosting
the effectiveness of ideological work in the drive to speed up socio-
economic development. But nobody should count on ideological,
political, labour, and moral education being thereby simplified. It
must always be borne in mind that however favourable it may be
the present situation has its own contradictions and difficulties. No
concession in its assessments should be allowed.

It is always a complex process to develop the social consciousness, but the distinctive character of the present stage has made
many pressing problems particularly sharp. First, the very magnitude
of the task of acceleration determines the social atmosphere, its

character and specific features. As yet not everybody has proved to be prepared to understand and accept what is taking place. Second, and this must be emphasised, the slackening of socio-economic development was the outcome of serious blunders not only in economic management but also in ideological work.

It cannot be said that there were few words on this matter or that they were wrong. But in practice purposeful educational work was often replaced by artificial campaigns leading propaganda away from life with an adverse effect on the social climate. The sharpness of the contradictions in life was often ignored and there was no realism in assessing the actual state of affairs in the economy, as well as in the social and other spheres. Vestiges of the past invariably leave an imprint. They make themselves felt, being reflected in people's consciousness, actions, and behaviour. The lifestyle cannot be changed in the twinkling of an eye, and it is still harder to overcome inertia in thinking. Energetic efforts must be made here.

Policy yields the expected results when it is founded on an accurate account of the interests of classes, social groups, and individuals. While this is true from the standpoint of administering society, it is even truer where ideology and education are concerned. Society consists of concrete people, who have concrete interests, their joys and sorrows, their notions about life, about its actual and sham values.

In this context I should like to say a few words about **work with individuals as a major form of education**. It cannot be said that it receives no attention, but in the ideological sphere the customary "gross" approach is a serious hindrance. The relevant statistics are indeed impressive. Tens and hundreds of thousands of propagandists, agitators, and lecturers on politics, the study circles and seminars, the newspapers and journals with circulations running into millions, and the audiences of millions at lectures. All this is commendable. But does not the living person disappear in this playing around with figures and this "coverage"? Do not ideological statistics blind us, on the one hand, to selfless working people meriting high recognition by society and, on the other, to exponents of anti-socialist morality? That is why maximum concreteness in education is so important.

An essential feature of ideological work today is that it is conducted in a situation marked by a sharp confrontation between socialist and bourgeois ideology. Bourgeois ideology is an ideology serving capital and the profits of monopolies, adventurism and social revenge, an ideology of a society that has no future. Its objectives are clear: to use any method to embellish capitalism, camouflage its intrinsic anti-humaneness and injustice, to impose its standards of life and culture; by every means to throw mud at socialism and misrepresent the essence of such values as democracy, freedom, equality, and social progress.

The psychological warfare unleashed by imperialism cannot be qualified otherwise than as a specific form of aggression, of information imperialism which infringes on the sovereignty, history, and culture of peoples. Moreover, it is direct political and psychological preparations for war, which, of course, have nothing in common with a real comparison of views or with a free exchange of ideas, about which they speak hypocritically in the West. There is no other way for evaluating actions, when people are taught to look upon any society uncongenial to imperialism through a gunsight.

Of course, there is no need to overestimate the influence of bourgeois propaganda. Soviet people are quite aware of the real value of the various forecasters and forecasts, they clearly see the actual aims of the subversive activities of the ruling monopoly forces. But we must not forget that psychological warfare is a struggle for the minds of people, for shaping their outlook and their social and intellectual bearings in life. We are contending with a skilful class adversary, whose political experience is diverse and centuries-old in terms of time. It has built up a mammoth mass propaganda machine equipped with sophisticated technical means and having a huge well-trained staff of haters of socialism.

The insidiousness and unscrupulousness of bourgeois propagandists must be countered with a high standard of professionalism on the part of our ideological workers, by the morality and culture of socialist society, by the openness of information, and by the incisive and creative character of our propaganda. We must be on the offensive in exposing ideological subversion and in bringing home truthful information about the actual achievements of socialism, about the socialist way of life.

We have built a world free of oppression and exploitation and a society of social unity and confidence. We, patriots of our homeland, will go on safeguarding it with all our strength, increasing its wealth, and fortifying its economic and moral might. The inner sources of Soviet patriotism are in the social system, in our humanistic ideology. True patriotism lies in an active civic stand. Socialism is a society with a high level of morality. One cannot be ideologically committed without being honest, conscientious, decent, and critical of oneself. Our education will be all the more productive, the more vigorously the ideals, principles and values of the new society are asserted. Struggle for the purity of life is the most effective way of promoting the effectiveness and social yield of ideological education and creating guarantees against the emergence of unhealthy phenomena.

To put it in a nutshell, comrades, whatever area of ideological work we take, life must be the starting point in everything. Stagnation is simply intolerable in such a vital, dynamic, and multifaceted matter as information, propaganda, artistic creativity, and amateur art activity, the work of clubs, theatres, libraries, and museums—in the entire sphere of ideological, political, labour, moral, and atheistic education.

In our day, which is dynamic and full of changes, the **role of the mass media** is growing significantly. The time that has passed since the April Central Committee Plenary Meeting has been a rigorous test for the whole of the Party's work in journalism. Editorial staffs have started vigorously tackling complex problems that are new in many respects. Newspapers, journals, and television programs have begun to pulse with life, with all its achievements and contradictions; there is a more analytical approach, civic motivation, and sharpness in bringing problems to light and in concrete criticism of shortcomings and omissions. Many constructive recommendations have been offered on pressing economic, social, and ideological issues.

It is even more important today to make sure that the mass media are effective. The Central Committee sees them as an instrument of creation and of expression of the Party's general viewpoint, which is incompatible with departmentalism and parochialism. Everything dictated by principled considerations, by the interests of improving our work will continue to be supported by the Party. The work of the mass media becomes all the more productive, the more thoughtfulness and timeliness and the less pursuit after the casual and the sensational there are in it.

Our television and radio networks are developing rapidly, acquiring an up-to-date technical level. They have definitely entered our life as all-embracing media carrying information and propagating and asserting our moral values and culture. Changes for the better have clearly appeared here: television and radio programs have become more diversified and interesting, and there is a visible aspiration to surmount established stereotypes, to take various interests of audiences into account more fully.

But can it be said that our mass media and propaganda are using all their opportunities? For the time being, no. There still is much dullness, inertia has not been overcome, and deafness to the new has not been cured. People are dissatisfied with the inadequate promptness in the reporting of news, with the superficial coverage of the effort to introduce all that is new and advanced into practice. Justified censure is evoked by the low standard of some literary works, television programs, and films that lack not only ideological and aesthetic clarity but also elementary taste. There has to be a radical improvement of film distribution and of book and journal publishing. The leadership of the Ministry of Culture, the State Television and Radio Committee, the State Film Committee, the State Publishing Committee of the USSR, and the news agencies have to draw practical conclusions from the innumerable critical remarks from the public. The shortcomings are common, but the responsibility is specific, and this must be constantly in the minds of ideological cadres.

The Party sees the main objective of its **cultural policy** in giving the widest scope for identifying people's abilities and making their lives intellectually rich and many-sided. In working for radical changes for the better in this area as well, it is important to build up cultural-educational work in such a way as to fully satisfy people's cultural requirements and interests.

Society's moral health and the intellectual climate in which people live are in no small measure determined by the state of **literature and art**. While reflecting the birth of the new world, our literature has been active in helping to build it, moulding the citizen of that world—the patriot of his homeland and the internationalist in the true meaning of the word. It thereby correctly chose its place, its role in the efforts of the entire people. But this is also a criterion which the people and the Party use to assess the work of the writer and the artist, and which literature and Soviet art themselves use to approach their own tasks.

When the social need arises to form a conception of the time one lives in, especially a time of change, it always brings forward people for whom this becomes an inner necessity. We are living in such a time today. Neither the Party nor the people need showy verbosity on paper, petty dirty-linen-washing, time-serving, and utilitarianism. What society expects from the writer is artistic innovation and the truth of life, which has always been the essence of real art.

But truth is not an abstract concept. It is concrete. It lies in the achievements of the people and in the contradictions of society's development, in heroism and the succession of day-to-day work, in triumphs and failures, in other words, in life itself, with all its versatility, dramatism, and grandeur. Only a literature that is ideologically motivated, artistic, and committed to the people educates people to be honest, strong in spirit, and capable of shouldering the burden of their time.

Criticism and self-criticism are a natural principle of our society's life. Without them there can be no progress. It is time for literary and art criticism to shake off complacency and servility to rank, which erodes healthy morals, and to remember that criticism is a social duty and not a sphere serving an author's vanity and ambitions.

Our unions of creative workers have rich traditions, and they play a considerable role in the life of art and of the whole of society, for that matter. But even here changes are needed. The main result of their work is measured not by resolutions and meetings, but by talented and imaginative books, films, plays, paintings, and music which are needed by society and which can enrich the people's intellectual life. In this context, serious consideration should be given to suggestions by the public that **the standard for judging works nominated for distinguished prizes should be raised**.

Guidance of intellectual and cultural life is not a simple matter. It requires tact, an understanding of creative work, and most certainly a love of literature and art, and respect for talent. Here much depends upon the ability to propagate the Party's cultural policy, to implement it in life, on fairness in evaluations, and a well-wishing attitude to the creative work and quests of the writer, the composer, and the artist.

Ideological work is creative work. It offers no universal means that are suitable to all occasions; it requires constant quest and the ability to keep abreast of life. Today it is particularly important to have a profound understanding of the nature of present-day problems, a sound scientific world view, a principled stand, a high cultural level, and a sense of responsibility for work in any sector. **To raise society's level of maturity and build communism means steadfastly to enhance the maturity of the individual's consciousness and enrich his intellectual world.**

The Party thinks highly of the knowledge, experience, and dedication of its ideological activists. Here, at our Congress, a word of the highest appreciation must be said to the millions of Party members who have fulfilled and continue to fulfil honourably an extremely important Party assignment in one of the main sectors of its work. We must continue to assign to ideological work such comrades who by personal example have proved their commitment, are able to think analytically, and know how to hear out and talk with people, in short, highly trained in political and professional terms, and capable of successfully carrying out the new tasks of our time.

VI.
THE RESULTS OF THE DISCUSSION OF THE NEW EDITION OF THE PARTY PROGRAM AND OF THE AMENDMENTS TO THE PARTY RULES

Comrades, the Political Report of the CPSU Central Committee examines the Party's program goals, its present-day economic and political strategies, the problems of improving inner-Party life, and the style and methods of work, that is, all that constitutes the core of the drafts of the new edition of the Program and of the amendments to the CPSU Rules. Therefore, there is no need to set them forth here in detail. Let me only dwell on some of the points of principle, taking into account the results of the Party-wide and nationwide discussion of the drafts of these documents.

What are these results? First of all, the conclusions and provisions of the CPSU Program and Rules have met with widespread approval. The Communists and all Soviet people support the Party's policy of accelerating the country's socio-economic development and its Program's clear orientation towards the communist perspective and the strengthening of world peace. They point out that the new historical tasks are based on in-depth analysis of the urgent problems of the development of society.

The new edition of the Program has also evoked a wide response abroad. Progressives take note of its profoundly humanist character, its addressing itself to man, its passionate call for mutual understanding among nations and for ensuring a peaceful future to mankind. Our friends abroad are inspired by the Soviet Union's unremitting striving for lasting comradely relations and all-round cooperation with all the countries of the socialist world system and its firm support of the peoples' anti-imperialist struggle for peace, democracy, social progress, and the consolidation of independence. Many of the sober-minded public figures in bourgeois countries take note of the peaceful orientation of our Program, of the CPSU line for disarmament and for normal, sound relations with all the countries.

The preparation and discussion of the pre-Congress documents have incorporated the Party's ideological and political work and furthered the social activity of millions of working people.

The drafts of the new edition of the Program and of the Rules have been thoroughly discussed at meetings of primary Party organisations, at district, city, area, regional and territorial election conferences, and at congresses of the Communist parties of Union Republics. Since the beginning of the discussion, over six million letters were received in connection with the draft Program alone. They came from workers, collective farmers, scientists, teachers, engineers, doctors, Army and Navy servicemen, Communists and non-Party people, veterans and young people. Assessing the new edition of the Program as a document that meets the vital interests of the Soviet people, they made numerous proposals, and suggested additions and more precise wordings. I believe it would be useful to dwell on some of them.

Stressing the novelty of the draft under discussion, the authors of some of the letters suggest adopting it at the Congress as the fourth Party Program. It will be recalled that the adoption of new Party programs, initially the second and then the third, was necessitated by the fact that the goals set in the preceding Program had been reached. In our case, the situation is different.

The Party's basic tasks of developing and consolidating socialism, of improving it in every way on a planned basis, and of ensuring Soviet society's further advance to communism, remain in force. The document submitted for your consideration reiterates the theoretical and political guidelines which have stood the test of time.

At the same time, much has changed in our life in the quarter of a century since the adoption of the third Party Program. New historical experience has been accumulated. Not all of the estimates and conclusions turned out to be correct. The idea of translating the tasks of the full-scale building of communism into direct practical action has proved to be premature. Certain miscalculations were made, too, in fixing deadlines for the solution of a number of concrete problems. New problems related to improving socialism and accelerating its development, as well as certain questions of international politics, have come to the fore and become acute. All this has to be reflected in the Party's program document.

Thus, the assessment of the submitted document as a new edition of the third Party Program is justified in reality and is of fundamental importance. It affirms the main goals of the CPSU, the basic laws governing communist construction, and at the same time shows that the accumulated historical experience has been interpreted in a creative manner, and that the strategy and tactics have been elaborated in conformity with specificities of the present turning point.

The public has paid great attention to those provisions of the Program which describe the stage of social development reached by the country and the goals yet to be attained through its implementation. Various opinions were expressed on this score. While some suggest that references to developed socialism should be completely removed from the Program, others, on the contrary, believe that this should be dealt with at greater length.

The draft sets forth a well-balanced and realistic position on this issue. The main conclusions about modern socialist society confirm that our country has entered the stage of developed socialism. We also show understanding for the task of building developed socialism set down in the program documents of the fraternal parties of other socialist countries.

At the same time, it is proper to recall that the thesis on developed socialism has gained currency in our country as a reaction to the simplistic ideas about the ways and period of time for carrying out the tasks of communist construction. Subsequently, however, the accents in the interpretation of developed socialism were gradually shifted. Things were not infrequently reduced to just registering successes, while many of the urgent problems related to the switching over of the economy to intensification, to raising labour productivity, improving supplies to the population, and overcoming negative things were not given due attention. Willy-nilly, this was a peculiar vindication of sluggishness in solving outstanding problems. Today, when the Party has proclaimed and is pursuing the policy of accelerating socio-economic development, this approach has become unacceptable.

The prevailing conditions compel us to focus theoretical and political thought not on recording what has been achieved, but on substantiating the ways and methods of accelerating socio-economic progress, on which depend qualitative changes in various spheres of life. An incalculably deeper approach is wanted in solving the cardinal issues of social progress. The strategy of the CPSU set out in the new edition of the Program is centred on the need for change, for stepping up the dynamism of society's development. It is through socio-economic acceleration that our society is to attain new frontiers, whereupon the advantages of the socialist system will assert themselves to the fullest extent and the problems that we have inherited from the preceding stages will be resolved.

Divergent opinions have been expressed, too, concerning details of the Program provisions. Some people hold that the Program should be a still more concise document, a kind of brief declaration of the Party's intentions. Others favour a more detailed description of the parameters of economic and social development. Some letters contain proposals for a more precise chronology of the periods that Soviet society will pass through in its advance to communism.

According to Lenin's principles of drafting program documents and the traditions that have shaped up, the Program should present a comprehensive picture of the modern world, the main tendencies and laws governing its development, and a clear, well-argued account of the aims which the Party is setting itself and which it is summoning the masses to achieve. At the same time, however, Lenin stressed that the Program must be strictly scientific, based on absolutely established facts, and that it should be economically precise and should not promise more than can be attained. He called for maximum realism in characterising the future society and in defining objectives. "We should be as cautious and accurate as possible," Lenin wrote. ". . . But if we advance the slightest claim to something that we cannot give, the power of our Program will be weakened. It will be suspected that our Program is only a fantasy."

It seems to me that the submitted edition of the Program is meeting these demands. As for the chronological limits in which the Program targets are to be attained, they do not seem to be needed. The faults of the past are a lesson for us. The only thing we can say definitely today is that the fulfilment of the present Program goes beyond the end of this century.

The tasks that we are to carry out in the next 15 years can be defined more specifically, and have been set out in the new edition of the Program, and in greater detail in the Guidelines for the Economic and Social Development of the USSR until the Year 2000. And, of course, the 12th five-year plan, a big step in the economy's conversion to intensive development through the acceleration of scientific and technological progress, will occupy an important place in the fulfilment of our program aims.

Many of the responses and letters received by the CPSU Central Committee Commission which drew up the new edition of the CPSU Program are devoted to social policy. Soviet people approve and support measures aimed at enhancing the people's wellbeing, asserting social justice everywhere, and clearing our life of everything that is contrary to the principles of socialism. They make proposals that are aimed at ensuring an increasingly full and strict fulfilment of the principle of distributing benefits according to the quantity and quality of labour, and at improving the social consumption funds; at tightening control over the measure of labour and the measure of consumption, at doing away firmly with unearned incomes and attempts at using public property for egoistic ends; at eliminating unjustified distinctions in the material remuneration of equal work in various branches of the economy, at doing away with any levelling of pay, etc. Some of these proposals are reflected in the draft. Others must be carefully examined by Party, government and economic bodies, accounted for in legislative acts and decisions, and in our practical work.

The provisions of the Program concerning the development of the people's socialist self-government have aroused considerable interest during the countrywide discussion. Unanimous support is expressed for the all-round democratisation of socialist society and the maximum and effective enlistment of all the working people in running the economic, social and political processes. The concrete steps taken in this field have also been commended, and ideas expressed that the capacity of work collectives as the primary cell of immediate, direct democracy should be shown more clearly when dealing with the problems of improving the administration of the affairs of society and the state. These ideas have been taken into account.

Concern for enhancing the role of cultural and moral values in our society prompted suggestions that the education of Soviet people should proceed more distinctly in the spirit of communist ideals and ethical norms, and struggle against their antipodes. The Program Commission saw fit to accept these proposals, so that the principles of lofty ideological commitment and morality should imbue the content of the provisions of the Party Program still more fully.

About two million people expressed their ideas concerning the

CPSU Rules. Having examined the results of the discussion, the Central Committee of the Party has deemed it essential to introduce in the draft Rules a number of substantive additions and clarifications aimed at heightening the vanguard role of the Communists, the capability of primary Party organisations, at extending inner-party democracy, and at ensuring unflagging control over the activity of every Party organisation, every Party worker.

In support of the idea of making more exacting demands on Communists, some comrades suggest carrying out a purge to free the Party of those whose conduct and way of life contradict our norms and ideals. I do not think there is any need for a special campaign to purge the ranks of the CPSU. Our Party is a healthy organism: it is perfecting the style and methods of its work, is eradicating formalism, red tape, and conventionalism, and is discarding everything stagnant and conservative that interferes with our progress; in this way it is freeing itself of persons who have compromised themselves by their poor work and unworthy behaviour. The Party organisations will continue to carry out this work consistently, systematically, and unswervingly.

The new edition of the Program and also the proposed changes in the Party Rules register and develop the Bolshelvik principles of Party building, the style and methods of Party work and the behavioural ethics of Communists that were elaborated by Lenin and have been tried and tested in practice.

On the whole, comrades, the discussion of the CPSU Program and Rules has been exceptionally fruitful. They have helped to amplify many ideas and propositions, to clarify formulations and to improve wordings. Allow me, on behalf of our Congress, to express profound gratitude to the Communists and all Soviet people for their businesslike and committed participation in discussing the pre-Congress documents.

It is the opinion of the Central Committee of the Party that the submitted drafts, enriched by the Party's and people's experience, correspond to the spirit of the times and to the demands of the period of history through which we are now living. They confirm our Party's fidelity to the great doctrine of Marxism-Leninism, they provide scientifically substantiated answers to fundamental questions of domestic and international affairs, and they give the Communists and all working people a clear perspective.

* * *

Comrades, those are the program aims of our further development which have been submitted for the consideration of the 27th Congress.

What leads us to think that the outlined plans are feasible? Where is the guarantee that the policy of accelerating socio-economic progress is correct and will be carried out?

First and foremost, the fact that our plans rest on the firm foundation of Marxist-Leninist theory, that they are based on the inexhaustible riches of Lenin's ideas.

The CPSU draws its strength from the enormous potentialities of socialism, from the vigorous creative efforts of the masses. At crucial turning points in history the Leninist Party has on more than one occasion demonstrated its ability to find correct roads of progress, to inspire, rally and organise the many-million masses of working people. That was the case during the revolution, in the years of peaceful construction and in the years of wartime trials, and in the difficult postwar period. We are confident this will be the case in future, too.

We count on the support of the working class because the Party's policy is their policy.

We count on the support of the peasantry because the Party's policy is their policy.

We count on the support of the people's intelligentsia because the Party's policy is their policy.

We count on the support of women, young people, veterans, all social groups and all the nations and nationalities of our Soviet homeland because the Party's policy expresses the hopes, interests and aspirations of the entire people.

We are convinced that all conscientious, honest-minded Soviet patriots support the Party's strategy of strengthening the might of our country, of making our life better, purer, more just.

Those are the powerful social forces that stand behind the CPSU. They follow it, they have faith in the Communist Party.

The surging tide of history is now speeding towards the shallows that divide the second and third millennia. What lies ahead, beyond the shallows? Let us not prophesy. We do know, however, that the plans we are putting forward today are daring, and that our daily affairs are permeated with the spirit of socialist ethics and justice. In this troubled age the aim of our social and, I would add, vital strategy consists in that people should cherish our planet, the skies above, and outer space, exploring it as the pioneers of a **peaceful** civilisation, ridding life of nuclear nightmares and completely releasing all the finest qualities of Man, that unique inhabitant of the Universe, for constructive efforts only.

The Soviet people can be confident that the Party is fully aware of its responsibility for our country's future, for a durable peace on Earth, and for the correctness of the charted policy. Its practical implementation requires above all persistent work, unity of the Party and the people, and cohesive actions by all working people.

That is the only way we will be able to carry out the behests of the great Lenin—to move forward energetically and with a singleness of will. History has given us no other destiny. But what a wonderful destiny it is, comrades!

(Mikhail Gorbachev's report was heard with great attention and repeatedly punctuated with prolonged applause.)

Mikhail Gorbachev—
Speech at the Closing of the 27th Congress

Dear Comrades,

The 27th Congress is about to close.

It is up to history to give an objective evaluation of its importance. But already today we can say: the Congress has been held in an atmosphere of Party fidelity to principle, in a spirit of unity, exactingness, and Bolshevik truth; it has frankly pointed out shortcomings and deficiencies, and made a profound analysis of the internal and external conditions in which our society develops. It has set a lofty moral and spiritual tone for the Party's activity and for the life of the entire country.

Coming to this rostrum, delegates put all questions frankly, and did not mince words in showing what is impeding our common cause, what is holding us back. Not a few critical statements were made about the work of all links of the Party, of government and economic organisations, both at the centre and locally. In fact, not a single sphere of our life has escaped critical analysis. All this, comrades, is in the spirit of the Party's finest traditions, in the Bolshevik spirit.

More than sixty years ago, when summing up the discussion on the Political Report of the RCP(B) Central Committee to the 11th Party Congress, Lenin expressed a thought that is of fundamental importance. He said: "All the revolutionary parties that have perished so far, perished because they became conceited, because they failed to see the source of their strength and were afraid to discuss their weaknesses. We, however, shall not perish, because we are not afraid to discuss our weaknesses and will learn to overcome them."

It is in this way, in Lenin's way, that we have acted here at our Congress. And that is the way we shall continue to act!

The Congress has answered the vital questions that life itself has put before the Party, before society, and has equipped every Communist, every Soviet citizen, with a clear understanding of the coming tasks. It has shown that we were right when we advanced the concept of socio-economic acceleration at the April 1985 Plenary Meeting. The idea of acceleration imbued all our pre-Congress activity. It was at the centre of attention at the Congress. It was embodied in the Political Report of the Central Committee, the new edition of the Party Program, and the amendments to the Party Rules, as well as in the Guidelines for the Economic and Social Development of the USSR for the 12th Five-Year Plan Period and for the Period Ending in the Year 2000. These documents were wholeheartedly endorsed and approved by the delegates to the Congress.

The adopted and approved general line of the Party's domestic and foreign policy—that of the country's accelerated socio-economic development, and of consolidating world peace—is the main political achievement of the 27th CPSU Congress. From now on it will be the law of life for the Party, for its every organisation, and a guide to action for Communists, for all working people.

We are aware of the great responsibility to history that the CPSU is assuming, of the huge load it has taken on by adopting the strategy of acceleration. But we are convinced of the vital necessity of this strategy. We are confident that this strategy is a realistic one. Relying on the inexhaustible potentials and advantages of socialism, on the vigorous creative activity of the people, we shall be able to carry out all the projected objectives.

To secure the country's accelerated socio-economic development means to provide new powerful stimuli to the growth of the productive forces and to scientific and technological progress through the improvement of socialism's economic system, and to set in motion the tremendous untapped potentials of our national economy.

To secure acceleration means conducting an active and purposeful social policy by closely linking the improvement of the working people's well-being with the efficiency of labour, and by combining all-round concern for people with the consistent implementation of the principles of social justice.

To secure acceleration means to provide scope for the initiative and activity of every working person, every work collective, by deepening democracy, by steadily developing the people's socialist self-government, and by ensuring more openness in the life of the Party and society.

To secure acceleration means to bring ideological and organisational work closer to the people and direct it towards the elimination of difficulties and the practical solution of our tasks by associating this work more closely with the actual problems of life, by getting rid of hollow verbiage and didacticism, and by increasing people's responsibility for their job.

Comrades, we can and must accomplish all this!

The CPSU is entering the post-Congress period better organised, more cohesive, more efficient, with a well-considered long-term policy. It is determined to act with purpose, aware of all the complexity, the great scope and novelty of the tasks it faces, undaunted by difficulties and obstacles.

It is up to us to reach every Soviet citizen and bring home the essence and spirit of the Congress decisions. Not only must we explain the basic concepts of the Congress; we must also organise in practice all work in line with present-day demands.

Very many interesting proposals were made and many profound thoughts expressed at our Congress and in the pre-Congress period. They must be carefully examined, and everything valuable and useful should be put into effect.

The most important thing now is to convert the energy of our plans into the energy of concrete action. This idea was very well expressed by a delegate to our Congress, Vasily Gorin, chairman of a Belgorod collective farm.

"All over the country," he said, "in every work collective, a difficult but, we are sure, irreversible process of renovation and reconstruction is now under way. It passes through the hearts and minds of Soviet people and calls for complete dedication on the part of each and everyone. Above all in their work."

Yes, comrades, acceleration and radical changes in all spheres of our life are not just a slogan but a course that the Party will follow firmly and undeviatingly.

Many delegates noted that departmentalism, localism, paper work, and other bureaucratic practices are a big obstacle to what is new and progressive. I wish to assure you, comrades, that the Central Committee will resolutely eliminate all the obstacles standing in the way of accelerating socio-economic progress, strengthen discipline and order, and create the organisational, moral and material prerequisites for the maximum development of creative activity, bold search, and socialist enterprise. I am confident that this will meet with broad and active support on the part of the entire Party and of all working people.

The Party committees, from top to bottom, are the organisers of the work of implementing the instructions of the Congress. What we now need are a concrete, businesslike and consistent style of work, unity of words and deeds, use of the most effective ways and means, a thorough consideration of people's opinions, and efficient coordination of the actions of all social forces.

Sluggishness, formalism, indifference, the habit of letting good ideas get bogged down in empty and endless roundabout discussions and attempts to "adjust to readjustment" must be completely overcome.

One of the main conclusions of the Congress is that all Party committees should act as genuine bodies of political leadership. In the final analysis, the success of all our efforts to implement the general line of the 27th Party Congress will be determined by the conscious participation of the broadest masses of the people in building communism. Everything depends on us, comrades! The time has come for vigorous and united actions. The Party calls on every Communist, every Soviet citizen, to join actively in the large-scale work of putting our plans into practice, of perfecting Soviet society, of renovating our socialist home.

Comrades, the Congress has strongly reaffirmed that socialism and peace, and peace and constructive endeavour, are indivisible. Socialism would fail to carry out its historic mission if it did not lead the struggle to deliver mankind from the burden of military threats and violence. The main goal of Soviet policy is security and a just peace for all nations. We regard the struggle against war and military preparations, against the propagation of hatred and violence as an inseparable part of the democratisation of all international relations, of the genuine normalisation of the political climate in the world.

In one respect the nuclear danger has put all states on an equal footing: in a big war nobody will be able to stand aside or to profit from the misfortunes of others. Equal security is the imperative of the times. Ensuring this security is becoming increasingly a political issue, one that can be resolved only by political means. It is high time to replace weapons by a more stable foundation for the relations among states. We see no alternative to this, nor are we trying to find one.

Unfortunately, however, in the international community there are still some who lay claims to a special security, one that is suited only to themselves. This is illustrated by the thinking in Washington. Calls for strength are still in fashion there, and strength continues to be regarded as the most convincing argument in world politics. It looks as though some people are simply afraid of the possibility that has appeared for a serious and long-term thaw in Soviet-American relations and in international relations as a whole.

This is not the first time we have come up against this kind of situation. Now, too, the militaristic, aggressive forces would of course prefer to preserve and perpetuate the confrontation. But what should we do, comrades? Slam the door? It is possible that this is just what we are being pushed into doing. But we very clearly realise our responsibility for the destinies of our country and for the destinies of the world. We do not intend, therefore, to play into the hands of those who would like to force mankind to get used to the nuclear threat and to the arms race.

Soviet foreign policy is oriented towards a search for mutual understanding, towards dialogue, and the establishment of peaceful coexistence as the universal norm in relations among states. We have both a clear idea of how to achieve this and a concrete program of work for maintaining and consolidating peace.

The Soviet Union is acting and will continue to act in the world arena in an open and responsible way, energetically and in good faith. We intend to work persistently and constructively to eliminate nuclear weapons, radically to limit the arms race, and to build reliable international security that is equal for all countries. A mandate to preserve peace and to curb the arms race resounded forcefully in speeches by delegates to our Congress. The Party will unswervingly carry out this mandate.

We call on the leaders of countries that have a different social system to take a responsible approach to the key issue of world politics today: the issue of war and peace.

The leadership of the CPSU and the Soviet state will do its utmost to secure for our people the opportunity to work under the conditions of freedom and a lasting peace. As reaffirmed by the Congress, our Party and the Soviet Union have many allies, supporters and partners abroad in the struggle for peace, freedom, and the progress of mankind.

We are sincerely happy to see here the leaders of the socialist countries. Allow me, on behalf of the Congress, wholeheartedly to thank the Communist Parties and peoples of these countries for their solidarity with the CPSU and the Soviet Union!

For a number of the fraternal parties in socialist countries this is also a congress year. The problems and tasks that the very course of history has set before the ruling Communist Parties are similar in many respects. And by responding to them, each party contributes to the treasure-chest of world socialism's combined experience. We wish you every success, dear friends!

The CPSU is grateful for the warm greetings addressed to it by the representatives of communist, revolutionary-democratic, socialist and social-democratic parties, of democratic, liberation, and anti-war forces and movements. We highly appreciate their understanding and support of the idea advanced by the Congress of establishing a comprehensive system of international security and the plan for eliminating nuclear arms before the end of the century. The CPSU is convinced that they are consonant with the true interests of all nations, all countries and all humanity.

Comrades, our Congress has shown that at the present stage, which is a turning point in our country's social development, the Leninist Party is equal to its historic tasks. On behalf of the delegates representing our entire Party

I should like to say from this rostrum that we Communists set great store by the confidence placed in us by the workers, the farmers, the intelligentsia, by all Soviet people. We put above all else the interests of the people, of our Motherland, of socialism and peace. We will spare neither effort nor energy to translate into life the decisions of the 27th Congress of the Communist Party of the Soviet Union.

THE PARTY CONGRESS: HOPE AND CONFIDENCE
Notes of a Delegate

VADIM ZAGLADIN*

On March 1 [1986] the 27th Congress of the CPSU passed its half-way point. Discussion of the first points on the agenda was completed, a resolution approved on the political report of the Central Committee, and the new text of the Party Program and amendments to the Party Rules were adopted. On March 3, Soviet Premier Nikolai Ryzhkov delivered his report on the basic guidelines for economic and social development of the country, and at this writing the debate on it is in full swing.

The deliberations at the congress have differed in some rather important essentials from debates at previous congresses. Of course, formerly too the delegates dicussed in detail the proposals put forward by the Central Committee, amendments and new considerations were advanced, and wishes for the future voiced. All this is traditional at our Party forums.

A new departure at this congress has perhaps been the markedly businesslike, sharply critical and at the same time optimistic character of the discussion. There is less [of the] ceremonial (although the atmosphere is one of uplift, even festive) and the tone is more matter-of-fact and concrete. Clearly, the very spirit of the political report of the Central Committee, its frankness, clarity in posing issues and emphasis on purposefulness and the unity of words and deeds, was communicated to the delegates.

The speakers deal with unresolved problems and criticize shortcomings. As a rule, they are **self-critical**. The stress is laid on what has to be done not only to rectify mistakes, but to give new impetus to all our efforts. Not only on doing what has been left undone, but on forging ahead more vigorously. Speaking of the significance of what has been achieved, delegates are not carried away by the successes, but seek to find in them points of departure for further purposeful advance.

The keynote is **acceleration**. This is in the center of attention. Naturally,

*D.Sc. (Philosophy); First Deputy Chief, International Department, CPSU Central Committee

domestic affairs are linked with external, international affairs. On the one hand, the speakers invariably support the Party's plans to help ensure all-embracing international security. On the other, they are clearly aware that the most reliable groundwork for our successes in the foreign policy arena is our own labor, the performance of each on the job.

It should perhaps be noted that the speeches of the delegates this time are, so to say, more individual than at previous congresses. This too is understandable, for the more concrete and businesslike the approach, the more clearly expressed are individual thoughts and opinions.

Indeed, one can only marvel at the diversity of our great Party. Each of its 19,000,000-odd members is a personality, with his own unique individuality. Only to our opponents does it occur to talk of stereotyped uniformity of Communists.

The Party, of course, is close-knit and strong by virtue of its unity. But this is not the unity of some mechanically contrived giant, but the unity of the living organism, the collective inspired by single-minded determination to work towards lofty, high-minded goals. The unity of the Party is the unity of **people** working towards a common goal. It is a unity of thought and quest, of joint conclusions and bold creative endeavor.

It was this creative unity that was manifest in the discussion of the previous items on the agenda and is manifest now in the debate on the guidelines for economic and social development of the country.

Nikolai Ryzhkov's report, like the report of the CPSU General Secretary, was strictly realistic, critical and self-critical, and at the same time deeply optimistic.

It, of course, dealt first of all with the country's development since the previous congress. The results are something we can only be proud of. Our opponents abroad maintain that "the Russians are having to revise their program inasmuch as it has proved a failure during the past stage." This is something that has been repeated latterly in the West scores, if not hundreds of times. This one-sided appraisal is, of course, utterly false.

True, we have not achieved all the targets we set ourselves in the past. This was clearly stated in the report of the Soviet Premier, as it had been in the political report of the Central Committee. But how can anyone belittle the achievements registered in the quarter-century since the adoption of the first text of the Party's Third Program [1961]? National income increased nearly fourfold and industrial production nearly five times over, while the productivity of social labor more than trebled. All this made it possible to take a substantial stride forward in resolving socio-economic problems. The per capita real income of the Soviet people increased 2.6 times in these 25 years, and 267 million people were provided with better housing. The country went over to compulsory secondary education and a far-reaching reform of our secondary school system was initiated, and is now being carried forward.

All this momentous progress is what enables the Soviet Union to play a weighty role in both the world economy and in world politics.

Nevertheless, the fact remains that we accomplished less than we had planned and of course less than we wanted. The report of the head of the Soviet government gives a concrete, matter-of-fact account of why this happened—in order to point the way to a real acceleration of our further development.

One of the foreign guests at the congress told me that he had tangibly sensed the delegates' awareness of the dialectical interconnection between pride in past achievements and dissatisfaction with failure to achieve all that had been planned, the dialectic of successes and problems. This meaningful evaluation indeed offers the key to an understanding of the tasks facing the country.

The targets set for the future are truly impressive. In the 15 years until the year 2000 the object is to double the country's economic potential. Here is a relevant figure from Ryzhkov's report: the aggregate national income in 1986-2000 is to amount to 12 trillion rubles, more than in all the preceding years of Soviet power. This is essential in order to resolve the pressing domestic political, and primarily social, tasks, and to safeguard the country's security.

A very important step in this direction is to be taken in the 12th five-year-plan period. In the coming five years the accent is to be replaced on effectiveness, on higher productivity of labor, which is to lay the basis for the further rapid advance of the country.

Suffice it to say that during the 12th five-year-plan period the national income is to rise 3.5-4 per cent annually, as against 3.1 per cent during the 11th five-year plan. Anyone acquainted in the slightest with economic problems will appreciate how far from simple it will be to achieve such an acceleration of the growth of the national income.

I shall not go into the details. It is plain to see that the tasks facing the country are tremendous and far from simple. This is clearly stated in the documents submitted to the congress. Awareness of the fact is palpably felt in the delegates' speeches.

Our opponents in the West are taking a rather equivocal stance these days. On the one hand, no one ventures to deny the magnitude and significance of the tasks posed by the congress or that the fulfilment of the projected plans will result in a qualitative change in Soviet society as a whole. The well-known American scholar, Professor R. Schlesinger of the University of California, has observed that it can be said without exaggeration that this is the beginning of a fundamentally new stage in the life of Soviet society. The Japanese Tokyo Shimbun writes: "Congresses of the Communist Party are important landmarks in the life of the Soviet Union. The present congress may be described as an 'epochal congress,' ushering in a new historic stage in the life of the country." On the other hand, few Western commentators have not sought to cast a shadow of doubt on our plans. This is done in different ways. Some say pointblank that they do not believe our plans are feasible, others in one or another way qualify the tasks we have set as "excessive." And all sorts of advice is offered us.

What kind of advice?

On the first day of the congress I had occasion to take part in a direct Moscow-Paris radio hookup sponsored by the French Europe-1 broadcasting station. I had two collocutors. One was the well-known radio commentator Jean Pierre Elkabbach, the other, former U.S. ambassador to France, Evan Galbraith. The latter bluntly declared: "You will get nowhere. If something comes out of it, it will happen only if you restore freedom in the economy, renounce state planning, and give free rein to private initiative."

Galbraith was crude about it. Other advisers of the same order use more moderate language. To believe them, socialism in the U.S.S.R. can be saved only if it ceases to be socialism.

A touching picture! Diehard opponents of socialism advising us on how to improve it! It would appear that socialism can be improved only by being destroyed. . . .

No, we cannot take such "advice" seriously. Look back at the history of our country. In less than seven decades it has developed from a poverty-stricken land into an advanced power. Thanks to what? To socialism. We stood our ground in that most destructive of wars—World War II. It may be confidently said that no other country, had it been placed in the situation we found ourselves in 1941, could have withstood the onslaught of the nazi war machine. The countries of continental Europe were unable to withstand it. But we withstood it. And not only withstood it, but won. Thanks to what? To socialism. In particular to the fact that the socialist planned economy based on public ownership of the means of production enabled us to re-structure the economy within an unprecedentedly short period of time—

moreover, at a time when the industrially most developed part of the country was under enemy occupation—and to build up an economic potential that ensured our victory.

During the celebration of the 40th anniversary of Victory a great deal of weighty data was published showing the relative potentialities of socialism and capitalism as revealed by the war. It was pointed out, for instance, that for its effectiveness the Soviet economy in those years surpassed not only the economy of nazi Germany, but also that of the United States and Britain. With equal expenditure of primary materials we produced more machinery, and of higher quality than, say, the United States whose territory in general was not touched by the hostilities.

Or take postwar restoration, which it would be more correct to call the rebirth of the country. This too was accomplished in a historically brief span of time, and again thanks to socialism. Or the achievement of such summits as the first sputnik, the first man in space, the first atomic electric power station, the first nuclear icebreaker. . . . We indeed have no reason to renounce socialism.

That there have been shortcomings and difficulties in our way is not the fault of socialism. The objective circumstances and, of course, subjective failings and mistakes are to blame.

Now too our Party is firmly steering a course aimed not at narrowing down the field of action of socialism in our country but at further strengthening its foundations, at making fuller use of the potential and advantages of our system. In this we see the key to success, a key to the communist morrow.

*   *   *

There is still another angle to the comment on the congress decisions relating to the internal political evolution of the country and its economic development. The reference is to those Western commentators who have discerned in our economic plans a "Soviet threat." In what precisely do they see this threat?

The logic of their reasoning (if it can be called that) is this: the Soviet plans envisage a growth of the country's economic potential, hence its military potential and, consequently, the "Soviet military threat" will also grow. Add to this the diverse, utterly unfounded discourses on the subject of the possible "expansionist" plans of Soviet policy in one or another region of the world.

All this could be dismissed as sheer invention. However, since views of this order are being vigorously and persistently circulated, a few more words should be added.

First of all, no attentive reader of the political report of the Central Committee, the report delivered by Ryzhkov, and the guidelines for the economic and social development of the country can fail to see that the emphasis in all our plans is on **peaceful construction**. The main stress is placed on the creation of the groundwork for meeting the material and spiritual requirements of man, his all-round development.

As a matter of fact, much has been said on this score at the congress. It has been pointed out that not enough attention was paid to the social and cultural sphere and that now this omission has to be rectified and attention to this area sharply increased.

Incidentally, these are not merely wishes voiced by the delegates. The problem has already been tackled in practice. Even before the congress, following the April 1985 plenum of the CPSU Central Committee, our Party took a number of decisions on focusing more attention on social and cultural problems. Additional funds, materials and manpower—in a word, everything needed to get things going properly—have have been allocated for this purpose.

Thus, our plans are not projected at the militarization of the country, but at its peaceful development. Where, then, does the "military threat" come in?

Needless to say, the growth of our economic potential increases our capability to protect our interests, to keep our defenses at the necessary level.

Here too it is a matter of defense, not of aggressive designs. The political report of the Central Committee clearly declared that the importance we attach to ensuring our security is only natural. We could not act otherwise. For it is nobody's secret that the Pentagon already has plans for the militarization of the United States all the way to the 21st century. Nor is it a secret that there exist old plans for war against our country and that new ones are being drawn up.

It is enough to read the U.S. President's February 26 address to the nation to see that, as distinct from what is happening at our congress, Washington is orienting not on the new realities, but on the outdated and dangerous positions-of-strength concept.

We regard the Soviet-American contacts that have begun with a high sense of responsibility and have no intention of closing the doors to them. This was underscored at the Party forum. But we cannot ignore the fact that, although we now and again hear words about peace—and words, even the finest, are only words—the material preparation of war goes on, with the Soviet Union named as the potential enemy. We see all this and shall never close our eyes to it.

As regards the military sphere, our intentions are defensive and our object is to ensure the security of our country and nothing more. Our military potential is limited to reasonable adequacy, but "the character and level of the ceiling," Mikhail Gorbachev said, "continues to be limited by the attitude and actions of the U.S.A. and its bloc partners. In these circumstances we repeat over and over again: the Soviet Union **lays no claim to greater security than that enjoyed by others, but it will not settle for less.**"

Thus, all talk about our country presenting a "military threat" is sheer nonsense. Nonsense that has essentially only one purpose: to justify the further escalation of war preparations by the United States and some of its allies.

* * *

Besides the "Soviet military threat" angle, there is another aspect to the talk about the growth of our economic strength presenting a threat to someone. And to some extent this aspect acquires ever greater significance as time goes on. What do I have in mind?

The growth of the might of the socialist countries virtually dooms to failure any attempt at military confrontation with socialism. In these circumstances the center of gravity in the contest between the two systems in the world arena is shifting towards peaceful competition. Needless to say, competion primarily in the economic sphere, but also in the social sphere.

Socialism has already chalked up a good many points in this competition. Indeed, if in the early postwar years the Soviet Union lagged far behind the United States, at present the levels of development of the two countries have come closer together. On many counts we are catching up with the Americans and in some, have outstripped them.

We know very well, of course, that much more has still to be done, primarily as regards productivity of labor, the speed with which the achievements of science and technology are introduced in production, and so on. Nevertheless the dynamics of competition in the economic sphere is working in favor of socialism.

As for the social sphere, here socialism long ago left capitalism behind. Full employment, free education, free medical services, social security and low rents are something working people in the West can only dream of.

Moreover, it is clear that with the acceleration of the rate of development the social advantages of socialism are revealed ever more fully. Our plans on this score are very definite and will be carried out.

But this is precisely what our opponents in the West are afraid of. The Soviet Union's striving to strengthen its peace economy and heighten popular well-being can seem frightening and dangerous only to those who tremble at the thought of socialism revealing more and more fully its potential and advantages, those who fear that all this taken together could expose to the eyes of the working people in the West the limited potential of the capitalist system, its inability to meet the interests of the overwhelming majority of the people.

"As we see it," the political report of the Central Committee says, "the main line of struggle in present-day conditions is to create worthy, truly human material and spiritual conditions of life for all nations, to see to it that our planet should be habitable and to deal with its riches rationally. Above all to deal rationally with the greatest value of all—with people and all their potentialities. That is exactly where we offer the capitalist system to compete with us in a setting of lasting peace."

It is precisely this competition that certain Western quarters fear. For, contrary to what they say as a rule, they know full well that the basic mission of their system is to ensure not the well-being of the people but maximum profits for the monopolies.

Open admission of the existence of such fears occurs rarely, but there is no dearth of indirect admissions. For instance, it has been said or written time and again that it is in the interests of the West to create difficulties for the Soviet economy, that there should be no growth of popular well-being in our country. How many times, especially in the recent period, have there been hints that the escalation of the arms buildup by the West pursues not only purely military but also economic objectives—the weakening of the Soviet economy, the creation of additional difficulties in the matter of meeting the needs of the population. In short, the object is to stop the improvement of living standards, of the quality of life, in the Soviet Union.

* * *

While some Western commentators see dangers and even threats in our plans and intentions, wide sections of the world public derive from them hope for the strengthening of peace and democracy, for social renewal.

Here it is in place to mention the guests of the congress. This time there are more of them than ever before. Communist, workers', revolutionary democratic, socialist, social democratic and labor parties and national liberation movements from 113 countries of all continents sent their envoys to Moscow. This fact alone is testimony to the keen interest evinced in the deliberations of the congress, to recognition of the role of the CPSU and the Soviet state in the international arena.

Still more striking evidence of this are the speeches delivered by our guests and the views they have voiced in the course of numerous conversations and talks.

It is of course impossible to give even an approximate account of all these talks and speeches. But there are some basic aspects common to them all that should be mentioned.

For one thing, our guests have naturally made particular note of the critical and self-critical character of the supreme Party forum. As many of them observed, it was as if the truth itself, the unvarnished truth, were speaking out from the congress rostrum. This is seen as an encouraging sign, a token of the intrinsic strength of socialism.

What our guests consider most important is the fact that the criticism has been constructive, aimed not simply at correcting one or another mistake, but at finding the most effective avenues for the further development of Soviet society. The trail-blazing, pioneering character of the congress and its thrust to the future has impressed our foreign visitors.

The fact that both the criticism and the positive proposals at the congress are not of a pragmatic nature but are substantiated theoretically, commands attention. Many of our friends qualify the new generalizations and arguments advanced in the political report of the Central Committee and the report of the Soviet Premier as further development of Marxist-Leninist theory. In this most see proof that the Party's present conclusions are well-grounded and that it will continue its theoretical quest in the process of its practical work.

The main point made by our friends is that the congress decisions will help to reveal more fully the potential of socialism, its possibilities. And this in turn will instil in ever new sections of the popular masses faith in socialism, in social progress, in the possibility of effective advance along new lines, and thereby heighten the potential of social progress the world over.

It is no secret that the problems and difficulties encountered in recent years in socialist countries, including our country, have been seized upon by anti-socialist propaganda to undermine faith in the possibility of advance along lines other than capitalist. Our weaknesses and shortcomings have been played up to make it appear as if the striving for social changes is futile, that it can produce no results. The advance of socialism in the Soviet Union, the tapping of its vast intrinsic potential, will expose the falseness of such contentions.

Our friends and comrades from the other socialist countries have naturally underscored the fact that successes in perfecting socialism in the U.S.S.R. will strengthen the socialist world system as a whole and above all consolidate the positions of the socialist community.

The communist movement as a whole and primarily the fraternal parties of the socialist countries have long been fully aware that mechanical copying of one another's experience, the devising of some sort of abstract models, is a futile exercise. But as time goes on it becomes increasingly clear that it is necessary to make a careful study of one another's experience and to utilize the most valuable results of creative Marxist thinking in the various countries to accelerate one's own progress. In view of this, our friends from the other socialist countries have been listening with keen interest to the conclusions drawn by our congress, to the views on ways and means of giving added impetus to the development of socialism voiced at our Party forum.

Our comrades from the capitalist countries are interested in everything. In particular, they point to the experience and example of socialism as serving the purpose of exposing the long current Western propaganda contention that technical progress, the scientific and technological revolution, are bound to have negative consequences. Indeed, in the West it has become a standard argument that scientific and technological progress creates nothing short of a threat to people irrespective of the social system they live under. The fact is, however, that both our achievements to date and our plans for the future convincingly show that this is not so.

Scientific and technological progress in itself presents no threat to man. The threat emanates from improper use of technical progress. The capitalist approach to it leads to negative consequences, primarily growing unemployment, social insecurity, poverty and want. In the socialist society technological progress serves humanity, improves living and working conditions.

All our friends from the capitalist world and the newly independent countries, of course, are impressed by the social plans of our Party, by the fact that the policy of the CPSU is a policy that serves the people's interests.

The representatives of newly independent countries have underscored the significance of the solution of the national question in the U.S.S.R., the fact that socialism, through the example of the Soviet Union, has conclusively shown that the new social system can ensure the rapid development of the nations. And not only by enabling them to overcome the backwardness inherited from the past, but also by making it possible for formerly under-developed regions to move to the forefront of economic, technological and social progress.

Needless to say, they also point to the importance of the support given by socialism to the struggle of the peoples of the newly independent countries to strengthen their independence and to speed up their economic develop-ment.

As I have mentioned above, the number of guests representing socialist, social democratic, and labor parties at this congress is greater than at any previous Party forum. The social democratic delegates attach much impor-tance to the very fact that they were invited to attend. They evince a keen interest in many of the points in the political report of the Central Committee as well as the report on the basic guidelines of economic and social devel-opment of the country. Particular attention is commanded by the formulations of the political report relating to the further development of relations between the Communists and the Social Democrats. "It is a fact that the ideological differences between the Communists and the Social Democrats are deep, and that their achievements and experience are dissimilar and not equiva-lent," the political report says. "However, an unbiased look at the standpoints and views of each other is unquestionably useful to both the Communists and the Social Democrats, useful in the first place for furthering the struggle for peace and international security." Our social democratic guests see in these formulations a good groundwork for the fruitful promotion of contacts between the CPSU and the social democratic, socialist and labor parties.

All our foreign guests have of course underscored the significance of the platform advanced by Mikhail Gorbachev for the creation of a comprehensive system of international security.

"This is a congress of hope and confidence," one of the guests observed in the course of a conversation during a recess between sessions.

On this score the representatives of the international working-class and liberation movements and Soviet people are at one. We too look to the future with hope. This outlook of hope was the keynote of the April 1985 plenum of the CPSU Central Committee and now it has been strengthened by the congress. We too are confident, confident of the correctness of the Party's line and the consistency and dedication to principle of its leadership, of the purposefulness and feasibility of our plans.

Every civic-minded Soviet citizen knows that realization of the congress decisions depends also on his own labor, on his personal contribution. The personal and the public are closely intertwined in our society. This is an inexhaustible source of strength for our system. It strengthens our confidence in the future, in the success of the plans outlined by the Party.

New Times #10, 1986

SOCIALISM ON THE EVE
OF THE TWENTY-FIRST CENTURY

IVAN T. FROLOV*

Until quite recently attempts to envisage the world in the year 2000 were regarded merely as a bold projection which, although based on certain elements of scientific prognostication, contained a fair admixture of fantasy and utopianism. We recall the "futurological boom" in the West in the early sixties, born of a breakthrough in science and technology. It was accompanied by social utopianism of a reformist kind which "slotted" capitalism into the third millennium.

This trend in capitalist futurology has not substantially altered today, except for some changes in terminology and nomenclature. At the same time it tries increasingly to invoke science and high technology—microelectronics, information science, robotics, biotechnology and the global problems of civilization. This results in futurological concepts of two kinds—either extremely pessimistic, or technocratically optimistic, heralding the advent of a "new civilization," the "information society" of the 21st century in which new technology will, it is claimed, eliminate the social distinctions between capitalism and socialism.

The Marxist View of the Future

On the other hand, Marxism has always sought to determine the **real social** directions leading to the future. It proceeds from the principles that underlie **dialectical materialist** methods of cognition of the objective laws and trends of historical development. Their extrapolation into the future (allowing, needless to say, for the corrections and elaboration inevitable in

*Corresponding Member, USSR Academy of Sciences; editor of *The Dictionary of Philosophy* (1980, 1984).

the course of progress) amounts, in fact, to a scientific forecast which excludes in any form the utopianism the founders of Marxism warned against.

While pointing out that communism was the future of man's historical development, Marx and Engels stressed that "we are for continuous unbroken development, and it is not our intention to dictate any final laws to mankind. Preconceived notions of the future society's organization? You won't find a hint of them in our works." Here is a more definite statement: "But, if constructing the future and settling everything for all times are not our affair, it is all the more clear what we have to accomplish at present." Lenin also warned against going into excessive detail and giving imagination free play in visualizing the future society of socialism and communism.

Such a profoundly scientific and realistic approach to the future, to the prospects of socialism and its development into communism, imbues all the theoretical works of present-day Marxists as well. It found its full embodiment in the draft of the new text of the CPSU Program that defined—as Mikhail Gorbachev put it in his report at the October 1985 plenary meeting of the CPSU Central Committee—the pivotal points of the Party's general line, its economic strategy in the extremely complex and responsible present historical period which marks a turning point in both domestic and international development. Consequently, the turn of the 21st century is a milestone in the development of socialism as well.

Guided by the Marxist principle of steady, continuous development through contradictions and conflict of opposites, and adhering to the Marxist practice of giving systematic and historical analysis to social phenomena, our Party has worked out a comprehensive concept for accelerated socio-economic progress and the attainment of a qualitatively new state of socialist society on this basis.

In the Guidelines for the economic and social development of the U.S.S.R. for 1986-90 and the period of up to 2000 these objectives are translated into the language of concrete target figures. In this way the prospects of socialism are outlined in real and practical terms. Consequently, what we have here is the **planning** rather than just the scientific forecasting of the future.

As a result, the year 2000 has drawn closer to us, as it were, and become an immediate concern of the present generation, "a matter to be dealt with today," as Marx put it. The drafts of the new text of the CPSU Program and the above-mentioned Guidelines formulate the objectives of the present with an eye to the future.

Topping the list of priorities are certainly those directly connected with attaining a qualitatively new state in our society in the economic, social and political spheres, as well as in the spiritual life, and molding the new man. What is to take shape on the basis, and as an extension, of our present achievements will constitute, in outline, the socialism of the turn of the 21st century (continuously improving in the process of its transition to communism), civilization of a historically new type surpassing capitalist civilization on all counts. This process constitutes the essence of the present epoch ushered in by the Great October Revolution.

The prospect of building communism, and our immediate objectives which make necessary an acceleration of the socio-economic progress of socialism, presuppose profound and substantial changes in all spheres of life. The draft documents to be submitted to the 27th CPSU Congress emphasize, above all, radical transformations in the material and technical base of society and in the productive forces through continued scientific and technological advance, and the wide-scale introduction of highly efficient machinery and production processes which ensure, along with the all-round development of society and the individual, a harmonious interaction between man and nature. By the year 2000 we are to have doubled our economic potential, to have increased national income and industrial output nearly 2 times and labor productivity 2.3-2.5 times.

The Party's economic strategy is aimed, in this connection, at accelerating scientific and technological progress as the chief means of raising production efficiency. This presupposes a major reorganization of production, and the improvement of socialist production relations and economic management practices and techniques.

Humanism at Its Loftiest

New—or "high"—technology calls not only for superior production and management structures, but also for high standards of social relations, culture and environmental ethics. Under socialism, however, this is not merely a "technological" demand. As it gears the entire social process to the good and interests of man and makes his all-round development the **aim in itself**—i.e., places the main emphasis on **humanist values**, socialist society—which is developing into communist society in the course of its improvement—subordinates all spheres of life to this objective. The Party's program documents point out that in terms of social progress this means the promotion of socialist self-government and its advance towards communist self-government—the highest form of social organization.

There is still a long way to go in this direction. But we dismiss as absurd assertions by bourgeois ideologists to the effect that our system is "non-democratic" and "authoritarian." We criticize the concepts of "state socialism" afflicted with "bureaucratic-etatist" metastases as concepts directed against Soviet, socialist democrary.

The new text of the CPSU Program gives an objective assessment to what has been done and clearly outlines the prospects for the process in the course of which "the activity of state organs will assume an increasingly non-political character, and the state as a specific political institution will gradually become redundant." At the same time the draft notes the complexity of this process and the need, under present-day conditions, for the development and strengthening of the Soviet socialist state, and an ever fuller disclosure of its democratic and popular character along with promoting the people's self-government in every way. This calls for the optimum functioning of the Soviets of People's Deputies, which constitute the political foundation of the U.S.S.R. and the chief link in the people's socialist self-government. The working people, work collectives and mass organizations must be more actively and effectively involved in dealing with state and social questions and democratization of management and decision-making at the state level through selecting the best suggestions, considering and comparing various opinions, and so on.

All this is a tangible demonstration of the humanist nature of socialism and its advantages over capitalism, which to an ever greater extent alienates man both on the production and social planes and makes him the object of ever more refined exploitation.

This further aggravates the main contradiction of our time, that between socialism and capitalism, in its new manifestations. These relate to the social systems' potential, and its ability to offer immediate and real solutions to the global problems on which mankind's very existence and development depends. On the eve of the 21st century socialism will assert itself more and more as a social system capable, in the highest degree, of solving the global problems of civilization for the good of humanity.

The program documents pay due attention to these problems. This is especially true of global problem No. 1—safeguarding peace and ending the arms race. Note is taken of the fact that no **scientific** forecasts of what socialism will be like on the eve of the 21st century are possible without tracing its wider relationships and interdependencies on a global scale.

In his statement of January 15 [1986], Mikhail Gorbachev, General Secretary of the CPSU Central Committee, specially underscored the need for a change for the better in the international arena. The Soviet Union has come up with a program of stage-by-stage consecutive action to **free the**

**world from nuclear weapons within the next fifteen years, i.e., before
this century is out.** This program contains concrete and realistic proposals
taking into account many aspects of the contemporary political situation and
the prospects for its development up to the year 2000.

The changeover to vigorous action aimed at ending the arms race and
reducing armaments is tied up with the need to solve the ever more urgent
global problems involved in protecting the environment, searching for new
energy sources, combating economic backwardness, famine and disease. A
future without wars, and without arms—this is the prospect opened up by
the Soviet proposals aimed at achieving a lasting peace and nuclear disarmament towards the end of the 20th century.

Internal Growth Potential

In drawing up its strategy for peace and social progress in the international
arena, the CPSU attaches prime importance to the further promotion of
friendly links between our country and the other socialist states in all spheres:
economic, scientific, technical, ideological, interparty relations and international activity. The new text of the CPSU Program lays special emphasis
on the activization of all forms of political cooperation, the deepening of
socialist economic integration, "the pooling of the fraternal countries' efforts
in all key areas involved in the intensification of production and the speeding
up of scientific and technological progress so as to accomplish together an
objective of historic importance—the advancement to the forefront of science
and technology with a view to raising still higher their nations' living standards and strengthening their security."

The Comprehensive Program of scientific and technological progress of
the CMEA member states in the period of up to 2000, adopted by the 41st
(special) CMEA session in December 1985 (which is to become the basis
of a coordinated and, in many cases, joint scientific and technological policy),
sets the following priority lines of scientific and technological progress:
electronization of the national economy, comprehensive automation including
the introduction of flexible automated systems, atomic power engineering,
the development of new materials and the techniques of their production
and treatment, and biotechnology.

In perspective, economic, scientific and technological cooperation among
the CMEA member states will be assuming new forms and tendencies characteristic of socialism which, as the new text of the CPSU Program points
out, "is to increase socialist countries' technological and economic immunity

against the hostile actions of imperialism and the impact of economic crises and other negative processes characteristic of capitalism."

This does not mean, of course, that the countries of the socialist community will refrain from promoting extensive economic, scientific and technological relations with the countries of the capitalist system. The world economy and world science are a reality, and there is no ignoring it if maximum results and the highest possible standard of research are to be attained. Therefore our Party's main program documents stress the need for promoting and improving the forms of cooperation with capitalist countries on the basis of mutual benefit and equality. The latter condition is of substantial importance, the idea being that socialism cannot allow its further development to become dependent in any way on external circumstances, including not only hostile actions on the part of imperialism, but the world economic, research and technological situation in general.

Depending on its own growth potential, world socialism will increasingly reveal, on the eve of the 21st century, the wealth and variety of its advantages and its possibilities for improvement. Extremely important in this connection are the theses and conclusions found in the new text of the CPSU Program which have to do with the accomplishment of such international objectives as strengthening the unity, building up the might and increasing the influence of the socialist community, with due account taken, at the same time, of the uneven levels of its countries' economic and political development, their historical and cultural traditions and the conditions obtaining in them.

Noting the fact that their social development does not always follow a straight line and that its every major stage poses new complex problems— the solution of which involves struggle, creative quests and the surmounting of certain contradictions and difficulties—the CPSU stresses the need for all-round cooperation lest there should appear grounds for differences capable of doing damage to common interests. "The experience of the CPSU and of world socialism as a whole shows that the vital factors for its successful advance are: loyalty of the ruling Communist and Workers' parties to the teaching of Marxism-Leninism, creative application of this teaching, close ties between the Party and the broad masses of the working people, the consolidation of the parties' authority and leading role in society, strict observance of Leninist norms of Party and state life, the promotion of socialist government of the people; due regard for the real situation, the timely and scientifically substantiated solution of problems that arise; basing relations with the other fraternal countries on the principles of socialist internationalism," says the new text of our Party's Program.

Special importance attaches in this connection to the pooling of the fraternal parties' efforts in the study and application of the experience gained in socialist construction, communist education of the working people, in the development of Marxist-Leninist theory, the deepening of its creative character, and upholding its revolutionary essence. The activization of collective thinking, a steady expansion of intellectual exchanges, and cooperation in the fields of science and culture contribute to the further deepening of friendship amongst the socialist countries.

This activity in the sphere of ideology has many components and presupposes a higher degree of coordination. "Disseminating the truth about socialism, exposing imperialist policy and propaganda, repulsing anti-communism and anti-Sovietism, fighting dogmatic and revisionist views—all this is achieved more successfully when the Communists act as a united front." This is not merely a wish for the future but a conclusion drawn from the vast positive (and, most unfortunately, negative) experience accumulated in the course of the development of world socialism and its theory.

The Pluralists' Gordian Knot

Today we witness numerous attempts—made not only beyond but, in a number of cases, within the bounds of Marxist socialist thought—to prove that there is such a thing as "the crisis of Marxism." Our Party's program documents and works by Marxist scholars analyzing the problems of today give the lie to this allegation which, more often than not, merely reveals the theoretical sterility of certain Marxists.

Many modern discussions on socialism on the eve of the 21st century have created a kind of Gordian knot (in addition to the real problems and contradictions). This knot cannot be untied by means of abstract theoretical discussion. It must be cut using facts drawn from life, which means identifying new and positive trends and problems in socialism on which its future depends.

Goethe said in his time: "In the beginning was the Deed!" And more: "Dear friend, all theory is grey, but the tree of life is green." In the beginning was the deed of the Great October Revolution. Today its word and thought and the strength of the advanced class that saw it through have not spent themselves as it is sometimes alleged, but have enhanced their creative potential and are the guiding force of the socialist nations and the progressives across the world. Creative Marxism is alien to dogmatism, scholastic theorizing and didacticism, which are rooted in the past, and to the manipulation of notions and ideas, behavior stereotypes and patterns of thought overcome by the very course of socialist development.

A look at present-day practice and at the future of Marxism and socialism will show that the concept of "pluralizing Marxist and socialist thought" is groundless. It is beneath serious scientific and theoretical criticism. Indeed, its adherents concentrate on just one aspect of the process—the need for a difference of opinion—which calls for dialogue, and so on. They fail to take account of the fact that all this is merely the external manifestation of the scientific pursuit of the objective truth which is indivisible and independent of subjective opinions, geographical and national characteristics.

The concept of "pluralizing Marxist and socialist thought," which leads to the distortion of the scientific principles of the dialogue on the problems of socialism on the eve of the 21st century is attended by direct attacks against socialism—as is unfortunately the case in a number of publications on the subject "Socialism on the Eve of the 21st Century" under discussion here.

The new text of the CPSU Program points out that "while remaining fully equal, and respectful of each other's national interests, the socialist countries will move towards ever greater mutual understanding and draw ever closer together. The Party will facilitate this historically progressive process." The course taken by the competition between socialism and capitalism and the future of world civilization depend on the successes of each socialist country's creative work and on the unity, might and influence of the socialist community as a whole.

New Times #7, 1986

Commentary

ACCELERATION STRATEGY—LENINISM IN ACTION

EDWARD A. SHEVARDNADZE*

Comrades,

On the birth anniversary of Vladimir Ilyich Lenin we would like to express in some special way our attitude to his personality, activity and heritage. But all limits are too narrow for Lenin's life. The best way to express our feelings is to be loyal to his example and his behests in our deeds. This is the sole criterion for any Leninist.

Memory is not a monument. It leads us into a future where Lenin's thought is applied creatively, in the context of the day. While marching forward, we ever more deeply come to understand the intransient force of Lenin's ideas.

This force was given to Lenin by Russia, his native land, the Russia of the people's rebels and Decembrists, Lomonosov and Radishchev, Pushkin and Gogol, Chernyshevsky and Herzen, Dostoyevsky and Tolstoi, the Russia of People's Freedom and the first Marxists. The phenomenon of Lenin was prepared by the life and struggle of the Russian proletariat and of all generations of revolutionaries, by their elan to win happiness for the people. But he, a truly Russian genius, processed immense layers of world thought, creatively developed the doctrine of Marx and Engels, and became a recognized leader of the nations, of all working people in the world.

Deep knowledge and practical use of the laws of social development underlie the entire activity of the Party of Bolsheviks which he founded and which mobilized the masses of people to a selfless revolutionary struggle and led them to the triumph of the Great October Revolution.

To continue Lenin's cause today means to us to undeviatingly follow the spirit of Leninism in our day-to-day work, in all our accomplishments. The changes which are now taking place in the country's affairs are inseparable from the methods of Lenin's analysis of reality and of the innovatory employment of them at a time most crucial for the world. In the new historic

*Speech by the Foreign Minister of the USSR at a gala observance of the 116th anniversary of Lenin's birth (April 23, 1986).

conditions the Party consults Lenin and finds in his works clear answers to the complex problems of the present day.

Like at the dawn of the revolutionary era, Lenin's theory illuminates our road to the aims set; the Leninist policy helps us pursue a correct line, and the crystally pure and integral life of Lenin gives us an ethic example.

Our anniversary meeting is not a tribute to ritual but a deep spiritual demand to collate our work with Lenin's ideas. The Party and the people are marking his birthday anniversary by an upsurge of new energy in which the deeds and words are at one.

Following the Course of the 27th Party Congress Means Following Lenin's Course

Comrades,

We feel an unbreakable intrinsic connection between the present Lenin commemorations and the 27th Party Congress. As an event that best carried forward Lenin's traditions, it demonstrated loyalty to the heritage of Vladimir Ilyich in all of its components. The major ones of them are the full-scale formulation of bold, revolutionary priorities and the innovative strategy for their solution. No less important in the characterization of the Congress was the climate of the Bolshevik fidelity to principle and truth due to which it responded by its very substance to the most burning social requirements.

This direction and this turn for the Congress were set by Mikhail Gorbachev in the Political Report which combined allegiance to our fundamental principles with the novelty of views and revolutionary optimism—with the courage of criticism and accuracy of political vocabulary—with striking imagery. Every priority as it was set and every conclusion as it was made induced thinking and equipped it with a fresh vision of the problems.

The Political Report, the updated Party Program, the Guidelines for the Economic and Social Development of the USSR, the resolutions of the Congress and its other documents are the latest achievement of creative Marxist-Leninist thought and a major contribution to the theory and practice of scientific Communism.

It took political will, audacity of ideas and resolute action to raise and discuss the issues the way they were raised and discussed at the 27th Congress. It took thorough knowledge of life, and an ability to assess the situation realistically as Lenin would and to drop what had outlived itself. It was necessary to determine clearly and unerringly how the outstanding problems had to be resolved and what forces and instruments had to be brought into action.

Let us say straight: such a Congress would have been impossible without the March Plenary Meeting of the Central Committee, without the new line hammered out by the Party at the April Plenary Meeting, without remanning key offices. In this respect, too, the Party has been true to Lenin who held success to depend on the way the Party could promote "its advanced representatives capable of organizing and leading the movement."

The concept of acceleration, formulated at the April Plenary Meeting and carried forward through the decisions of the Congress, reposes on the proper consideration of our achievements and reserves.

The ground for the present renewal has been laid by the entire previous development of Soviet society. The nation has an extensive productive and scientific potential at its disposal. In the last quarter century, Soviet industry advanced at twice the rate of the advanced capitalist countries. The living standards increased considerably. The USSR has strengthened its world positions. Its defense capability has grown, and the Soviet people's constructive work is under dependable protection.

Yet, the building of a new society is not a one-line process. Against the background of overall progress, occasional fall-offs and let-ups in the rates of growth may occur for various reasons. The Party has learned a good lesson from past failures and mistakes and at the Congress analyzed, in depth and with a sense of responsibility, the past and cleared the way to the future.

We have embarked upon a long-term policy of accelerating the country's social and economic development. The main elements of this policy are a strong economy oriented on scientific and technological progress and the highest level of labor productivity, mobile and flexible management of the economy, broad democratization of the political and economic sphere, and vigorous and integral social policy. A key to the implementation of this policy is creative activity of the masses, which, at the new stage of social development, can and must reveal its vast potential to the fullest extent.

A year has passed since the April Plenum. What has changed? The trend, above all. The atmosphere, the pace of life and people's attitudes are changing. It is highly significant that we have received the first answer to the question about whether the acceleration policy is realistic or not. We now have a clear program of action and we know how to go about it. The Party has succeeded in bringing about a change for the better in the economy. A series of crucial decisions have been taken to restructure the production, social and other spheres of life. The style of work of Party, government and economic bodies is changing. Bold, innovative approaches are being adopted in foreign policy.

Comrades, it is the same with nature: spring does not come overnight, though people want to feel its renovating strength everywhere. The ambitious reconstruction program launched in the country is projected for years to come, but people want changes now. They are right when they demand that things be set to rights and discipline be fostered everywhere; in industrial plants, in city streets, in transport, on collective farm markets, in shops, in hospitals, in cultural institutions and in the services. People want to be treated with consideration and concern everywhere. In this we should invest not only billions of rubles but also our heart and soul.

As Lenin said, "what we need now is practical work and practical results." That was how Mikhail Sergeyevich formulated our tasks in his address to the residents of Togliatti. We want people to see that the decisions of the Congress are being put into practice.

Comrades, you know the rates of acceleration we are to achieve. It is an extremely difficult task; in a matter of 15 years we are to double the country's production potential and national income and we must do so on a qualitatively new basis. A mighty and advanced economy is the initial base of our future and of the implementation of all our long-term projects. Lenin emphasized that economic development "is our most correct cause from the point of view of both principle and practice . . . and also from the international point of view." We must win in peaceful competition with capitalism by economic means. We have no alternative. The future of socialism depends on this. And the future of humankind.

Having put the task this particular way, the Congress has stressed that we must get into the swing of it at once. Reconstruction must be done quickly, at high rates and, just as importantly, in a competent and intelligent manner. Lenin had repeatedly emphasized the importance of the time factor when dealing with drastic changes in the life of the country. Winning time, he said, means winning everything.

The Congress has given practical meaning to Lenin's formula about a higher standard of labor productivity compared to capitalism. This has provided a clear working criterion for the contemporary scientific and technical, structural and investment policies and has indicated a precise measure for evaluating the end results of all our work to implement the decisions of the Congress.

If one is to recall the unprecedentedly short historical terms within which we have created a powerful industry, accomplished collectivization and Lenin-designed cultural revolution, restored the economy ravaged by the war, developed the virgin lands and started peaceful exploration of space, despite all its complexity the task set by the Congress appears quite feasible. Everything accumulated by the previous generations provides a foundation for the projected acceleration. On this powerful basis we will move on to new frontiers.

The opening year of the 12th Five-Year Plan has started succesfully, but the Central Committee warns that there are no grounds for complacency. In this five-year period we must lay a firm foundation for production intensification so that we could proceed faster in all the directions of social and economic development. That is why the project rates of economic growth for 1986 are very high indeed. This also presupposes a higher standard of economic thinking. This is because, to put it frankly, there are also people who think as follows; let us wait for the arrival of new-generation equipment, and then we will speed up everything. This is an erroneous view. Concentrating efforts on rapid development and introduction of advanced technology, the Party calls for maximum efficiency in the use of the available production potential, for the actuation of all reserves and for the improvement of labour discipline and work organization.

The principal yardstick here is quality. Product quality. Work quality. This multi-faceted category is an organic fusion of economics and design, technology and conscience, worker's prestige, state authority and consumers' interests. As it has been aptly put, an article bearing a trademark is not only a visiting card but also a credit book of each particular enterprise.

All too often the Soviet people put low marks in that book. Why so? Some managers and executives are stubbornly beckoning to objective reasons. In the meantime, the example of the enterprising and resourceful people and works indicates that these causes often have a personal, subjective character.

The things of the past are the products of foregoing mentality.

In broader terms, no major economic or social issue can be resolved as long as the problem of quality is unresolved. It would be unrealistic not to link it with transition to the cost accounting system, self-financing of enterprises and a steady growth of profitability.

So those work collectives which do care about the prestige of their products, both at home and abroad, are to be praised and encouraged. It would be in line with the principles of social justice to allow them to profit in one way or another from their good work.

Bad management and incompetence, productive expenses and working time wastes inflict enormous damage. But no account is to be made of the damage inflicted by wasting talent, stifling initiative and innovation and curbing people's desire to think and live in a new way.

The decisions of the Congress mark a decisive turn in this field, too. The system of management is being drastically reformed. The idea behind it is this: the central agencies shall spell out key economic issues to be tackled by local bodies with greater autonomy and responsibility. Departments shall not hamper regional development, while regions shall promote the development of economic sectors. A skillful blend of centralized management with local initiative, of sectoral development with territorial affairs and removal of unnecessary links will make management flexible.

It is impossible to run the affairs the old way under new conditions. The old system of economic management, largely based on all kinds of limits and bans, fails to meet the requirements of the time. The Congress said it in no uncertain terms and ruled that progressive forms of management be consolidated in all possible ways and that enterprises and associations be encouraged to depend on self-financing and self-sufficiency.

Man will be in the focus of the profound and sophisticated processes of renovation. Unless his conscience, mentality and thinking are transformed, other changes would be impossible. We ought not to remain blind to obstacles we may encounter on the way. There is the danger of a simplistic approach to the decisions already taken and their primitive interpretation.

The quest is understood to involve risk and failures, but this should not be feared. The dangerous things are stagnation, ossification and lack of movement, without which, as is known, any organism will necessarily die away.

The tasks set by the Congress imply as high a level of intellect, knowledge, competence and Party-style devotion to work as to make education, training, search for and promotion of gifted people a most important political need.

The country does have people of this sort. It is perhaps one of the greatest achievements of the Congress that it has moved them to the foreground. A great undertaking calls for outstanding workers. A talented person in the right place is the best guarantee of success if he is given an opportunity to work to the full of his capacity. The task is to give scope to his energies, experience, and desire to work in a new way. An innovator should not be worse off than a mediocrity who never takes risks and makes up for the lack of skills with toadying and subservience.

Transformation of mentality is a most difficult, sometimes painful, process; it is concomitant with tremendous overloads. These are made easier by attention to people, adherence to principle, justice, warm-heartedness and sincerity in human relations. How significant today are moral help and support, how dramatically grows the value of a warm word that lends people wings! Short of genuine humaneness, all talk about the human factor is mere verbiage.

We need beauty—beauty everywhere and in everything. In production. In designing and in the building practice. In arts. In relations between people. Aspiring for the highest world economic, scientific and cultural standards, the Party pins its hopes on a concerned participation of the working people in the intended changes—talented, educated, civilized, beautiful, strong, and capable of inspiring others with their example.

We are exceptionally rich and our riches have many components. These are the indestructible Leninist union between the working class, the collective farmers, and the intellectuals and professional people. This is the indissoluble international fraternal friendship between the ethnic groups and republics.

Internationalism as Lenin saw it is a policy of action. Lenin's ethnic policy allowed the once backward peoples to catch up with world culture. The concept for the nation's faster growth, endorsed by the Congress, calls for building up the economic and cultural potentialities of every nationality, republic and region and increasing their contribution to the common wealth of the country. We have tremendous inexhaustible resources here and the task is to maximize the contribution of all republics, territories and regions to the progress of the nation's integrated economy and its multi-ethnic culture. On the other hand, it is obvious that more flexible and stimulating approaches should take over from unwarranted overregimentation in planning their activities.

The Congress highlighted the social aspect of the economy. Of course, goods and services should be distributed fairly. However, it is important for the volume of these goods to be as great as possible and for the wealth of the nation to grow. In other words, society must give more to the individual who, in turn, must do more for society. It is only in this case that the principle of social justice will receive material confirmation.

Further, social justice will not triumph unless we combat all anti-social phenomena such as heavy drinking, parasitism, rowdyism and plain disregard for others at home and in public places. Social justice will not triumph unless we eliminate private-owner psychology, bribery, embezzlement and dishonest incomes. As Lenin said, if there is such a thing as bribery, if this is possible, there is no politics as such.

Local government can do and is doing much to combat negative practices. To consider that such things should be eliminated by the federal authorities means to capitulate before vice where it persists. Inversely, the uncompromising and resolute character of measures taken to combat such practice is an indicator of the political well-being and effectiveness of the Party organizations.

The course of the April Plenary Meeting of the CPSU Central Committee for resolutely combating things which run against the socialist way of life has met with full support on the part of workforces and the great majority of Soviet citizens. We shall follow this course steadily and firmly.

Comrades, the 27th Congress approached the development of Soviet democracy in an innovative way as Lenin did. The decisions of the Congress constitute a practical program for the growing involvement of working people in running society and the state, effectively using all forms of representative and direct democracy, perfecting the electoral system, and improving the activities of state and community organizations and all political institutions.

Further democratization of community, political and economic activity directly depends on the growth of the political awareness of the people. Today's level of political awareness is conducive to socialist self-government by the people.

Its main unit is the Soviets of People's Deputies. The measures being worked out must raise, on the one hand, the responsibility of local governments, and on the other—ensure in practice their full power.

The Party is for an order which would make the Soviets directly and intimately interested in achieving the best end performance of all the enterprises within their jurisdiction. When the Soviets really influence their production activity and bear their share of responsibility for it, everybody gains; the enterprise and the industry, the village and the city, their residents.

A test model of such cooperation has been succesfully applied in a number of districts of the country. The first results show that departmentalism and parochialism can be overcome, the conflicts in interests removed, and— most importantly—the local Soviets can be vested with required economic autonomy.

Counterposed to real democracy is bureaucratism. The Party has always fought against it. A bureaucrat is especially dangerous now, because today's bureaucrat is better educated, if you like—more qualified, better accommodates himself, more easily changes his spots and more seriously harms the cause.

The Congress named effective remedies against bureaucratism. They include a further democratization of management in the first place. Citizens' participation in the decision making process, the course for extending the electivity of leading employees, the regular accountability of managements to staffs, consideration of public opinion in executive appointments, and the universal certification of the staff—these and many other rules are gradually becoming standard. Not all of the sailing is smooth, but the Congress decisions stimulate the process.

The Party establishes a direct link between the democratization process and publicity. Lenin's thesis on the masses, who must know everything and be consciously involved in all undertakings, today becomes a rule of social practice. A healthy society is not afraid of publicity, criticism or self-criticism, of a sharp presentation of issues. We fundamentally disagree with those who advocate a "dosing" of social information; there can't be too much to truth.

The Party has abolished the once off-limits zones for criticism, the "privileges" of being protected from it. Suppression of criticism is being prosecuted, without respect of persons or ranks. Not a single honest man should suffer for truth. But while encouraging criticism, securing broad publicity and combating the shortcomings, we must put up a barrier to slander and the slanderers. This is also a matter of political principle.

The nature of socialist self-government is such that democracy in it is inseparable from discipline and order, freedom from responsibility, initiative from good organization, and rights from duties. Herein, in this dialectical unity, lies the guarantee of real self-government which gives a major outlet to civic energy and to the Soviet people's social activity.

Comrades,

Lenin and our historic experience teach us that the key to success is first of all that the Party and all its detachments and elements influence the social processes and the course of developments not by force of power but by force of prestige, energy, experience and conviction, that they show their efficiency as bodies of exactly political guidance. Among the many questions in this field the main one is the question of personnel, above all, managers.

As a rule, after the April Plenary Meeting of the Central Committee more energetic and initiative people, who are less subject to the habitual stereotypes and who better understand the spirit and requirements of our time, take leading posts. Among them are many young workers and quite a number of experienced personnel who have won great authority in the past, so to speak, high-ranking senior officials who can think and act in a new way.

At the same time, the Party is getting rid of inert and incompetent workers. As Lenin said, reappraisal is taking place of the high-ranking cadres, a certain reshuffle of them, because it is impossible for them to adjust themselves to the new conditions and to the new objective.

Society pays a dear price for the errors in the personnel policy. An atmosphere ruling out any possibility of errors in the field of the cadre policy, an atmosphere allowing to bare them, is necessary. It is exactly such a climate that is now being established in the Party and the country after the history-making April Plenary Meeting. Today, every Communist, no matter what post he holds, bears full responsibility for his deeds, first of all, to his primary Party organization. And we do not need Party members "for show," as Vladimir Ilyich said.

To guard, like the apple of our eye, the honor of the Party and the purity of its ranks, and the honest and untainted image of a Party member—this is what Lenin bequeathed to us and what the Congress has called for.

We shall always be loyal to his behest and shall undeviatingly follow this call.

Today, when the Congress ideas are coming home to the masses, it is essential to prevent devaluation of new notions and emasculation of their essence, to prevent a situation when words are new but deeds are old. It is particularly necessary to take this into account in the ideological, educational work in which fundamental reorganization is also taking place. And the main stress is laid in this field on qualitative indicators, on the maximal connection with life, on individual work with people, and on a non-formal, clever and honest dialogue with the individual. It is necessary to respect him and not to repulse him by instructive phrasemongering.

Verbal stereotypes and hackneyed phrases do not stimulate a sense of patriotic duty. Active and effective Soviet patriotism today has finer and deeper inducements behind it. True patriotism is in the everyday hard work of brain and soul, in workaday courage rejecting easy ways and solutions. It is not satisfied with average levels, but strives for the greatest possible summits in any business—whether at the bench or on the farm, on operational duty or in the designing office, in research laboratory or in the world of art.

What molds a patriot is not only knowledge of the nation's glorious past but realization of his involvement in its movement towards the most advanced frontiers of time.

The decisions of the Congress appeal to young people in a special way. Their moral flair has unerringly detected in them the dynamic quality, novelty of views and clarity of value options that attract them so much. Young people like to be talked to on equal terms, with respect for, and confidence in them, without grumbling or patronizing tone.

Ours is fine youth. In the long run, all that we are undertaking to do today is for the sake of our children and grandchildren. They are to be the nation's full masters in the upcoming 21st century. And we want them to build their future together with us and to be happy. While creating optimal conditions for their work, studies and leisure, the Party has the right to expect that young people will put all of their creative powers into the energy of acceleration.

The Congress set much store by the family. It is very important to see that young couples should be solid, close-knit and hard-working. Let them take as the model to emulate the fine family of the Ulyanovs which produced outstanding fighters for the cause of the people.

We, Communists, are encouraged by Lenin's words: "We are a Party of the future, and the future belongs to youth. We are a Party of innovators, and youth are always most willing to follow the innovators. We are a Party of self-sacrificing struggle against the old rotten order, and youth will always be the first to rise for a self-sacrificing struggle."

Our Party is a Party of trail-blazers, and for that reason it is always young. Its youth is in the daring search for new ways into the future, in the boldness of its accomplishments renovating life in the name of human happiness and welfare.

The 27th Congress: Leninist Philosophy of Peace and Security

Comrades, Lenin said that old diplomacy was unable to talk straightforwardly and openly.

Straightforward and open talk with peoples and governments is an intrinsic feature of new, socialist, Leninist diplomacy and the 27th Party Congress has just demonstrated this. The Political Report to the Congress and the Basic Provisions for a Comprehensive System of International Security and a program for the elimination of nuclear and other weapons of mass destruction, which were formulated in it, embody the Leninist principle: "Let's have as few general statements, solemn promises and high-flown phrases as possible and as many . . . clearest decisions and measures that would really lead to peace."

The Soviet Union has proposed the clearest measures and solutions leading to peace and the complete removal of war danger.

A clear proposal requires a clear reply. The West, however, replies in the traditional manner which, as Lenin said, is designed to distract attention "to minor things and particular aspects of events . . . and dim the essence of a whole process."

The unwillingness to talk sincerely, diplomatic casuistry and nit-picking, the "art" of complicating the simplest problems and deadlocking issues— all these are the concrete manifestations of the reactionary ideology which allows imperialism to regard the world only as a sphere of furthering its anti-popular egotistic interests and an arena of confrontation between antagonistic and hostile forces.

The fundamentally new concept formulated in Mikhail Gorbachev's January 15 statement and in the Political Report to the Congress rests upon the vision of the world as a complex, contradictory but, at the same time, increasingly inter-related entity. The course of its development has led to a review of the traditional political concepts such as "war" and "victory in war" and showed that these concepts are unacceptable or, to be more exact, senseless in the nuclear and space age.

The new political philosophy of the world puts the equals sign between the prevention of war and the survival of humankind. It emphasises that the level of security is now inversely proportional to the rate of accumulation and modernization of nuclear weapons. It is based on the view that the security of each state is directly proportional to the security of all. National security is fiction if it does not fit in with universal security.

This leads to a conclusion of vital importance for the destiny of humanity; the only way that does not involve the risk of suicide is that of renouncing force as a method of tackling international problems and settling them by political means only.

This philosophy places the task of preserving civilization above bloc, national and other interests. At the beginning of the century Lenin was farsighted enough to see in the development of military technology the threat to life on Earth and formulated a practical policy of peaceful co-habitation and co-operation of states with different social systems. In the nuclear and space age, this is imperative for all countries and peoples.

The concept of a comprehensive security system contains necessary pre-requisites for the materialization of the ideas of the new political philosophy of peace. The whole complex of international relations and each of their component spheres; the military-political, economic, cultural or humanitarian, can be rebuilt on its basis. It is a key to the settlement of global problems and regional conflicts and to the eradication of terrorism.

Our ideology categorically rejects terror. It was still at its 2nd Congress in 1903 that the party decisively ruled it out as a means of political struggle.

The Soviet Union is a principled and convinced opponent of terrorism in all forms and especially of its most revolting variant which is state-backed terrorism. Imagine what will happen if in response to individual or group terrorist acts states make it a rule to perpetrate armed aggression against other states accused of terrorism. This would jeopardize peace and security of nations not only in individual regions but on the whole planet. But can these conditions allow successful pursuit of the line at arms reduction, consolidation of international security and peaceful coexistence in general? Just like the governments of other countries and many foreign statesmen and politicians, we are strongly opposed to bullying in international relations, which poses an irrevocable threat to peace on Earth. We are prepared to cooperate on a sensible basis with all countries and with all peace-loving forces in the struggle against terrorism no matter what forms it may take.

Our concept of peace and security meets the basic aspirations of all nations.

There is a historical parallel which comes to mind here. At one time, Lenin's slogan of peace without annexations and contributions was rejected by the capitalist governments but accepted by the peoples. Today, we once again see a common aspiration of peoples for the new political philosophy of peace and the refusal of certain governments to accept it.

Does this lead to the fatal conclusion that this century-old scheme of things cannot be changed? The April Plenum and the 27th Congress of the CPSU have clearly and unequivocally said: no, it doesn't! So we have no pessimism over the fact that the first steps in the practical materialization of our proposal have been rejected by some Western states. We understand that this is just the beginning of the road. Everything is still ahead, and we are fully determined to go patiently, consistently and purposefully, implementing step by step the course at all-round development of international cooperation and genuine detente. We are prepared for this in any sphere, in any form and at any level; from panel discussions to summit meetings. This course is distinguished by high dynamics and activity, assertiveness, realism and scientific approach to the formulation and settlement of problems. The whole period after the April Plenum attests to our loyalty to this course.

We shall never miss a single political chance to attain the aims set. We shall refine the negotiations mechanisms, strengthen the treaty-legal base of relations, raise the efficiency of our foreign policy, and enrich it with all the best that has been accumulated by socialist diplomacy. We shall conduct a direct and honest dialogue with the partners in search of mutually-acceptable results.

This is one of the directions of the Party's foreign-policy activity.

Another direction is an open talk with the world public. The theoretical premise for it is Lenin's idea that one of the causes of the immense acceleration of the world development is the involvement of ever new hundreds of millions in it. The time when deals were struck behind the peoples' backs is gone never to return. The right to know and understand what is taking place in the world is a vital right of the peoples. And we shall continue to satisfy the thirst for truth, no matter what it is.

Let the West call it propaganda. We understand the meaning of this word in different ways. They view it as putting smokescreens of lie and deception, camouflaging their designs and actions, whereas we regard it as explaining the true aims and combining words with deeds and deeds with words.

Last but not least, we have no right to forget security, our own security and that of our allies and friends.

We have given more than enough proofs of the seriousness of our intentions. Our country has not conducted nuclear explosions for eight months, and is now in no hurry to resume them. It is not we that are trying the will of the world community expressed by the leaders of six states of Europe, Africa, Asia and Latin America. It is not we that have responded to their appeal with new nuclear blasts.

All the peoples, including the majority of the American people, stand for ceasing the nuclear weapon tests.

We again call upon the leaders of the United States to heed the voice of mankind, of their own people, the voice of reason. Failing this, they will assume a heavy responsibility before the world.

The Soviet Union is doing everything in its power to stop the nuclear train which is going downhill. But no one should have any illusions. We can meet any challenge, including a military-space one.

But this is not our choice. We are convinced that not only we but all other peoples do not need it.

Let us look at this issue from the viewpoint of the world's socio-economic problems.

The leaders of the United States of America readily boast of their powerful economy. Common justice would require saying that it largely lives off other, primarily developing, nations and peoples. It is also known that militarization, allocating huge sums for war programs give shots-in-the-arm for the crisis-ridden economy of the wealthiest capitalist state.

So called Strategic Defense Initiative, to keep the US military-industrial complex at a level wanted by its bosses, generals and advocates, of course, features among those sums. As was noted in the Political Report to the Congress, the 200-plus billion dollars annually pumped out of the developing countries and practically the same US arms budget size in recent years are not a mere coincidence. And this involves both a money and brain drain.

Nations must realize that the Star Wars program will also be financed by them, but with graver consequences for their economic and sociopolitical health, and their cultural and intellectual potential. But not only that, as economic security and political freedom, the sovereignty of nations are indivisible.

Our concept of peace highlights the economic, social and other aspects of disarmament. For if today's rate of military spending of the nonsocialist states continues, then before the end of the century this spending will equal approximately another 9 trillion dollars, according to experts.

Implementing the Soviet proposals would open up real opportunities for cutting the military budgets of the nuclear weapon states. Renouncing fresh nuclear-missile and chemical arms programs would save the Western European states alone some 300 billion dollars.

Disarmament is vital to the newly-free countries where the number of starving people has reached 500 million.

No, a just economic order won't be established in the world unless the physical preparations for war are stopped.

Our important proposals to curb the arms race and to promote disarmament and military detente are well known.

The other day Mikhail Gorbachev spelled out in Berlin the practical aspects of the Basic Provisions for a Comprehensive System of International Security. He presented the essence of the new initiative by the socialist countries, aimed at consolidating European security and bringing down, fairly and gradually, the levels of conventional armaments.

A new approach to international affairs was molded in the course of collective debates of global political problems with our allies and friends. This joint creative effort was highlighted by meetings between top party and state leaders of fraternal countries. Cooperation within the framework of the Warsaw Treaty and the council for Mutual Economic Assistance was elevated to a new level.

Meanwhile, the new approach set a different pace for the development of our relations with all socialist states. After the April Plenum of the Central Committee cooperation with these states, based on Marxism-Leninism and socialist internationalism, reached a qualitatively new level. Every facet of these relations has been marked by growing dynamism, comradely openness, proper coordination and a sense of purpose. Some positive changes in the Soviet-Chinese interstate relations are heartening.

By pooling their efforts the socialist countries provide a fresh impulse, stronger than the one given by a mere sum total. Herein lies the decisive factor toward paving the way for the concept of peace based on a civilized attitude being translated into reality.

The communist and workers' parties, the Social Democrats, the nonaligned movement and the powerful peace movements of the world increasingly favor a drastic reform of international relations on a fair and democratic basis. The ruling quarters of the U.S.-led imperialist powers, with their claims for hegemony and the role of self-proclaimed rulers of the peoples' destinies, are alone in opposing it.

So at one end of the scales there is a policy of peace and security, while at the other end that of militarism and expansion inherent in the doctrine of neoglobalism. The very lexicon of this doctrine—"to punish," "to penalize," "to teach a lesson," "to avenge"—speaks for its essence and bias.

It is nothing but a revised version of colonialism expected to justify the right to topple legitimate governments by exporting counterrevolution and employing hired bandits, and in so doing to achieve social revenge. The undeclared wars against Afghanistan, Lebanon, Nicaragua, Angola, Mozambique, and subversive activities against the governments of several other sovereign states are the cases in point.

The US aggression against Libya has shown how dangerous this policy is. The bomb explosions in the residential quarters of Tripoli and Benghazi are organically connected with the nuclear explosions in Nevada. The nations have seen rabid chauvinism, arrogance and a psychology of anything goes take the shape of a barbarous act of state terrorism, perpetrated with the latest in modern means of destruction. The nations have seen why US aircraft carriers are ploughing the seas and oceans, and why US military bases have been set up belting the globe with barbed wire from Japan and the Korean Peninsula to England and the Panama Canal.

The staunchness of the Libyan people, the resolute steps by the Soviet leadership, our country, and the principled condemnation by the world community of the act of state terrorism have prevented further growth of the threat to peace, and have frustrated this imperialist venture. But the danger of new imperialist intrigues remains. No one should doubt that the Soviet Union sides and sympathizes with those who defend their right to independent and free development, and their national and human dignity.

Our country is prepared to lead a constructive dialogue with all countries, the United States included, of course. We are for continuation of the process launched in Geneva. But by its actions Washington has seriously hindered possible improvement in Soviet-American relations, and more so practical preparations for a meeting of our two countries' leaders.

There are forces in Washington, eager to blow up the thaw which has started in Soviet-American relations, and to put an end to the "Geneva spirit." It is those forces' influence which is felt in the US policies of late, the events in Libya being a link in the chain.

The creation of conditions necessary for resuming a high-level direct dialogue depends on the US administration now. Practical steps are called for, capable of reducing the military danger and building confidence among states. We are prepared for that.

Lenin's companions-in-arms admired his political realism. G.V. Chincherin recalled that in critical moments this trait of Lenin's nature served as a reliable guarantee of the correctness of the Party's foreign policies. We adhere to the same stance. The Soviet leadership is convinced that political reason and realism shall take the upper hand over political madness.

The Communist Party and the Soviet Government will do everything necessary for our people to live in peace and work vigorously to implement the historic decisions of the 27th CPSU Congress. Creative work by the Soviet people is the most reliable guarantee of peace and security and of our readiness to reply to any challenge of the time and to rebuff any machinations of the enemies of socialism. We have tremendous natural resources and inexhaustible resources of will and knowledge, energy and talents and the ability to work and achieve success.

We have the people and the means to defend the constructive work and freedom of the Soviet people. We shall not allow anybody to upset the military and strategic parity which ensures our security and the security of our allies and friends, as well as peace worldwide.

We have an active foreign policy, an integral concept of lasting peace and universal security worked out by the Party Congress, and a firm will to materialize it.

We have weapons that make impotent any plans of achieving military superiority, any sophisticated military doctrines and any technology, weapons which the enemies of socialism will never be able to have. These weapons are firm confidence in our forces and in the historical rightness of our cause; the moral and political unity of Soviet society, our internationalist fraternity and unbreakable unity of the Party and the people.

Comrades, in all times and at turning points in history the working people believed in the Party. Jointly with the Party they went to the barricades, stormed the Winter Palace, rebuffed foreign invasions, built legendary projects under Five-Year Plans, fought the Great Patriotic War and won. The cause of the Party is invincible, because it has common aspirations with the people and is connected with them by thousands of living links. The cause of the Party is invincible because its plans and activity rest on firm unity of theory and practice. The most convincing example of this is the 27th Congress which has fulfilled Lenin's instructions; "to discard what is harmful, and to combine all that is valuable, in order to determine precisely a number of . . . practical measures and to carry out these measures at any cost."

We shall follow this line in the future, too.

Let the cause of Lenin live eternally in all our deeds!

Text from Novosti Press Agency

Editor's Note

The CPSU has grown from the first party of Communists organized by V.I. Lenin over 80 years ago to a Party of over 19 million members (one-tenth of the adult population of the USSR). The Communist Party of the Soviet Union encompasses a cross-section of the Soviet people with more than one hundred nationalities in its ranks and leadership.

The first Program of the Bolshevik Party was acted upon in 1903, with the goal of ending czarist rule and establishing working-class power. A second program, enacted after the October Revolution of 1917, set the basis for building the world's first socialist society. After the victory over fascism and reconstruction of the extensive war damage, a third program was adopted in 1961 for the advance to a communist society. This 1961 program has now been amended and recast as a new edition (not a new *program*), taking into account the experiences of the last twenty-five years and the pace of social development that is now possible.

Industrial workers comprise over 44% of the membership of the CPSU at the present time. Collective farmers are approximately 12%, and the professional-technical and white collar workers make up 43%. That many of the latter work directly in industrial enterprises is shown by the fact that 73.2% of the total party membership works in branches of material production. One member in six works in "science, education, public health or culture" while only 8.9% are in bodies of state administration, management, or Party or public organizational apparatus.

Over five million women are members of the CPSU and their percentage of the total grows at an increasing rate. Whereas women were 25.7% of new members in 1970, they were 34.3% in 1982 and this acceleration has continued. [Over one-third of the deputies to the Supreme Soviet of the USSR are women; more than half at the republic, regional and local levels.]

Workers in industry and on the farms account for over 42% of the members and alternate members of Party district, city and area committees; over 31% are members of similar bodies at the regional level or higher, including the Central Committee of the CPSU and of the Party in each republic.

The CPSU incorporates the Communist Parties of 14 constituent Soviet Republics. The 15th, the Russian Federation, has no party organization of its own but its major regions, territories and autonomous areas work under the direct guidance and assistance of the CPSU Central Committee.

There is hardly a workplace or community without a branch of the CPSU. As of 1983, the number of these primary Party organizations was nearly 426,000.

THE PROGRAM OF THE COMMUNIST PARTY OF THE SOVIET UNION
A New Edition

INTRODUCTION

Born of the Great October Socialist Revolution, the Soviet land has traversed a long and glorious road. Victories of worldwide historic importance have been scored under the leadership of the Communist Party. Consistently expressing the interests of the working class, of all working people, and armed with Marxist-Leninist teaching, with a wealth of experience in revolutionary struggle and the building of socialism, the CPSU is confidently leading the Soviet people along the course of communist creative endeavour and peace.

The Party emerged on the political scene as a worthy successor to the ideas of the socialist transformation of society proclaimed in the first program document of the Communists—the *Communist Manifesto*, to the unfading exploit of the heroes of the Paris Commune, and to the revolutionary traditions of the international working class and of the Russian revolutionary democratic movement.

Relying on the historical experience of the class struggle and the best that was achieved by human thought, Karl Marx and Frederick Engels, founders of scientific communism, discovered the objective laws of social development, theoretically proved the inevitability of the collapse of capitalism, and substantiated the world historic mission of the proletariat as the creator of the new, communist system. Their passionate call—"Workers of all countries, unite!"—remains to this day the fighting slogan of the working-class movement.

In new historical conditions Vladimir Ilyich Lenin, who brilliantly continued the cause of Marx and Engels, comprehensively developed their teaching, provided answers to vital questions of the times and armed the working-class movement with the theory of socialist revolution and the building of socialism, with a scientific system of views on problems of war and peace.

Marxism-Leninism is an integral revolutionary teaching. Created by the great Lenin, the Party has become the living embodiment of the fusion of scientific socialism with the working-class movement, of the unbreakable unity of theory and practice. It has been and will be a party of Marxism-Leninism, a party of revolutionary action.

At each stage in history the CPSU accomplished the tasks that were scientifically formulated in its programs.

Having adopted its First Program at the 2nd Congress in 1903, the Bolshevik

Party led the working class, the peasantry, all the working people of Russia in the struggle to overthrow the tsarist autocracy and then the capitalist system, and passed through the flames of three Russian revolutions. In October 1917 the working class took political power into its hands. A state of workers and peasants came into being for the first time in history. **The creation of a new world began.**

In the Second Program, adopted at the 8th Congress in 1919, the Party set the task of building socialism. Following untrodden paths, overcoming incredible difficulties, and displaying unprecedented heroism, the Soviet people under the leadership of the Communist Party implemented the plan for building socialism worked out by Lenin. **Socialism in our country became a reality.**

With the adoption of the Third Program at the 22nd Congress in 1961, the Party undertook enormous work in all areas of the building of communism. The Soviet society achieved great successes in developing productive forces, economic and social relations, socialist democracy, and culture, and in moulding the new man. **The country entered the stage of developed socialism.** The role of the Soviet Union grew as a powerful factor in the struggle against the imperialist policy of oppression, aggression and war, for peace, democracy and social progress.

The time that has elapsed since the Third Program was adopted has confirmed the correctness of its main theoretical and political propositions. At the same time, accumulated experience and scientific understanding of the changes in the country's domestic life and in the world arena provide an opportunity to define more accurately and concretely the prospects for Soviet society's development, the ways and means of attaining the ultimate goal—communism, and the tasks of international policy in new historical conditions.

The Third Program of the CPSU in its present updated edition is a program for the planned and all-round perfection of socialism, for Soviet society's further advance to communism through the country's accelerated socio-economic development. It is a program of the struggle for peace and social progress.

PART ONE

THE TRANSITION FROM CAPITALISM TO SOCIALISM AND COMMUNISM—
THE MAIN CONTENT OF THE PRESENT EPOCH

I. The Great October Socialist Revolution and the Building of Socialism in the USSR

Mankind's history-making turn towards socialism, begun by the October Revolution, is a natural result of social development.

Capitalism is the last exploiter system in human history. Having given a powerful impetus to the development of productive forces, it then became an obstacle to social progress.

The history of capitalism is the history of the aggravation of its main contradiction—the contradiction between the social nature of production and the private capitalist form of appropriation, of the growing exploitation of the working class and all working people, of the aggravation of the struggle between labour and capital, the oppressed and the oppressors, of economic crises, socio-political upheavals, wars of conquest and conflicts bringing endless hardships to working people.

Early in the 20th century the process of the concentration and centralisation of capital resulted in the emergence of powerful capitalist monopoly associations that seized the main levers in the whole of economic and political life. Capitalism entered its highest and last stage—the stage of imperialism. In the words of Lenin, "capitalism in its imperialist stage has turned into the greatest oppressor of nations," the primary source of wars of aggression.

The material conditions for replacing capitalist production relations by socialist ones took shape and the objective and subjective prerequisites for a victorious socialist revolution mature at the stage of imperialism. **History has entrusted the working class with the mission of the revolutionary transformation of the old society and the creation of the new one.** In fulfilling this mission the working class serves not just its own class interests, but those of all working people.

Aggravated by tsarist oppression and the vestiges of serfdom, imperialism's contradictions manifested themselves in Russia with exceptional force. Russia turned out to be the weakest link of world imperialism, the focal point of its contradictions. It was to Russia that the centre of the world revolutionary movement shifted, and the Russian proletariat faced the most difficult and important task of being the first to break the chain of the bourgeoisie's world domination. This could be done only under the leadership of a party of a new type—a fighting revolutionary organisation of the proletariat.

The formation of the Bolshevik Party became the turning point in the history of the Russian and international working-class movement. This was an expression of an objective requirement of social development, of the proletariat's class struggle, the fruit of scientific foresight, a result of the untiring political and organisational activity of Lenin and the Marxists who had rallied round him. Lenin's ardent call "Give us an organisation of revolutionaries and we will overturn Russia" found fervent response in the hearts and minds of workers, the progressive-minded people in Russian society, the best representatives of the working people. Lenin worked out the ideological, political and organisational principles of the Party, and the methods for its work among the masses. The party of the new type was being formed and growing stronger in the course of implacable clashes with revisionism, right-wing opportunism, dogmatism and leftist adventurism.

The revolution of 1905–1907, the first people's revolution of the imperialist epoch, showed the strength of the working class and was a prologue to the proletariat's coming victories. The bourgeois-democratic revolution of February 1917 eliminated tsarism, but it did not deliver the popular masses from social and national oppression, from the hardships of imperialist war, nor did it resolve the contradictions that were tearing Russian society apart. Socialist revolution became an urgent demand of the times.

The working class of Russia was known for its fervent revolutionary spirit and high level of organisation. It was led by the Bolshevik Party, steeled in political battles and armed with progressive revolutionary theory. Lenin gave it a clear perspective of struggle by evolving the theory that a victorious proletarian revolution in conditions of imperialism was possible initially in one or several countries.

At the call of the Bolshevik Party and under its leadership the working class began a decisive battle against the power of capital. The Party brought together into one powerful stream the proletarian struggle for socialism, the peasants' struggle for land, the national liberation struggle of Russia's oppressed peoples, and the nationwide movement against imperialist war and for peace, and directed that stream towards overthrowing the bourgeois system.

The Great October Socialist Revolution became a landmark in world history, determined the general direction and main trends of world development, and initiated the irreversible process of the replacement of capitalism by the new, communist socio-economic formation.

A state with the dictatorship of the proletariat emerged and became established for the first time in history. Rallying together all working people, the working class set about resolving the most complex problems of the period of transition from capitalism to socialism, and creating the foundations of the new society.

The winning of political power, victories on the Civil War fronts, the rout of foreign military interventionists, and prospects for building a new life generated a powerful upsurge of strength and revolutionary energy among the working people. They overcame the privations and difficulties caused by economic dislocation, the counterrevolutionary plots and sabotage by the bourgeoisie, and the country's technical, economic and cultural backwardness. In the transition period, the class struggle at times took the form of bitter clashes. The Soviet Union was subjected to fierce attacks by the hostile capitalist encirclement, to numerous military and political provocations.

Relying on the enthusiasm of the masses, repulsing the attacks by right-wing and leftist opportunists, and strengthening its ideological, political and organisational unity, the Party undeviatingly pursued the Leninist general line aimed at building socialism.

The basic means of production passed into the hands of the people. The **nationalisation** of land, factories, plants and banks ensured the preconditions necessary for asserting and developing socialist ownership and organising a system of planned economy. **Industrialisation** turned the Soviet Union into a powerful industrial state. **Collectivisation** of agriculture was a breakthrough in economic relations, in the entire life of the peasantry. The alliance of the working class and the peasantry was placed on a solid socio-economic foundation. As a result of the **cultural revolution**, illiteracy was stamped out, broad vistas were opened for the development of creative forces and the intellectual flourishing of the working man, a socialist intelligentsia emerged, and Marxist-Leninist ideology became dominant in the minds of the Soviet people.

The solution of the **nationalities question** is an outstanding accomplishment of socialism. The victory of the October Revolution forever put an end to national oppression and inequality among nations and ethnic groups. A tremendous role was played here by the voluntary unification of the free and equal peoples into a single multinational state—the Union of Soviet Socialist Republics. In the course of building socialism rapid economic, social and cultural progress of the former national outlands was ensured. Ethnic conflicts became a thing of the past, and fraternal friendship, close cooperation and mutual assistance of all peoples of the USSR became a way of life.

All this signified that a social transformation of worldwide historic importance had been accomplished—the age-old dominance of private ownership was eliminated and exploitation of man by man abolished forever. Socio-political and ideological unity of Soviet society took shape on the basis of the common interests of the working class, the collective farmers, people's intelligentsia, and the working people of all nationalities. The working man became the full master of the country. **A socialist society in the USSR was essentially built.**

The Great Patriotic War was a severe trial for the new system. The Soviet people and its armed forces rallied round the Party and, displaying unprecedented heroism, inflicted a crushing defeat on German fascism—the strike force of world imperialist reaction. By its victory the Soviet Union made the decisive contribution to the liberation of European peoples from Nazi slavery, to saving world civilisation. The rout of Nazi Germany and militarist Japan opened up new possibilities for peoples' struggle for peace, democracy, national liberation and socialism. The Soviet people's victory raised high the Soviet state's international prestige.

Within a short period the USSR healed the deep wounds of war, considerably strengthened its economic, scientific, technological and defence potential, and consolidated its position internationally. **The victory of socialism in our country was final and complete.**

In its economic, socio-political and cultural development, Soviet society, relying on its achievements, continued to advance confidently. An integral national economic complex took shape in the country. Large new areas in the North and East of the country were developed, and nature management became more efficient. National income and productivity of social labour grew considerably. The level of the people's well-being was raised substantially and a huge housing construction program was carried out. The people's cultural wealth increased, the transition to universal secondary education was completed, and Soviet science and technology achieved outstanding successes. The Soviet Union built the first atomic power station and the first atomic-powered icebreaker; it also launched the first artificial satellite of the Earth and the first manned spaceship.

The socialist social relations gained in strength, a new social and international community—the Soviet people—emerged. The state with the dictatorship of the proletariat grew into a socialist state of all people.

Displaying Bolshevist fidelity to principle and a self-critical approach, and relying on the support of the masses, the Party did a great deal to eliminate the consequences of the personality cult, deviations from the Leninist norms of party and state guidance, and to rectify errors of a subjectivist, voluntaristic nature. Soviet democracy was further developed and socialist legality consolidated.

The Soviet people's persistent work, great achievements in the economic, social and political spheres, science and culture have brought our country to new historical frontiers that marked the beginning of the stage of developed socialism.

The establishment of military-strategic parity between the USSR and the USA, between the Warsaw Treaty Organisation and NATO was a historic accomplishment of socialism. It strengthened the positions of the USSR, the countries of socialism and all progressive forces, and dashed the hopes cherished by aggressive imperialist circles of winning a world nuclear war. Preservation of this balance is vital for ensuring peace and international security.

The experience of the USSR and other socialist countries convincingly demonstrates the indisputable socio-economic, political, ideological and moral advantages of the new society as a stage in mankind's progress that is superior to capitalism, and provides answers to questions that the bourgeois system is incapable of solving.

Socialism is a society on whose banner are inscribed the words "Everything for the sake of man, everything for the benefit of man." It is a society in which:

— the means of production are in the hands of the people, an end has been put forever to exploitation of man by man, social oppression, the rule of a privileged minority, and the poverty and illiteracy of millions of people;

— the broadest vistas have been opened for the dynamic and planned development of productive forces, and scientific and technological progress brings not unemployment but a steady growth in the well-being of the entire people;

— the equal right to work and pay in conformity with the principle "From each according to his ability, to each according to his work" is ensured, and the population enjoys such social benefits as free medical service and education, and housing with a minimum rent;

— the inviolable alliance of the working class, the collective farmers and the intelligentsia has been affirmed, men and women have equal rights and guarantees for exercising them, the young generation is offered a reliable road into the future, and social security for veterans of labour is guaranteed;

— national inequality is abolished, the juridical and factual equality, friendship and brotherhood of all peoples and nationalities are established;

— genuine democracy—power exercised for the people and by the people— has been established and is developing, and broad and equal participation of citizens in the management of production, public and state affairs is ensured;

— the ideas of freedom, human rights and dignity of the individual are filled with real content, unity of rights and duties is ensured, uniform laws and norms of morality and a single discipline apply to each and all, and increasingly favourable conditions are taking shape for the all-round development of the individual;

— the truly humanistic Marxist-Leninist ideology is dominant, the popular masses have access to all sources of knowledge, and an advanced socialist culture has been created which absorbs all that is best in world culture;

— a socialist way of life which gives working people confidence in the future, spiritually and morally elevates them as creators of new social relations and of their own destiny has taken shape on the basis of social justice, collectivism and comradely mutual assistance.

Socialism is a society whose deeds and intentions in the international arena are directed towards supporting the peoples' striving for independence and social progress, and are subordinated to the main task of preserving and consolidating peace.

At the new stage of historical development our Party and the Soviet people are faced with the task in all its magnitude of the all-round perfection of socialist society and a fuller and more effective utilisation of its possibilities and advantages for further advance towards communism.

II. Struggle Between the Forces of Progress and Reaction in the Modern World

After the rout of German fascism and Japanese militarism the worldwide historical process of social liberation, which began with the Great October Revolution, was marked by the overthrow of the power of exploiters in several countries in Europe and Asia and then America. **Socialism, which first became a reality in our country, has turned into a world system.** The Marxist-Leninist theory of building the new society has been verified in practice on an international scale, socialism has asserted itself on vast expanses of the earth, and hundreds of millions of people are following the road of creating a communist civilisation. More and more nations are losing their confidence in capitalism; they do not wish to associate their prospects of development with it and are persistently searching for and finding ways of socialist transformation of their countries.

The successes of socialism are all the more impressive because they have been achieved within very short time spans, in conditions of imperialism's unceasing pressure—from economic pressure and ideological subversion to direct attempts to stage counterrevolutionary coups and launch military aggression.

The experience accumulated in socialist countries is of lasting significance. The past decades have enriched the practice of the building of socialism and clearly demonstrated the diversity of the world of socialism. At the same time the experience of these decades shows the immense importance of the **general laws of socialism**, such as: the power of working people, with the working class playing the leading role; guidance of society's development by the Communist Party armed with the ideology of scientific socialism; establishment of social ownership of the basic means of production and on this basis the planned growth of the economy in the interests of the people; implementation of the principle "From each according to his ability, to each according to his work"; development of socialist democracy;

equality and friendship of all nations and nationalities; and defence of revolutionary gains from encroachments by class enemies.

The use of the general laws in the specific conditions of each of the socialist countries forms the basis of their confident advance, the overcoming of the growing pains and the resolving in good time of contradictions that arise; it is a real contribution of the ruling Communist parties to the general process of socialist development.

Socialism has brought forth a new, previously unknown type of international relations, which are developing between socialist states. Their firm foundation consists of a uniform socio-economic and political system; Marxist-Leninist ideology; class solidarity; friendship, cooperation and mutual assistance in carrying out tasks of building and defending the new society; the struggle for peace, international security, social progress; and equality and respect for the independence and sovereignty of each state.

Relations of socialist internationalism have been most fully embodied in the **socialist community**. The countries belonging to the community—member states of the Council for Mutual Economic Assistance and the Warsaw Treaty Organisation—are united by common fundamental interests and aims and by ties of extensive multifaceted cooperation, and coordinate their actions in international affairs. History has not known such a community of countries in which no one country has or can have special rights and privileges, in which international relations have really become relations between peoples, and in which fruitful ties at various levels have taken shape and are developing—from the highest level of Party and state leadership to work collectives. The community multiplies the strength of the fraternal states in the building of socialism and helps reliably to ensure their security.

The objective requirement of the socialist countries' drawing ever closer together stems from the very essence of socialism. Whereas in the capitalist world the law of uneven economic, socio-political and cultural development operates, and strong countries enrich themselves by plundering weak ones and prolong in every way the backwardness of the latter, socialism creates the necessary conditions for raising the less developed countries to the level of the developed ones. The higher and the more similar the levels of social development of socialist countries, the richer and deeper their cooperation, the more organic the process of their drawing together.

The establishment of the world socialist system, the formation and strengthening of the socialist community have brought about a **fundamental change in the alignment of forces in the international arena** in favour of the peoples fighting for social progress, democracy, national freedom and peace. The socialist community is the most authoritative force of our time and without it no issue in world politics can be solved; it is a firm bulwark of peace on earth, the most consistent champion of sound, peaceful, democratic principles in international relations, the main force opposing imperialist reaction.

The young, forward-looking world of socialism is opposed by the exploiter world of capitalism which is still strong and dangerous, but which has already passed its peak. **The general crisis of capitalism is deepening.** The sphere of its domination is shrinking inevitably, its historical doom becoming ever more obvious.

Modern capitalism differs in many ways from what it was at the beginning and even in the middle of the 20th century. In conditions of state-monopoly capitalism, which combines the strength of the monopolies and the state, the conflict between the vastly increased productive forces and capitalist production relations is becoming ever more acute. The inner instability of the economy is growing, which is seen in the slowing down of the overall rates of its growth, in the intertwining and deepening of cyclical and structural crises. Mass unemployment and inflation have become a chronic disease, and budget deficits and state debts have reached a colossal scale.

The strengthening of transnational corporations, which make huge profits by exploiting working people on a world scale, is a direct result of capitalist concentration and internationalisation of production. They not only undermine the sovereignty of newly free states, but also encroach on the national interests of developed capitalist countries.

The monopoly bourgeoisie is constantly manoeuvring in an attempt to adjust itself to the changing situation. A capitalist state redistributes, in particular through the budget, a considerable part of the national income in favour of big capital and tries to place at its service the latest achievements in science and technology. The mechanism of exploitation has become more complex, more sophisticated. The skills, intellectual powers and the energy of the worker are being exploited for gaining more and more profit.

With the growing influence of world socialism, the class struggle of working people at times compels the capitalists to make partial concessions, to agree to certain improvements as regards working conditions, remuneration for work and social security. This is being done to preserve the main thing—the domination of capital. Such manoeuvring, however, is being increasingly combined with violent actions, with a direct assault by the monopolies and the bourgeois state on the living standards of working people.

Under capitalism the scientific and technological revolution has grave social consequences. Millions of working people, thrown out of the factory gates, are doomed to losing their skills and to material hardships, and can have no confidence in the future. A considerable proportion of young people cannot find application for their energy and knowledge and suffer from the hopelessness of their condition. Mass unemployment remains regardless of the economic situation, while the real prospect of its further growth is fraught with the most serious upheavals for capitalism as a social system.

The monopolies have seized the dominant positions in the agrarian sector of the economy. Large numbers of farmers are being forced out of the production sphere while those who survive do so at the cost of excessive work and privations. The fate of farmers' families depends entirely on market fluctuations and the arbitrariness of monopolies. The plight of the peasantry is especially grave in the former colonies and semi-colonies. The small and middle businessmen in cities are being increasingly exploited by big capital and are caught in the net of financial dependence.

Even in the most developed capitalist countries a great number of people are deprived, homeless, illiterate and without medical care. Shameful discrimination against ethnic minorities persists and the rights of women are infringed upon.

A tendency towards an all-round intensification of reaction is characteristic of imperialism in the political field. Wherever the working people have achieved certain demócratic rights as a result of determined struggle, state-monopoly capitalism is conducting a persistent, at times cunningly camouflaged offensive against those rights. In situations that pose a danger to state-monopoly capitalism, it resorts without hesitation to political blackmail, repression, terror and punitive actions. Neo-fascism is becoming increasingly active in the political arena. When the usual forms of suppressing working people fail, imperialism implants and backs tyrannic regimes in order directly to suppress progressive forces by military means. Striving to weaken the international solidarity of working people, imperialism stirs up and abets national egoism, chauvinism and racism, and scorn for the rights and interests of other peoples and their national cultural and historical heritage.

The inhumane ideology of modern capitalism is inflicting ever greater damage on the spiritual world of people. The cult of individualism, violence and permissiveness, rabid anti-communism and exploitation of culture as a source of profit give rise to spiritual callousness, to moral degradation. Imperialism has given rise to large-scale crime and terrorism that have engulfed capitalist society. Ever more pernicious is the role of the bourgeois mass media which befuddle people in the interests of the ruling class.

The uneven nature of the development of countries within the capitalist system is deepening. Three main centres of interimperialist rivalry have formed: the United States, Western Europe and Japan. Competition is mounting between them for markets, spheres of capital investment, sources of raw materials and superiority in the key areas of scientific and technological progress. New centres of economic and political rivalry are forming, particularly in the Pacific basin and in Latin America. Contradictions between bourgeois states are deepening. The imperial ambitions and selfish policy of the US monopolies and their readiness, for egoistic reasons, to sacrifice the interests and security of other, even allied, states are giving rise to growing indignation and alarm throughout the world.

Imperialism is responsible for the huge and widening gap between the economic development levels of the industrial capitalist countries and the majority of the newly free states, for the continued existence on earth of vast zones of hunger, poverty and epidemic diseases.

As the course of historical development more and more weakens the positions of imperialism, the policy of its more reactionary forces becomes increasingly hostile to the interests of the peoples. Imperialism is putting up fierce resistance to social progress, and is trying to stop the course of history, to undermine the positions of socialism, and to avenge itself socially on a world scale. The imperialist powers strive to coordinate their economic, political and ideological strategy, to create a common front of struggle against socialism, against all revolutionary, liberation movements.

Imperialism refuses to face the political realities of today's world. Ignoring the will of sovereign peoples, it tries to deprive them of their right to choose their road of development and threatens their security. Herein lies the main cause of conflicts in various parts of the world.

The citadel of international reaction is US imperialism. The threat of war comes chiefly from it. Claiming world domination, it arbitrarily declares whole continents to be zones of its "vital interests." The US policy of hegemony, the imposition of its will and unequal relations on other states, support for repressive anti-popular regimes and discrimination against countries that do not suit the United States, disorganises inter-state economic and political relations and prevents their normal development.

The bloody war against Vietnam, the blockade of Cuba for many years, the flouting of the lawful rights of the Palestinian people, the intervention in Lebanon, the armed seizure of defenceless Grenada, and the aggressive actions against Nicaragua—these are only some of the countless crimes that will remain forever the most shameful pages in imperialism's history.

The race unleashed by imperialism in the manufacture of nuclear and other arms on a scale that knows no precedent is its gravest crime against the peoples. It brings the monopolies huge profits. The colossal military expenditures weigh heavily on the shoulders of working people. The monopolies that manufacture arms, the military, the state bureaucracy, the ideological machinery and militarised science, that have merged to form the military-industrial complex, have become the most zealous advocates and makers of policies of adventurism and aggression. The sinister alliance of the death merchants and imperialist state power is a pillar of extreme reaction, a constant and growing source of war danger, and a convincing confirmation of the capitalist system's political, social and moral untenability.

No "modifications" and manoeuvres by modern capitalism have rendered invalid or can render invalid the laws of its development, or can overcome the acute antagonism between labour and capital, between the monopolies and society, or can bring the historically doomed capitalist system out of its all-permeating crisis. The dialectics of development are such that the very same means which capitalism puts to use with the aim of strengthening its positions inevitably lead to an aggravation of all its deep-seated contradictions. Imperialism is parasitical, decaying and moribund capitalism; it marks the eve of socialist revolution.

The working class was and is the main revolutionary class of the present age. In the capitalist world, it is the main force struggling for the overthrow of the exploiting system and for building a new society.

Practice confirms the Marxist-Leninist concept of the increasing role of the working class in society. As science is being applied in production on an ever larger scale, the ranks of the working class are being replenished with highly skilled workers. In the course of class battles, the working class becomes more cohesive, creates its own political parties, trade unions and other organisations, and wages economic, political and ideological struggle against capitalism. The scale of that struggle is growing, its forms are becoming more diverse and its content is being enriched. The basic interests of the proletariat make it more and more imperative to achieve unity in the working-class movement and concerted actions by all its contingents.

The young and rapidly growing working class in the countries of Asia, Africa and Latin America is facing difficult tasks. It is opposed both by foreign capital and local exploiters. Its political maturity and degree of organisation are growing in the course of struggle.

The vanguard of the working-class movement, of all the forces of the world revolutionary process is the international communist movement. Communists are working for both the immediate and the long-term goals of the working class, for the interests of all the working people, for social progress, national liberation of peoples, disarmament and peace. The communist movement is the most influential ideological and political force of our time.

The revolutionary parties of the working class are guided by the scientific theory of social development, Marxism-Leninism, and are pursuing a principled working-class policy. They are characterised by a conviction in the historical inevitability of the replacement of capitalism by socialism, a clear understanding of the objective laws of socialist revolution in whatever form—peaceful or non-peaceful—and an ability to apply the general principles of struggle for socialism in the specific conditions of every country.

The strength of revolutionary parties lies in the fact that they firmly uphold the rights and vital aspirations of the working people, point out ways of leading society out of the crisis situation of bourgeois society, indicate a real alternative to the exploiter system and provide answers, imbued with social optimism, to the basic questions of our time. They are the true exponents and the most staunch defenders of the national interests of their countries.

A consistently class-oriented course enhances the authority of the Communist parties, despite the fact that the political and ideological machinery of imperialism is operating in an increasingly subtle way. It is combining discrimination against and persecution of Communists and outright anti-communist propaganda with support for those elements in the working-class movement that are opposed to working-class policy and international solidarity, and that endorse social reconciliation and partnership with the bourgeoisie. The monopoly bourgeoisie and reactionary forces attack the Communists so fiercely precisely because the latter represent a movement that has deep roots in social development and that expresses the most vital interests of the mass of the people.

A characteristic feature of our time is **an upsurge of mass democratic movements in the non-socialist world.** The antagonism between the monopolies and the overwhelming majority of the population is deepening in capitalist countries. Professionals and office employees, farmers, representatives of the urban petty bourgeoisie and national minorities, women's organisations, young people and students are taking an ever more active part in the struggle against the dominance of the monopolies and against the reactionary policy of the ruling classes. People of different political views are demanding an end to the militarisation of society and to the policy of aggression and war, an end to racial and national discrimination, to infringements on the rights of women, to the deterioration in the condition of the younger generation, to corruption, and to the predatory attitude of the monopolies towards the use of natural resources and the environment. These movements are objectively directed against the policy of the reactionary circles of imperialism and merge with the overall struggle for peace and social progress.

The anti-imperialist struggle of the peoples and countries that have cast off the yoke of colonialism for the consolidation of their independence and for social progress is an integral part of the world revolutionary process. The disintegration of the colonial system of imperialism and the emergence of dozens of independent states from its ruins are an historic achievement of the national liberation revolutions and movements, an achievement that has considerably influenced the alignment of forces in the world.

Since independence many of those countries have made appreciable progress in economic and cultural development and in consolidating national statehood.

Collective forms of struggle by those countries for their rights in the international arena have taken shape. Practice has shown, however, that their way to the consolidation of political independence and to economic and social rejuvenation is being seriously hampered by the legacy of their colonial and semi-colonial past and by the actions of imperialism.

Conducting a policy of neo-colonialism, imperialism is seeking to reduce to naught the sovereignty won by the young states and to retain and even tighten control over them. It is trying to drag them into a militarist orbit and to use them as springboards for its aggressive global strategy. In pursuing these goals, the imperialists resort to military pressure, impose their economic diktat and support internal reaction. Even countries that won state independence long ago, for instance, Latin American countries, have to wage a resolute struggle against the dominance of the monopolies of the United States and other imperialist powers.

Taking advantage of the economic and technological dependence of the newly free countries and their unequal status in the world capitalist economy, imperialism mercilessly exploits them. It is exacting tributes that run into billions of dollars, and which are exhausting the economies of those states. The huge indebtedness of the countries of Asia, Africa and Latin America to the industrially developed capitalist states has become an important lever for the exploitation of these countries by imperialism, and primarily US imperialism. At the same time, the resistance of the peoples of these countries to the policy of plunder and robbery is growing. They are continuing their determined, just struggle against neo-colonialism, against interference in their internal affairs, and against racism and apartheid. This resistance objectively links up with the overall anti-imperialist struggle of the peoples for freedom, peace, and social progress.

The non-capitalist way of development, **the way of socialist orientation,** chosen by a number of newly free countries, is opening up broad prospects for social progress. The experience of these countries confirms that in present-day conditions, with the existing world alignment of forces, the formerly enslaved peoples have greater possibilities for rejecting capitalism and for building their future without exploiters, in the interests of the working people. This is a phenomenon of immense historic importance.

Overcoming the resistance of external and internal reaction, the ruling revolutionary-democratic parties are pursuing a course of abolishing the dominance of imperialist monopolies, tribal chiefs, feudal lords and the reactionary bourgeoisie; of strengthening the public sector of the economy; of encouraging the cooperative movement in the countryside; and of enhancing the role of the mass of the working people in economic and political life. Defending their independence against the onslaught of the imperialists, these countries are broadening their cooperation with socialist states. The road chosen by them meets the genuine interests and aspirations of the mass of the people, reflects their desire for a just social system, and coincides with the mainstream of historical development.

The most acute problem facing mankind is that of war and peace. Imperialism was responsible for two world wars that claimed tens of millons of lives. It is creating the threat of a third world war. Imperialism is using the achievements of man's genius for the development of weapons of awesome destructive power. The policy of the imperialist circles, which are prepared to sacrifice the future of whole nations, is increasing the danger that these weapons may actually be put to use. In the final count it threatens mankind with a global armed conflict in which there would be no winners or losers and in which world civilisation could perish.

The question of what goals the achievements of the scientific and technological revolution should serve has become pivotal in the present-day socio-political struggle. Contemporary science and technology make it possible to ensure abundance on earth and to create material conditions for the flourishing of society and the development of the individual. These creations of the human mind, and human hands, however, are being turned against humanity itself owing to class selfishness, for the sake of the enrichment of the elite, which dominates the capitalist world. This is a glaring contradiction which confronts mankind as it approaches the threshold of the 21st century.

It is not science and technology in themselves that pose a threat to peace. This threat is posed by imperialism and its policy, the policy of the most reactionary militarist, aggressive forces of our time. The threat can be averted only by curbing those forces.

In the present-day world, which is riddled with acute contradictions, and in the face of impending catastrophe, the only sensible and acceptable way out is **the peaceful coexistence of states with different social systems.** This does not merely mean the absence of wars. It is an international order under which good-neighbourliness and cooperation rather than armed force would prevail, and a broad exchange of the achievements of science and technology and cultural values would be carried out for the good of all nations. When vast resources are no longer used for military purposes, it would be possible to use the fruits of labour exclusively for constructive purposes. States that have embarked on the road of independent development would be protected from external encroachments, and this would facilitate their advance along the path of national and social revival. Favourable opportunities would also arise for solving the global problems by the collective efforts of all states. Peaceful coexistence meets the interests of all countries and peoples.

The danger looming over mankind has never been so awesome. But then the possibilities for safeguarding and strengthening peace have never been so real. By uniting their efforts the peoples can and must avert the threat of nuclear annihilation.

The aggressive policy of imperialism is being countered by the growing potential of the forces of peace. This means the vigorous and consistently peaceful policy of the socialist states and their growing economic and defensive capacity. This means the policy of the overwhelming majority of states of Asia, Africa and Latin America which have a vital interest in safeguarding peace and ending the arms race. This means the anti-war movements of the broadest mass of the people on all continents, movements that have become a long-lasting and influential factor in the life of society. A realistic assessment of the actual alignment of forces is leading many statesmen and politicians in capitalist states, too, to an understanding of the danger involved in continuing and extending the arms race.

The CPSU proceeds from the belief that, however grave the threat to peace posed by the policy of the aggressive circles of imperialism, **world war is not fatally inevitable. It is possible to avert war and to save mankind from catastrophe. This is the historical mission of socialism, of all the progressive and peace-loving forces of the world.**

The entire course of world development confirms the Marxist-Leninist analysis of the character and main content of the present epoch. **It is an epoch of transition from capitalism to socialism and communism, and of historical competition between the two world socio-political systems, an epoch of socialist and national liberation revolutions and of the disintegration of colonialism, an epoch of struggle of the main motive forces of social development—world socialism, the working-class and communist movement, the peoples of the newly free states, and the mass democratic movements—against imperialism and its policy of aggression and oppression, and for peace, democracy, and social progress.**

The constant growth of these forces and their interaction are a pledge that the hopes of the peoples for a life of peace, freedom, and happiness will be fulfilled. The advance of humanity towards socialism and communism, despite all its unevenness, complexity and contradictoriness, is inevitable.

PART TWO

THE CPSU'S TASKS IN PERFECTING SOCIALISM AND MAKING A GRADUAL TRANSITION TO COMMUNISM

I. The Communist Perspective of the USSR and the Need to Accelerate Social and Economic Development

The ultimate goal of the CPSU is to build communism in our country. Socialism and communism are two consecutive phases of one communist formation. There is no distinct line dividing them: the development of socialism, an ever fuller revelation and use of its possibilities and advantages, and the consolidation of the general communist principles characteristic of it—this is what is meant by the actual advance of society to communism.

Communism is a classless social system with one form of public ownership of the means of production and with full social equality of all members of society. Under communism, the all-round development of people will be accompanied by the growth of the productive forces on the basis of continuous progress in science and technology, all the springs of social wealth will flow abundantly, and the great principle "From each according to his ability, to each according to his needs" will be implemented. Communism is a highly organised society of free, socially conscious working people, a society in which public self-government will be established, a society in which labour for the good of society will become the prime vital requirement of everyone, a clearly recognised necessity, and the ability of each person will be employed to the greatest benefit of the people.

The material and technical foundation of communism presupposes the creation of those productive forces that open up opportunities for the full satisfaction of the reasonable requirements of society and the individual. All productive activities under communism will be based on the use of highly efficient technical facilities and technologies, and the harmonious interaction of man and nature will be ensured.

In the highest phase of communism the directly social character of labour and production will become firmly established. Through the complete elimination of the remnants of the old division of labour and the essential social differences associated with it, the process of forming a socially homogeneous society will be completed.

Communism signifies the transformation of the system of socialist self-government by the people, of socialist democracy into the highest form of organisation of society—communist public self-government. With the maturation of the necessary socio-economic and ideological preconditions and the involvement of all citizens in administration, the socialist state—given appropriate international conditions—will, as Lenin noted, increasingly become a transitional form "from a state to a non-state." The activities of state bodies will become non-political in nature, and the need for the state as a special political institution will gradually disappear.

The inalienable feature of the communist mode of life is a high level of consciousness, social activity, discipline, and self-discipline of members of society, in which observance of the uniform, generally accepted rules of communist conduct will become an inner need and habit of every person.

Communism is a social system under which the free development of each is a condition for the free development of all.

The CPSU does not attempt to foresee in detail the features of complete communism. As society advances towards communism and more experience is accumulated in building it, scientific notions of the highest phase of a new society will become enriched and more concrete.

The growth of socialism into communism is determined by the objective laws of the development of society, laws which cannot be disregarded. Any attempts to move ahead too fast and to introduce communist principles without taking into consideration the level of material and spiritual maturity of society are, as experience has shown, doomed to failure and may cause both economic and political losses.

At the same time, the CPSU believes that there must be no delay in effecting the necessary transformations and solving new tasks. The Party takes into account the fact that along with undeniable successes the 1970s and early 1980s saw certain unfavourable trends and difficulties in the country's development. To a great extent these were due to the failure to assess appropriately and in good time changes in the economic situation and the need for profound transformations in all spheres of life, and to a lack of persistence in carrying them out. This prevented fuller use of the possibilities and advantages of the socialist system and impeded onward movement.

The CPSU believes that under the present domestic and international conditions, the all-round progress of Soviet society, its onward movement towards communism can and must be ensured by **accelerating the country's socio-economic development**. This is the strategic line of the Party aimed at qualitatively transforming all aspects of life in Soviet society: a radical renewal of its material and technical foundation on the basis of the achievements of the scientific and technological revolution; perfection of social relations, above all economic ones; profound changes in the content and nature of labour and in the material and cultural conditions of the life of people; and invigoration of the entire system of political, social, and ideological institutions.

The Party links the successful solution of the tasks set with an **increase in the role of the human factor**. Socialist society cannot function effectively without finding new ways of developing the creative activity of the people in all spheres of life. The greater the scope of the historical goals, the more important the interested, responsible, conscious and active participation of millions of people in achieving them.

Soviet society is to reach new heights on the basis of accelerating its social and economic development. This means:

in the economic sphere—raising the national economy to a basically new scientific-technological and organisational-economic level, gearing it towards intensive development; achieving the world's highest level in productivity of social labour, quality of output, and efficiency of production; ensuring an optimal structure and balance for the integral national economic complex of the country; significantly raising the level of the socialisation of labour and production; drawing collective-farm and cooperative property and the property of the people as a whole closer together, with the prospect of their merging in future;

in the social sphere—ensuring a qualitatively new level of people's well-being while consistently implementing the socialist principle of distribution according to work; the establishment of an essentially classless structure of society, the gradual elimination of substantial differences in the socio-economic, cultural, and living standards of town and countryside; an ever more organic combination of physical and mental labour in production activities; further cohesion of the Soviet people as a social and international community; a high level of creative energy and initiative on the part of the masses;

in the political sphere—the development of socialist self-government by the people through ever greater involvement of citizens in running state and public affairs, the perfection of the electoral system, the improvement of the activities of elective bodies of people's power, the enhancement of the role of the trade unions, Komsomol, and other mass organisations of the working people, and an effective use of all forms of representative and direct democracy;

in the sphere of cultural life—the further consolidation of socialist ideology in the minds of Soviet people; full establishment of the moral principles of socialism, of the spirit of collectivism and comradely mutual assistance; bringing the achievements of science and cultural values within the reach of the broadest masses of the population; moulding a harmoniously developed man.

These transformations will bring about a qualitatively new state of Soviet society, which will fully reveal the enormous advantages of socialism in all spheres of life. Thus a historic step will be made on the road to the highest phase of communism. The Party always correlates its policy, economic and social strategy, and the tasks of its organisational and ideological work with the communist perspective.

II. The Economic Strategy of the Party

The task set by the Party to accelerate the social and economic development of the country calls for profound changes primarily in the decisive sphere of human activity—the economy. A sharp turn is to be made towards the intensification of production; every enterprise and every sector is to be reoriented towards the utmost and top-priority use of qualitative factors of economic growth. A transition must be ensured to an economy of supreme organisation and efficiency with comprehensively developed productive forces and production relations, and a smoothly functioning economic mechanism. The country's production potential should double and be renewed fundamentally and qualitatively by the year 2000.

These tasks are being tackled by the Party and the people under the conditions of the further development of the scientific and technological revolution, which is exerting strong influence on all aspects of present-day production, on the entire system of social relations, on man and his environment, and is opening up new prospects for considerably raising labour productivity and for the progress of society as a whole. The historical mission of socialism is to apply the achievements of science, the most advanced and efficient technology, and the growing force of people's creative and collective labour in the building of communism.

Acceleration of Scientific and Technological Progress—the Main Lever for Raising Efficiency in Production

The basic issue in the Party's economic strategy is the acceleration of scientific and technological progress. **A new technical reconstruction of the national economy is to be carried out** and the material and technical foundation of society thereby transformed.

Of primary importance is a rapid **renewal of the production apparatus through extensive introduction of advanced technology**, of the most advanced technological processes and flexible production lines that make it possible quickly to put out new products with maximum economic and social effect. It is necessary to complete comprehensive mechanisation in all sectors of the production and nonproduction spheres and to take a major step to promote the automation of production, involving a transition to automated shops and enterprises and automated control and design systems. Electrification, chemicalisation, robotisation, and computerisation of production will be effected and biotechnology used on an increasingly large scale.

The Party will facilitate in every way the further growth and effective use of the country's **scientific and technological potential** and the development of scientific research which opens up new opportunities for major, revolutionary changes in the intensification of the economy. The introduction of the latest achievements of science and technology in production, management, public services, and everyday life must be ensured everywhere. Science will become in full measure a force directly involved in production.

A considerable **increase in labour productivity** is to be achieved on the basis of accelerating scientific and technological progress, radical changes in machinery and technology, and mobilisation of all technical, organisational, economic and social factors. Without this, as Lenin taught, "the full transition to communism is impossible." Labour productivity is to be increased by 130–150 per cent in the coming fifteen years as an important stage on the way to the highest productivity.

Reserves for growth in labour productivity must be used to the utmost at every association, every enterprise, and every work-place. It is necessary to reduce the labour intensity of products, to cut the waste of working time, to introduce up-to-date machinery and technology, strengthen order and discipline, improve norm-setting, broadly apply advanced forms of scientific organisation of labour, raise production standards, make work collectives more stable, and encourage the efforts of inventors and innovators.

Scientific and technological progress should be aimed at a radical improvement in the **utilisation of natural resources, raw and other materials, fuel and energy** at all stages—from extracting and comprehensive processing of raw materials to the output and use of end products. The rates of reduction of material intensity, metal intensity and power intensity per unit of national income must be increased. Saving of resources will become the decisive means of meeting the increase in the requirements of the national economy in fuel, energy, and raw and other materials.

Utmost **improvement in the technical level of products** is at the centre of the Party's economic policy and all practical work. Soviet products should incorporate the latest achievements of scientific thought, meet the highest technical, economic, aesthetic and other consumer demands, and be competitive on the world market. Improving product quality is a reliable way of more fully meeting the country's requirements in commodities and the population's growing demand for a variety of goods. Poor quality and rejects mean wasted material resources and labour. The Party will actively support efforts to maintain the reputation of the Soviet trade mark. The quality of products should be a matter of professional and patriotic pride.

The effectiveness of scientific and technological progress depends not only on an increase in the output of the latest technical facilities, but also on the **better use of fixed assets**, and an increase in the output of products per unit of equipment, per square metre of production space. The present downward trend in output-assets ratio is to be overcome, and in the long run this ratio is to be increased.

Accelerated scientific and technological progress is making greater demands on the general and vocational education of working people. The course of improving the entire system of training personnel and raising its skills, of ensuring, on a planned basis, a balance between the number of workplaces and manpower resources in all economic sectors and regions of the country will be pursued.

The drive for all-round intensification and rationalisation of production, for its highest efficiency on the basis of scientific and technological progress is being organically combined, under the socialist system of planned economy, with the implementation of the humanitarian goals of Soviet society, with full employment and the steady improvement of all aspects of life.

Structural Reorganisation of Social Production

The switchover to intensification calls for serious **structural changes in the economy**. The national economy should be able to change flexibly and promptly in line with advances in science and technology, in social and individual requirements. There must be faster development of sectors essential for scientific and technological progress and for the successful solution of social tasks, an optimal correlation between consumption and accumulation, and a better balance between the manufacture of the means of production and consumer goods, between sectors in the agro-industrial complex. The social orientation of the economy will be strengthened and a turn will be made consistently to assure a more complete satisfaction of the Soviet people's growing requirements.

In this connection new demands are being made on **investment policy**. It is being called upon to ensure a higher effectiveness of capital investments, their concentration in the key sections that are essential for the prompt achievement of the highest economic effect and a balanced development of the economy, and the highest increment in output and national income per rouble spent. Emphasis must be shifted from new construction projects to technical re-equipment and reconstruction of existing enterprises, with a considerable increase in the share of funds spent on these purposes in the overall volume of productive capital investments, and with greater spending on equipment and machinery. The top-priority task is to improve the correlation between capital investments in resource-extracting, processing and consuming sectors and to redistribute funds in favour of the sectors which ensure the acceleration of scientific and technological progress.

Making the Soviet economy the most highly-developed and powerful one in the world calls for further development of **heavy industry** as the basis of economic strength.

The Party assigns to **machine-building** the key role in applying the latest achievements of science and technology. Higher growth rates in machine-building are the basis for scientific and technological progress in all sectors of the national economy and for maintaining the country's defences at a proper level, and represent the main trend in the long-range development of the economy. Machine-building is called upon to manufacture systems and sets of machinery, equipment and instruments of the highest technical and economic standards so as to ensure revolutionary changes in the technology and organisation of production, manifold increase in labour productivity, reduction in material intensity and power intensity, improvement in product quality, and higher returns on capital. Priority will be given to the development of machine-tool building, electrical engineering, the microelectronic industry, computer engineering and instrument-making, the entire branch of information science as the real catalysts for scientific and technological progress.

We must strengthen the potential of and effect a qualitative improvement in metallurgy, the chemical industry, and other sectors of heavy industry that produce **structural materials**, continuously broaden the range and improve the quality of materials, and increase the output of new, highly economical and advanced types.

The effective development of the **country's fuel-and-energy complex** is a most important task. Consistent satisfaction of the country's growing requirements for various types of fuel and energy requires improvement in the structure of the fuel-and-energy balance, accelerated development of the nuclear power industry, large-scale utilisation of renewable sources of energy, and vigorous and purposeful work to save fuel and energy resources in all sectors of the national economy.

An indispensable condition for social and economic progress is the further strengthening and improved efficiency of the **agro-industrial complex,** and a full satisfaction of the country's requirements in its produce. The task is to complete the transfer of agriculture to an industrial basis, introduce everywhere scientific systems of farming and intensive technologies, improve the utilisation of soil and raise its fertility, achieve a significant increase in the yield of agricultural crops and in livestock productivity, build up the fodder base, ensure stability in agricultural production, reduce its dependence on unfavourable natural and climatic conditions, and rule out losses in harvested farm crops and livestock produce. Agro-industrial integration and inter-farm cooperation will be consolidated; the machinery, technology and organisation of production, procurement, transportation, storage and processing of agricultural produce will be raised to a new level.

Collective and state farms, and agro-industrial associations and enterprises that form the backbone of socialist agriculture are called upon to contribute decisively to satisfying the country's requirements in agricultural produce. At the same time subsidiary farms run by enterprises and individual plots of citizens, as well as collective gardening, will be used to replenish the food resources.

The CPSU will direct efforts towards accelerated growth in the production of **consumer goods and the entire sphere of services** to satisfy completely the needs of the Soviet people. Enterprises, associations and organisations in all sectors of the national economy should be involved in this.

In perfecting the integral national economic complex of the country the Party assigns an important role to technical retooling and the more efficient performance of sectors of the **production infrastructure**—the systems of electric power, oil and gas supply, communications and information back-up. Special attention will be paid to developing an integrated transport system, upgrading all its links, and developing a ramified network of well-appointed roads.

The task is essentially to raise technical and economic standards in **construction**, turn construction work into an integral industrial process, improve the quality and reduce the cost of design and construction work, and cut down the time taken to complete construction projects and to bring them up to design capacity.

The Party will continue to devote undivided attention to improving the **distribution of the productive forces**, an effort which should ensure the economy of social labour and the comprehensive and highly efficient development of each region. The economies of all Union republics will develop further through the greater social division of labour, and their contribution to the satisfaction of the requirements of the country will grow. The task is further to improve the structure of the existing territorial-production complexes and of economic ties, and to bring enterprises that process raw materials as close as possible to the places where those materials are extracted. It is necessary to use to a fuller extent the possibilities offered by small and medium-sized towns and workers' settlements, to locate within them specialised production facilities linked to the manufacture of products under co-production arrangements with major enterprises, to the processing of agricultural and local raw materials, and to the provision of services to the population.

Accelerated development of the productive forces in **Siberia and the Soviet Far East** remains a component part of the Party's economic strategy. In developing new regions it is of special economic and political importance strictly to ensure the comprehensive fulfilment of production tasks and the development of the entire social infrastructure so as to improve people's working and living conditions.

In charting economic development prospects, the CPSU proceeds from the need to improve **foreign economic strategy** and more fully to utilise the possibilities offered by the mutually advantageous international division of labour and, above all, the advantages of socialist economic integration. Foreign economic, scientific and technical contacts will be extended, and progressive structural changes will be introduced in the sphere of export and import in order to raise the efficiency of the national economy and guarantee independence from capitalist countries in strategically important areas.

Improvement of Socialist Production Relations, the System of Economic Management and Its Methods

Constant improvement of production relations, which should always correspond to the dynamically developing productive forces, and identification and resolution in good time of non-antagonistic contradictions arising between them are vital prerequisites for accelerating socio-economic progress.

Consolidation and enhancement of social ownership of the means of production, which is the foundation of the economic system of socialism, will remain at the centre of the Party's attention. The task is to increase the degree to which production is socialised, to raise the efficiency of its planned organisation, and steadily to improve the forms and methods of utilising the advantages and potentials of the property belonging to all the people.

An upsurge of productive forces in agriculture, the development of inter-farm cooperation and agro-industrial integration will help bring about a further drawing together, and in the future a fusion, of collective-farm and cooperative property and the property of all the people. This will be a result of the all-round development and strengthening of both forms of socialist ownership, ever fuller utilisation of the possibilities of the collective-farm and cooperative sector of the economy.

The Party will persevere in fostering in work collectives and in every worker a sense of co-ownership of social property, take the necessary measures to protect socialist property, prevent all attempts to use it for self-serving ends, eradicate methods of appropriation of material benefits that are alien to socialism, and ensure the constitutional right of citizens to personal property.

The Party attaches great significance to **improvement of relations in the sphere of distribution** which have a notable effect on enhancing collective and personal interest in the development of social production and on the standards and mode of life of the people. A policy will be consistently implemented of ensuring the most effective distribution of the social product and national income, and making sure that the mechanism of distribution serves as a reliable barrier to unearned incomes and to levelling in pay, a barrier to everything that contradicts the norms and principles of socialist society. It is necessary to have strict control over the measure of work and the measure of consumption, to increase the interest of collectives and of every worker in achieving better national economic results, and skilfully to combine moral and material incentives in work.

An urgent task is further to develop **relations in the sphere of economic exchange**. It is necessary to increase the stability of economic ties, ensure a dynamic correlation between demand and supply, improve the circulation of material and money resources and accelerate the turnover of circulating assets.

To raise production efficiency and improve distribution, exchange and consumption it is important to use commodity-money relations more fully, in conformity with the new content inherent in them under socialism. It is necessary to promote greater economy and control over the amount and quality of work by using monetary means, to employ the whole arsenal of economic levers and incentives, to consolidate the state budget and to increase the buying power of the rouble.

The acceleration of the social and economic development of the country demands continuous **improvement in the guidance of the national economy**, reliable and effective functioning of the economic mechanism comprising diverse and flexible forms and methods of management, and their correspondence to changing conditions of economic development and the character of the tasks being fulfilled.

Improvement of management should be based on a more efficient and comprehensive use of the advantages and possibilities of the socialist planned economic system and economic laws, and take full account of the changes in productive forces and production relations and of the growth of educational standards, consciousness, qualifications and experience of the broad mass of the working people. It should ensure an optimal combination of personal interests and the interests of work collectives and of different social groups with the interests of the entire state, the interests of all the people, and in this way use them as the motive force of economic growth.

The entire system of management should be directed towards augmenting the contribution of every element of the national economy to attaining the supreme goal—to satisfy to the fullest extent the requirements of society. The all-round increase of this contribution with a minimum expenditure of all resources is an immutable law of socialist economic management, and the basic criterion for evaluating the performance of various sectors, associations and enterprises, of all production units.

There must be a consistent implementation of the Leninist principles of management and, above all, of the principle of **democratic centralism** which reflects the unity of both of its basic elements—enhanced efficiency of centralised guidance and a considerable broadening of the economic autonomy and responsibility of associations and enterprises.

The attention of central management bodies should be concentrated to an increasing degree on fulfilling the strategic tasks of economic and social development, and on implementing in practice a uniform policy in the spheres of scientific and technological progress and capital investments, of structural changes in the national economy, the proportionality of social production, the strengthening of the system of planned state reserves, distribution of the productive forces, payment for work, social security, prices, tariffs, finances, accounting and statistics.

The Party considers it necessary to raise the efficiency of **planning** as an instrument for carrying out its economic policy. Planning should be an active lever for accelerating the social and economic development of the country, for intensifying production on the basis of scientific and technological progress, implementing progressive economic decisions and ensuring balanced and dynamic economic growth. Qualitative indices reflecting the efficiency of utilisation of resources, the scale of output of new products and the growth of labour productivity on the basis of the achievements of science and technology should occupy a central place in plans. It is vital to tackle economic and social tasks comprehensively, organically combine long-term, five-year and annual plans, raise the scientific standards of planning, enhance discipline in carrying out plans, ensure priority of the interests of the entire state, and decisively put a stop to all manifestations of departmentalism and parochialism, red tape and voluntarism. The finance-and-credit system must be substantially improved, and its role in raising production efficiency and strengthening the money turnover system and cost accounting must be enhanced.

Developing the principles of centralised management and planning, the Party, in the fulfilment of strategic tasks, will vigorously carry out **measures to enhance the role of the main production element**—associations and enterprises, and consistently follow a line towards broadening their rights and economic autonomy and increasing their responsibility and interest in achieving good final results. Day-to-day management work should be concentrated at the local level—in work collectives.

The Party considers it necessary to develop and improve further the effectiveness of **cost accounting** and consistently to switch enterprises and associations over to full-scale cost accounting, while enhancing economic leverage and reducing the number of indices set by higher organisations. The activity of associations and enterprises will be regulated to an ever fuller extent by long-term economic norms which give scope to initiative and creativity in work collectives. Measures to improve management from above should be combined with the development of collective forms of organisation and stimulation of work at a grass-roots level. The system of levers and incentives should give real advantages to work collectives that are successful in accelerating scientific and technological progress, put out better products and increase the profitability of production. The opportunities and rights of associations and enterprises to use money earned to develop production, provide material incentives for the work force and resolve social questions will grow.

Wholesale trade will expand, the role of direct ties and economic contracts between the consumer-enterprises and manufacturers of products will grow, and so will the influence of the consumer on the technical standards and quality of products.

Price-formation must be improved to ensure that prices reflect more accurately the level of socially indispensable inputs and the quality of products and services, that they stimulate more actively scientific and technological progress, thrift in the use of resources, improvement of technical, economic and consumer qualities of products and introduction of all things new and advanced, and that they promote greater economy.

The CPSU sets the task of consistently improving the **organisational structure of the management** of the nationl economy at all levels, reducing the managerial apparatus and doing away with its excessive elements. It is necessary to improve the management of major national economic complexes and groups of interrelated and similar sectors; to achieve a rational combination of large, medium-sized and small enterprises, and of sectoral and territorial management; to extend the network and improve the performance of production and research-and-production associations; to deepen specialisation; and to develop integration and cooperation in production.

The attention of inter-sectoral and sectoral management bodies will be concentrated on the most important trends in the development of various sectors and on the introduction of scientific and technological achievements. They should be responsible for meeting fully the requirements of the national economy and the population for products of the range and variety that have been decided on. The role and responsibility of republican and local bodies in managing economic, social and cultural development and in meeting the needs of the working people will grow, and the powers of these bodies will be broadened.

In its work to improve economic guidance the CPSU will consistently pursue a line towards **developing the working people's creative initiative and their increased involvement in the process of managing production**, a line towards enhancing the role of work collectives in drafting plans and making economic decisions, in implementing measures in the field of social and economic development at enterprises, and in finding and mobilising the internal reserves of production. Thriftiness, the efficient use of public funds, rational use of every rouble, eradication of mismanagement, and elimination of various non-productive expenditures and losses—this is the cause of the entire Party, all the people, every work collective, every worker.

The development of **socialist emulation** is a subject to which the Party gives constant attention. It is one of the most important spheres for encouraging the creativity of working people, one of the chief means of self-expression and social recognition of the individual. Guided by the Leninist principles of openness and the possibility to compare results and to draw on advanced experience, we must improve the organisation and enhance the efficiency of emulation, root out formalism and stereotypes, and develop the spirit of initiative, comradely cooperation and mutual assistance. Of great significance is all-round support for the initiative and creativity of the people in accelerating scientific and technological progress, increasing labour productivity, ensuring the thrifty use of resources, improving production efficiency and output quality while reducing output costs, ensuring an efficient work rhythm with timely fulfilment of contractual obligations and achieving better national economic results.

III. The Social Policy of the Party

The Party regards social policy as a powerful means of accelerating the country's development, heightening the labour and socio-political activity of the masses, moulding the new man, and affirming the socialist way of life, and as a major factor of political stability in society. It proceeds from the belief that the influence of social policy on growing economic efficiency—on all aspects of public life—will intensify. The CPSU considers undiminishing concern for solving the social questions of labour, everyday needs and culture, for meeting the interests and requirements of the people to be the supreme aim of the activity of all state and economic bodies and public organisations.

The Party defines the **principal tasks of social policy** as follows:

— a steady improvement of the living and working conditions of Soviet people;

— the implementation to an ever fuller extent of the principle of social justice in all spheres of social relations;

— a drawing closer together of all classes and social groups and strata, overcoming essential distinctions between mental and physical work, between town and countryside;

— the perfection of relations between nations and ethnic groups; strengthening the fraternal friendship of the peoples and nationalities of the country.

Raising the Well-Being and Improving the Living and Working Conditions of Soviet People

The production and intellectual potential created in the Soviet Union, and the tasks of accelerating the country's social and economic development make it necessary and possible to achieve notable progress in attaining "**full** well-being and free, **all-round** development for **all** the members of society" (Lenin).

The CPSU sets the task of improving the well-being of Soviet people so as to give it a qualitatively new dimension, of ensuring that the level and structure of consumption of material, social and cultural benefits will correspond most fully to the aim of moulding a harmoniously developed, spiritually rich individual and creating the necessary conditions for the full application of the abilities and talents of Soviet people in the interests of society.

Already in the next fifteen years it is planned to double the volume of resources channelled into meeting the requirements of the people.

The Party attaches special importance to enhancing the creative content and collective character of work, improving its efficiency, and encouraging highly skilled and highly productive labour for the good of society. All this will help make work a prime vital necessity for every Soviet person.

The task ahead is to continue to carry out a series of scientific, technological, economic and social measures aimed at ensuring full and effective employment of the population, and granting to all able-bodied citizens the possibility to work in their chosen sphere of activity in accordance with their inclinations, abilities, education and training, with due account of the needs of society.

A consistent policy will be carried out to decrease considerably the amount of manual work, reduce substantially, and in the future eliminate altogether, monotonous, arduous physical and low-skilled work, ensure healthy, hygienic conditions and introduce better production safety norms in order to prevent industrial accidents and occupational diseases. Intensification and increased efficiency of production and labour productivity will open up in the future new possibilities for reducing working hours and extending the period of paid holidays.

The Party will continue to do everything necessary to raise steadily the real incomes of working people and further to improve the well-being of all strata and social groups in accordance with the country's economic possibilities.

Payment according to work done remains the principal source of working people's incomes during the first phase of communism. The system of wages and salaries must be improved constantly so that it fully corresponds to the principle of payment according to the amount and quality of work done, with due account of the conditions and results of work, stimulates the upgrading of workers' skills and labour productivity, and promotes better output quality and the rational use and saving of all types of resources. It is on this basis that the wages and salaries of working people should grow and their living standards improve. As social wealth grows, the size of minimum wages will increase and the policy of reducing personal income taxes will be carried on. The Party attaches fundamental significance to the resolute elimination of unearned incomes, the eradication of all deviations from the socialist principles of distribution.

Accelerated growth and improvement of the distribution of **social consumption funds** will continue. These funds are to play an increasing role in the development of the state system of free public education and free public health service and social security, in improving the conditions of rest and recreation for working people, in lessening the differences that are objectively inevitable under socialism in the material status of citizens, families and social groups, in evening out socioeconomic and cultural conditions for the upbringing of children and in helping to improve radically the well-being of low-income groups of the population.

A task of foremost importance is **to meet completely the growing demand of the population for high-quality and diverse consumer goods**—foodstuffs, durable and beautiful clothing and footwear, furniture, commodities for cultural needs, and sophisticated household appliances and goods.

Domestic retail trade and public catering will be further developed. Their material and technical basis will be improved and the standards of service will be raised. Consumers' cooperatives, which are to improve trade in the countryside, organise the purchase of farm produce grown by the population and the marketing of agricultural products, will also be further developed. The collective-farm market will continue to play a significant role. A policy of retail prices will be pursued in the interests of increasing people's real incomes.

It is planned to carry out large-scale measures for the setting up of a **modern, highly developed service sector**. An increase in the volume of services, a broadening of their range and improvement of their quality will make it possible to meet more fully the growing demand of the population for various types of communal, transport, everyday, social and cultural services, to make housework easier, and to create better conditions for rest and a meaningful use of free time. The service industry will expand at an accelerated rate in the countryside and in the regions now being developed.

The Party considers as a matter of special social significance an accelerated solution of the **housing problem**, which will ensure that by the year 2000 practically every Soviet family will have their own living quarters—an apartment or an individual house. This end will be served by the large scale of state-funded housing construction, more extensive development of cooperative and individual house building, as well as reconstruction, renovation and better upkeep of the available housing and stricter control over its distribution. Special attention will be devoted to the quality of housing construction, to improving the standards of comfort, layouts and technical equipment of apartments and houses.

Higher demands will be made on the architecture, landscaping and planning of urban and rural settlements. Such population centres should be a well thought-out arrangement of production zones, residential districts, public, cultural, educational and child-care institutions, trade and service establishments, sports facilities, and public transport, ensuring the best conditions for work, everyday life and rest. The practice of encouraging people to contribute funds for the improvement of living conditions, cultural and recreation facilities, tourism and other activities will be broadened.

A matter of primary importance is **building up the health of Soviet people** and prolonging the period of their active life. The Party sets the task of satisfying completely the requirements of urban and rural residents everywhere for all types of medical services of a high standard, and of radically improving the quality of medical services. To this end it is planned: to introduce a universal system of medical check-ups for the population; to extend further the network of mother-and-child-care centres, clinics, hospitals and sanatoria and to equip them with modern medical facilities; and to ensure the necessary supply of medicines, medical equipment and sanitation and hygiene means.

Physical training and sports are a factor of everyday life. Their importance is growing in improving people's health, in the harmonious development of the individual and in preparing youth for work and the defence of their homeland. Efforts should be made to ensure that every person cares for his physical fitness from an early age, has a knowledge of hygiene and medical aid and has a healthy way of life.

The CPSU attaches great significance to **showing more care for the family**. The family plays an important role in building up the health of the younger generation and in its upbringing, in ensuring the economic and social progress of society and in improving demographic processes. It is in the family that one's basic character, one's attitude to work and to moral, ideological and cultural values take shape. Society is vitally interested in having families that are stable and spiritually and morally healthy. Proceeding from this, the Party considers it necessary to pursue a policy of strengthening the family and rendering assistance to it in the performance of its social functions and in the upbringing of children, a policy of improving the material, housing and living conditions of families with children and of newly married couples. There must be a more profound cooperation between the family, the school and the work collective; it is necessary to enhance the responsibility of parents for the upbringing of children, as well as the responsibility of children for the well-being of parents, for their secure old age.

A matter of continuing concern to the Party is **a further improvement of the status of mothers**. To this end favourable conditions will be created that will enable women to combine motherhood with active participation in work and social activities. Special attention will be devoted to mother-and-child care, and the period of pre-natal and child-care leave will be extended. The network of sanatoria, rest homes and boarding houses that accommodate families on holiday will be expanded. Diverse forms of employing women will be further developed. Sliding work schedules, a shorter working day, and work at home will be introduced on a wider scale in accordance with the wishes of women.

A broad range of measures will be implemented to create the necessary conditions for the upbringing of the younger generation. In the near future the demand of the population for child-care establishments will be met in full. The network of Young Pioneer and work-and-sports camps, Young Pioneer houses, and scientific and technical and creative arts centres and stations will be expanded. The norms of expenditures on catering in pre-school and vocational training establishments and in children's homes will grow.

The Party stresses the need to give considerably **more attention to the social problems of young people** and, above all, to develop and more fully satisfy those interests and requirements of young people that are socially significant, in the sphere of work and everyday life, education and culture, professional advancement and promotion, and rational use of free time.

The CPSU will continue to show constant **concern for improving the material status of labour and war veterans**, senior citizens, disabled persons, and the families of soldiers killed on duty, for providing social, medical and cultural services to them. The sizes of pensions and, above all, minimum pensions and those granted earlier will be periodically increased. The level of pensions provided to collective farmers will gradually approach that established for production and office workers. The network of homes for the aged and disabled will be further developed and the conditions of upkeep in such homes will be improved. Labour veterans with valuable experience will have more opportunities to work in accordance with their capabilities and to be involved in public life and educational work; this is a matter of major social and economic importance.

The harmonious interaction between society and nature, between man and the environment is acquiring ever growing significance in improving the life of the people. Socialist society, which consciously builds its future, manages the use of nature in a planned and thrifty manner and is in the vanguard of mankind's struggle to preserve and augment the natural wealth of our planet. The Party considers it necessary to exercise greater control over nature management and to conduct ecological education on a wider scale.

Overcoming Class Differences and the Formation of a Socially Homogeneous Society

An important law of the development of social relations at the present stage is the **drawing closer together of the working class, the collective-farm peasantry and the intelligentsia, and the establishment of a classless structure of society with the working class playing the decisive role in that process.**

The political experience of the working class, its high level of consciousness, organisation and will provide a rallying point for our society. The growth of the general educational and cultural standards and skills, and of the labour and socio-political activity of the working class enhances its vanguard role in perfecting socialism, in building communism.

In the course of consistently implementing the Party's agrarian policy, agricultural work is turned into a variety of industrial work and the substantial social differences and differences in cultural and service standards between town and country are being eliminated. The way of life and the character of work of the peasants are becoming increasingly similar to those of the working class. Overcoming the differences between these classes and establishing a classless society in our country will take place mainly in the historical framework of the first, socialist phase of the communist formation.

Revolutionary transformations of the productive forces are leading to an increase in the share of brain work in the activities of the broad mass of workers and collective-farm peasants. At the same time, the numerical strength of the intelligentsia is growing and its creative contribution to material production and other spheres of public life is increasing. This promotes a gradual elimination of the substantial differences between physical and brain work and the drawing closer together of all social groups. The complete elimination of these differences and the formation of a socially homogeneous society will take place at the supreme phase of communism. At the same time, as long as such differences exist, the Party considers it a matter of foremost importance to take careful account in its policies of the distinctive features characterising the interests of the classes and social groups. Much attention will be given to evening out the working and living conditions of the population in different regions of the country.

The role of work collectives in the social structure of Soviet society **is growing**. The Party is helping in every way to bring about a situation in which every work collective will become an effective social cell of socialist self-government by the people and day-to-day genuine participation of working people in the solution of questions related to the work of enterprises, institutions and organisations, and of the development and application of the creative energies of the individual. It considers it necessary to enhance in a purposeful manner the influence of work collectives on all spheres of the life of society, to extend their rights and at the same time to increase their responsibility for carrying out specific tasks of economic, social and cultural development.

Further Flourishing and Drawing Closer Together of Socialist Nations and Nationalities

The CPSU takes full account in its activities of the multinational composition of Soviet society. The path that has been traversed provides convincing proof that **the nationalities question inherited from the past has been successfully solved in the Soviet Union**. Characteristic of the national relations in our country are both the continued flourishing of the nations and nationalities and the fact that they are steadily and voluntarily drawing closer together on the basis of equality and fraternal cooperation. Neither artificial prodding nor holding back of the objective trends of development is admissible here. In the long-term historical perspective this development will lead to complete unity of the nations.

The CPSU proceeds from the fact that in our socialist multinational state, in which more than one hundred nations and nationalities work and live together, there naturally arise **new tasks of improving national relations**. The Party has carried out, and will continue to carry out such tasks on the basis of the tested principles of the Leninist nationalities policy. It puts forward the following main tasks in this field:

— all-round strengthening and development of the integral, federal, multinational state. The CPSU will continue to struggle consistently against any manifestations of parochialism and national narrow-mindedness, while at the same time showing constant concern for further increasing the role of the republics, autonomous regions and autonomous areas in carrying out countrywide tasks and for promoting the active involvement of working people of all nationalities in the work of government and administrative bodies. Through creative application of the Leninist principles of socialist federalism and democratic centralism, the forms of inter-nation relations will be enriched in the interests of the Soviet people as a whole and of each nation and nationality;

— a buildup of the material and intellectual potential of each republic within the framework of the integral national economic complex. Combining the initiative of the Union and autonomous republics, autonomous regions and autonomous areas with central administration at the countrywide level will make possible the more rational use of the country's resources and of local natural and other features. It is necessary consistently to deepen the division of labour between the republics, even out the conditions of economic management, encourage active participation by the republics in the economic development of new regions, promote inter-republican exchanges of workers and specialists, and broaden and improve the training of qualified personnel from among citizens of all the nations and nationalities inhabiting the republics;

— development of the Soviet people's integral culture, which is socialist in content, diverse in its national forms and internationalist in spirit, on the basis of the greatest achievements and original progressive traditions of the peoples of the USSR. The advancement and drawing together of the national cultures and the consolidation of their interrelationships make mutual enrichment more fruitful and open up the broadest possibilities for the Soviet people to enjoy everything valuable that has been created by the talent of each of the peoples of our country.

The equal right of all citizens of the USSR to use their native languages and the free development of these languages will be ensured in the future as well. At the same time learning the Russian language, which has been voluntarily accepted by the Soviet people as a medium of communication between different nationalities, besides the language of one's nationality, broadens one's access to the achievements of science and technology and of Soviet and world culture.

The Party proceeds from the belief that consistent implementation of the Leninist nationalities policy and a strengthening in every way of the friendship of the peoples are part of the effort to perfect socialism and a way that has been tested in social practice of ensuring the further flourishing of our multinational socialist homeland.

IV. Development of the Political System of Soviet Society

Established as a result of the socialist revolution, the dictatorship of the proletariat played the decisive role in creating the new society, and in the process it, too, underwent changes. With the abolition of the exploiter classes the function of suppressing the resistance of the overthrown exploiters gradually faded away and full scope was given to accomplishing its foremost, constructive tasks. Having fulfilled its historical mission, the dictatorship of the proletariat has evolved into a political power of all working people, while the proletarian state has become a state of the whole people. It is the main tool for perfecting socialism in our country, while on the international scene it performs the functions of upholding the socialist gains, strengthening the positions of world socialism, countering the aggressive policy of imperialist forces and developing peaceful cooperation with all nations.

The CPSU believes that at the present stage the strategic line of development of the political system of Soviet society consists in advancing Soviet democracy and increasingly promoting socialist self-government by the people on the basis of active and effective participation of working people, their collectives and organisations in decision-making concerning the affairs of state and society.

The leading force in this process is the Party, the nucleus of the political system of Soviet society. It exercises guidance over the work of all other parts of this system—the Soviet state, the trade unions, the Young Communist League, the cooperatives and other public organisations reflecting the common and specific interests of all sections of the population, of all the nations and nationalities of the country. Acting within the framework of the Constitution, the CPSU directs and coordinates the work of state and public organisations and sees to it that each of them fully carries out its functions. In all its activities the Party sets an example of serving the interests of the people and observing the principles of socialist democracy.

The Party makes sure that the principles of socialist self-government by the people are consistently applied in the administration of society and the state, that is, that the work of administration is not only carried out in the interests of working people but also becomes naturally, and to an ever greater extent, a direct concern of working people themselves, who, to use Lenin's words, know no authority except the authority of their own unity.

The Party will continue to work to ensure that the socio-economic, political and personal rights and freedoms of citizens are extended and enriched and that ever more favourable conditions and guarantees are created for their full exercise. Soviet citizens have every possibility to express and exercise their civic will and interests and enjoy all the benefits of socialism. Soviet citizens' exercise of their rights and freedoms is inseparable from the performance of their constitutional duties. It is an immutable political principle of socialist society that there are no rights without duties and no duties without rights. The CPSU will continue its persistent efforts to make sure that every Soviet citizen is educated in a spirit of awareness of the indivisibility of his rights, freedoms and duties.

It is a matter of key importance for the Party's policy to **develop and strengthen the Soviet socialist state** and increasingly reveal its democratic nature as a state of the whole people and its creative and constructive role.

The CPSU makes constant efforts to improve the work of the Soviets of People's Deputies—the political foundation of the USSR, the main element in socialist self-government by the people. The Party attaches great significance to perfecting the forms of the people's representation, to developing the democratic principles of the Soviet electoral system and to ensuring free, comprehensive discussion of the candidates' personal and professional qualities so that the most capable and re-spected representatives of the working class, collective-farm peasantry and the people's intelligentsia of all the nations and nationalities of the country are elected to the Soviets. In order to improve the work of the Soviets and infuse fresh blood into them, in order that more millions of people will go through the school of running the state, the composition of deputies to the Soviets will be systematically renewed at elections.

The CPSU makes a constant effort to facilitate the work of the Supreme Soviet of the USSR and the Supreme Soviets of the Union republics of consistently perfecting legislation, effectively resolving the key problems of home and foreign policy within their sphere of responsibilities, exercising vigorous guidance over the Soviets of People's Deputies and checking on the work done by the agencies under them. The role and responsibility of local Soviets in ensuring the compre-hensive economic and social development of their respective regions, in imple-menting tasks of local significance and in coordinating and checking on the activities of organisations in their areas will continue to grow.

All conditions should be created for the strict fulfilment of Lenin's instructions that the Soviets should be bodies that not only make decisions but also organise and check on their implementation. Soviets at all levels should apply ever more fully democratic principles of work, including collective, free and constructive discussion and decision-making; publicity; criticism and self-criticism; the deputies' regular reporting back to the constituencies and their accountability to them to the extent of being recalled before the expiration of their term of office for having failed to justify the voters' confidence; control over the work done by executive and other bodies; and extensive involvement of citizens in the work of administration.

The Party will unswervingly conduct a policy of **democratising administration, the process of working out and adopting decisions of state importance**, which ensures selection of optimal solutions and the consideration and comparison of different opinions and proposals put forward by the working people. The range of matters to be decided on only after discussion in work collectives, standing commissions of the Soviets, and trade union, YCL and other public organisations will broaden. The more important draft laws and decisions will be submitted for countrywide discussion and put to a popular vote. The task is to continue to improve the system of summing up and fulfilling mandates given by electors to their candidates in elections and other suggestions and proposals from citizens and of studying public opinion, and to enable the people to be better informed about the decisions taken and the results of their implementation.

Of particular importance is the broadening of the rights and a heightening of the activity of work collectives in all matters of managing production, social and cultural development and in the political life of society. Steps will be taken to enhance the role of general meetings and councils of work collectives and the responsibility of the management for the fulfilment of their decisions, and to introduce the election of foremen, heads of sections and leaders of other production units.

It is a matter of great importance to improve the performance of the state apparatus and all other administrative bodies. The Soviet apparatus serves the people and is accountable to the people. It should be highly competent and efficient. It is necessary to work for a streamlining of the administrative machinery, a reduction of costs and elimination of redundant jobs, persistently to eradicate manifestations of red tape, formalism, departmentalism and parochialism and get rid of incompetent and inert officials without delay. Careless work, abuse of office, careerism, striving for personal enrichment, nepotism and favouritism should be relentlessly rooted out and punished.

The Party considers it necessary to abide strictly by the principle of accountability of the staff of state bodies and extend the system of filling vacancies through election or competition. It is necessary persistently to implement the principle of collective decision-making, with each executive remaining personally responsible for the work done; members of the staff should be judged objectively by their practical work and there should be effective control over the actual fulfilment of the decisions taken.

The CPSU will actively help to raise the efficiency of state and public control. It regards the participation of working people in **People's Control** bodies as an important way of increasing their political maturity and heightening their activity in protecting public interests, and of fostering a statesmanlike approach to matters and a caring attitude to public property.

It has been and remains a matter of unremitting concern to the Party to **strengthen the legal foundation of the life of the state and society**, ensure strict observance of socialist law and order, and improve the work of judicial bodies, the work of supervision by agencies of the Procurator's Office, and the work of justice and internal affairs bodies. Relying on the support of work collectives, public organisations and all working people, state bodies are obliged to do everything necessary to ensure the safety and good condition of socialist property, protect the personal property of citizens, their honour and dignity, wage an unrelenting struggle against crime, drunkenness and alcoholism, prevent offences of any kind and remove their causes.

The Communist Party of the Soviet Union regards defence of the socialist homeland, a strengthening of the country's defences and the ensuring of state security as one of the most important functions of the Soviet state.

From the standpoint of the country's internal conditions our society does not need an army. But as long as there exists the danger of imperialism starting aggressive wars and military conflicts, the Party will be paying unflagging attention to enhancing the defence capacity of the USSR, strengthening its security and ensuring the preparedness of its Armed Forces to rout any aggressor. The Armed Forces and the state security bodies should display high vigilance and be always ready to cut short imperialism's intrigues against the USSR and its allies.

The leadership exercised by the Communist Party over the country's military development and the Armed Forces is the basis for strengthening the defences of the socialist homeland. It is under the Party's guidance that the country's policy in the field of defence and security and the Soviet military doctrine, which is purely defensive in nature and geared to ensuring protection against an outside attack, are worked out and implemented.

The CPSU will make every effort to ensure that the Soviet Armed Forces remain at a level that rules out strategic superiority of the forces of imperialism, that the Soviet state's defence capacity continues to be improved in every way and that military cooperation between the armies of the fraternal socialist countries is strengthened.

The Party will continue to make constant efforts to ensure that the combat potential of the Soviet Armed Forces is a firm union of military skill, a high level of technical capability, ideological staunchness, organisation and discipline of the officers and men and their loyalty to their patriotic and internationalist duty.

The CPSU considers it necessary in the future as well to increase its organising and directing influence on the Armed Forces' activities, strengthen the principle of one-man leadership, broaden the role and influence of the political bodies and Party organisations of the Army and the Navy and make sure that the Armed Forces' vital links with the people will become still stronger. It is the duty of every Communist, every Soviet citizen to do everything possible to maintain the country's defence capacity at an adequate level. **Defence of the socialist homeland and military service in the ranks of the Armed Forces are an honourable and sacred duty of Soviet citizens.**

The Party attaches foremost importance to enhancing the role of public organisations, which are important component parts of the system of socialist self-government by the people.

The CPSU regards it as its task to promote the continued growth of the prestige and influence of the **trade unions**, which are the most broadly-based organisations of the working people, a school of administration, a school of economic management and a school of communism. The trade unions are to discharge their main functions consistently; to do everything possible to help increase public wealth, improve the working people's working and everyday-life conditions and recreation facilities, protect their rights and interests, be constantly involved in the communist education of the people and draw them into the management of production and the affairs of society, and strengthen conscious labour discipline.

It is the task of trade-union organisations to take an even more active part in promoting socialist self-government by the people and in solving the fundamental questions of the development of the state, economy and culture, interact more closely with the Soviets and other organisations of the working people, raise the standards of the socialist emulation movement and of the effort to disseminate advanced experience and promote its wider application, develop social forms of control over the observance of the principles of social justice and help work collectives exercise the powers vested in them.

The CPSU justly regards as its active helpmate and dependable reserve the **All-Union Leninist Young Communist League**, a public political organisation whose membership of many millions represents the advanced section of Soviet youth. The Party will continue to increase the YCL's role in the education of the younger generation, in the improvement of the work of the Young Pioneer organisation, and in the practical implementation of the tasks of speeding up the country's social and economic development. Exercising guidance over the YCL, the CPSU pays special attention to strengthening its ranks organisationally and politically and enhancing the independent character of the youth league. The YCL should persistently promote the labour and social activity of young people, instill in them a Marxist-Leninist world outlook and high political and moral standards and help them become aware of their historical responsibility for the future of socialism and the world.

The Party helps to improve the work of the **cooperatives**— collective farms, consumer and home-building cooperatives and other cooperative organisations and associations, regarding them as an important form of socialist self-government and an effective means of developing the national economy.

The CPSU will facilitate a further heightening of the activity of the **unions of workers in the arts, of scientific, science and technology, cultural and educational, sport, defence and other voluntary societies and people's social activity bodies.** In fulfilling their functions, these organisations are to make an ever greater contribution to furthering the Party's policy and work for the all-round expression and satisfaction of the interests of the working people united in them, and for enhancing the Soviet people's civic initiative and sense of responsibility.

V. Ideological and Educational Work, Public Education, Science and Culture

The Party will do everything necessary for using in full measure the transforming force of Marxist-Leninist ideology to accelerate the country's social and economic development, and will conduct purposeful work for the ideological, political, labour and moral education of the Soviet people and for **moulding harmoniously developed, socially active individuals combining cultural wealth, moral purity and a perfect physique.**

The CPSU regards it as the main tasks of its ideological work to educate the working people in a spirit of high ideological integrity and dedication to communism, Soviet patriotism and proletarian, socialist internationalism, and a conscientious attitude towards work and public property, to make cultural and intellectual treasures ever more readily available to the people and to eradicate the morals that contradict the socialist way of life.

The Party proceeds from the conviction that a person's education is inseparable from his practical involvement in constructive work for the benefit of the people, in public life and in solving the tasks of social, economic, and cultural advancement. Detachment from reality and its problems dooms ideological and educational work to abstract instruction and empty rhetoric, leading it away from the pressing tasks of building communism. Ideological work should be characterised by close links with social practice, profound ideological and theoretical content and taking account fully and accurately of the realities of domestic and international life and of the growing intellectual requirements of the working people; it should be close to the people, truthful, well argued and comprehensible.

Unity of word and deed—the most important principle of all Party and state activities—is also an indispensable requirement of political and educational work. Active participation in this work is a duty of all leading cadres, a duty of every Communist.

The Party puts forward the following tasks:

In the Field of Ideological and Educational Work

The shaping of a scientific world outlook. Socialism has given Soviet society's intellectual and cultural life a scientific world outlook based on Marxism-Leninism, which is an integral and harmonious system of philosophical, economic and socio-political views. The Party considers it its most important duty to continue creatively developing Marxist-Leninist theory by studying and generalising new phenomena in Soviet society, taking into account the experience of other countries of the socialist community and the world communist, working-class, national liberation and democratic movements and analysing the progress in the natural, technical and social sciences.

The CPSU will work unremittingly so that all Soviet people can thoroughly study the Marxist-Leninist theory, raise their political awareness, consciously participate in the shaping of the Party's policy and actively implement it.

Labour education. In educational work the Party focuses its attention on instilling in all Soviet citizens deep respect and readiness for conscientious work for the common good, be it mental or physical work. Labour is the main source of society's material and cultural wealth, the principal criterion of a person's social status, his sacred duty and the cornerstone of his communist education. The Party will make continued efforts to increase the prestige of honest, efficient work, encourage labour initiative and innovation and strengthen the principles of the communist attitude towards work.

The affirmation of communist morality. In the gradual advancement towards communism the creative potential of communist morality, the most humane, just and noble morality, based on devotion to the goals of the revolutionary struggle and the ideals of communism, manifests itself ever more fully. Our morality has assimilated both universal moral values and the norms of conduct and norms governing relations between people, which have been established by the popular masses in the course of their centuries-old struggle against exploitation, for freedom and social equality, for happiness and peace.

The communist morality upheld by the CPSU is as follows:

— **a collectivist morality,** the fundamental principle of which is "One for all and all for one." This morality is incompatible with egoism and selfishness; it harmoniously blends the common, collective and personal interests of the people;

— **a humanistic morality,** which ennobles the working man, is filled with a deep respect for him and is intolerant of infringements upon his dignity. It asserts truly humane relations between people—relations of comradely cooperation and mutual assistance, good will, honesty, simplicity and modesty in private and public life;

—**an active, vigorous morality,** which stimulates one to ever new labour achievements and creative accomplishments, and encourages one to take a personal interest and be involved in the affairs of one's work collective and of the entire country, to be implacable in rejecting everything that contradicts the socialist way of life and to be persistent in the struggle for the communist ideals.

Patriotic and internationalist education. The Party will continue to work tirelessly so that in every Soviet citizen feelings of love for the country of the October Revolution where he was born and grew up, and pride for the historic accomplishments of the world's first socialist state are combined with feelings of loyalty to proletarian, socialist internationalism, of class solidarity with the working people of the fraternal countries, with all who are fighting against imperialism, and for social progress and peace.

The CPSU and the Soviet state want to see feelings of friendship and fraternity uniting all nations and nationalities of the USSR, a high standard of relations between nationalities and intolerance of any manifestations of nationalism, chauvinism, national narrow-mindedness or egoism, as well as attitudes and traditions that hinder the communist renovation of life become part of every Soviet citizen.

An important task of the Party in its ideological and educational work continues to be that of providing military-patriotic education and ensuring that everyone is prepared to defend the socialist homeland, to give it all his energies and, if necessary, to sacrifice his life for it.

Legal education. The Party attaches great importance to instilling in people a high sense of civic responsibility, respect for Soviet laws and the rules of socialist conduct, irreconcilability to any violations of socialist legality, and a readiness to take an active part in the maintenance of law and order.

Atheistic education. The Party uses ideological means for the broad dissemination of a scientific materialist world outlook, and for overcoming religious prejudices, while at the same time respecting the feelings of believers. While calling for the strict observance of the constitutional guarantees of freedom of conscience, the Party condemns attempts to use religion to the detriment of society and the individual. A highly important aspect of atheistic education consists in heightening the people's labour and public activity, raising their educational level, and the broad dissemination of new Soviet traditions and customs.

The struggle against manifestation of alien ideology and morals and all negative phenomena, connected with the vestiges of the past in the minds and behaviour of people as well as with shortcomings in the practical work in various fields of public life, with delays in solving urgent problems, is an integral part of communist education. The Party attaches paramount importance to the steady and consistent eradication of violations of labour discipline, embezzlement and bribery, profiteering and parasitism, drunkenness and hooliganism, private-owner psychology and money-grubbing, toadyism and servility. It is essential to make full use of both the power of public opinion and the force of law for combatting these phenomena.

Struggle against bourgeois ideology. The acute struggle between the two world outlooks on the international scene reflects the opposition of the two world systems—socialism and capitalism. The CPSU regards it as its task to tell people the truth about real socialism, about the domestic and foreign policy of the Soviet Union, actively to advocate the Soviet way of life and vigorously to expose in a well-argued manner the anti-popular, inhuman and exploitative nature of imperialism. It will instill in Soviet people a high level of political awareness, vigilance, and the ability to assess social phenomena and uphold the ideals and spiritual values of socialism from clear-cut class positions.

The mass information and propaganda media play a growing role in the life of society. The CPSU will make every effort to ensure that the media analyse trends and phenomena in domestic and international life as well as economic and social phenomena in depth, that they actively support everything new and advanced, and call attention to pressing issues of concern to the people and suggest ways of solving them. The press, television and radio networks should provide people with news coverage and commentary that are politically clear and purposeful, profound, prompt, informative, vivid and comprehensive. The Party will continue to render the press and all other mass media ready assistance and support in their work.

Special attention will be devoted to developing television broadcasting, ensuring that radio and TV programs are increasingly available to the population, making the broadcasts richer in content and more interesting and raising their ideological and artistical level.

It is essential to resolutely eliminate any manifestations of pompous verbosity and formalism in ideological, educational, and propaganda work. All the forms and means of this work must help mobilise the people for fulfilling the tasks facing the country by ensuring broad publicity of the work of the Party and state bodies and public organisations, direct and frank discussions with people, and by shaping public opinion and promoting its influence on practical matters. The CPSU will take constant care of strengthening the material foundation of ideological work.

In the Field of Public Education

The Party consistently pursues a policy of educating and training conscientious, highly-educated people fitted for both physical and mental work, for energetically accomplishing their jobs in the national economy, in various fields of public and state life, in science and in culture. The genuinely popular system of education established in the USSR has brought knowledge within the reach of all citizens and made it possible within a historically short span of time to eliminate widespread illiteracy and introduce universal secondary education.

The CPSU will continue improving the public education system, taking

into account the need to accelerate social and economic development, the prospects of communist construction and the requirements of scientific and technological progress. The reform of the general education and vocational training school now being effected in the country is based on the creative development of Lenin's principles of a uniform polytechnical labour school; it is aimed at raising still higher the standards of instruction and education of the young, and making them better prepared for their future labour activity, and geared toward gradually introducing universal vocational training. Schools are called upon to instill in their pupils love for their homeland, collectivism and respect for the elderly, for their parents and teachers, to impart to the younger generation a keen sense of responsibility for the quality of their study and work and for their conduct, and also to encourage student self-administration. As the planned measures are carried out, the vocational training and general education forms of schooling will continue to develop and draw closer together, with their eventual merging.

In keeping with the demands of scientific, technological and social progress, the system of secondary specialised and higher education will be further developed. It should respond readily and timely to the requirements of production, science and culture and meet the national economy's needs for specialists with high professional standards, ideological and political maturity and organisational and managerial skills. The Party attaches much significance to developing the system of advanced training which, combined with the system of correspondence and evening courses, will offer favourable opportunities for all working people to continue their education, steadily increase and refresh their knowledge and raise their general cultural and professional levels.

The Party will show unfailing concern for the teaching staff and for strengthening and extending the material foundation of the entire system of education.

In the Field of Science

Science is playing a growing role in developing the productive forces, perfecting social relations, creating fundamentally new kinds of equipment and technology, raising labour productivity, developing natural resources in the depths of the earth and the ocean, exploring outer space and protecting and improving the environment.

The Party's policy in the field of science is designed to create favourable conditions for dynamic progress in all areas of knowledge; concentrate personnel, and material and financial resources in the more promising areas of research called upon to accelerate the accomplishment of planned economic and social tasks and society's cultural advancement; and ensure a reliable defence capability of the country.

Dialectical materialistic methods have been and remain the chief, tried-and-tested basis for progress in the natural sciences and social studies. They should be creatively further developed and skilfully applied in research and in social practice.

Soviet science is called upon to take leading positions in the principle areas of scientific and technological progress and to provide effective and timely solutions to current and long-term production, social and economic problems. It is important to ensure priority development of fundamental, exploratory research and ensure prompt implementation of scientific ideas in the national economy and other fields of endeavour. The organisational and economic forms of the integration of science and production and of directing scientific and technological progress should be continuously updated; the scale of topical applied research and experimental design projects and their efficiency should be increased. It is essential to strengthen the interaction of scientific work collectives at research institutions, higher educational establishments and in production.

Social science workers should focus their attention on studying and thoroughly analysing the experience of world development and the building of the new society in the USSR and other socialist countries, the dialectics of productive forces and relations of production and of the material and cultural spheres under socialism, the general laws governing the formation of the communist system and the ways and means of ensuring gradual movement towards its highest stage. An urgent task facing social sciences at the present stage is to provide the scientific analysis of the objective contradictions in socialist society, work out sound recommendations on how to overcome them, and make reliable economic and social forecasts.

The processes under way in the communist, working-class and national liberation movements, as well as in capitalist society should be studied most thoroughly. The course of world development confronts mankind with quite a few questions of global importance. Science should furnish correct answers to these questions. Combatting bourgeois ideology, revisionism and dogmatism has been and remains an important task of the social sciences.

The Party supports bold exploration, competition of ideas and trends in science, and fruitful discussion. Scholastic discourses and passive recording of facts which do not provide scope for daring conclusions of a general theoretical nature are alien to science, as are time-serving and loss of touch with reality. The complex and multifaceted problems of today call for a broader integration of the social, natural and technical sciences. Forms of organisation of science that provide for an interdisciplinary study of pressing problems, necessary mobility of scientific personnel and a flexible structure of scientific centres as well as effectiveness of research and development must be introduced on a greater scale. It is vital to enhance their role in the elaboration and fulfilment of plans for economic and social development. An indispensable condition for scientific progress is a constant influx of fresh forces, in particular from the sphere of production, efficient use of the creative potentialities of scientists, and active support of their work according to their actual contribution to solving theoretical and applied problems.

In the Field of Cultural Development, Literature and Art

The development of the multinational and truly popular Soviet culture, which has won worldwide recognition, is a historic achievement of our system. The great influence exercised by Sovet culture is due to its faithfulness to the truth of life and to the ideals of socialism and communism, to its profound humanism and optimism, and its close links with the people.

The CPSU attaches much importance to a fuller and deeper assimilation by working people of the values of intellectual and material culture and to their active involvement in artistic creative work. Steadily applying the Leninist principles of cultural development, the Party will see to the aesthetic education of the working people, in particular of the young generations, based on the best works of national and world artistic culture. Implementation of aesthetic principles will provide an even greater inspiration to work, raise the stature of man and enrich his everyday life.

The sphere of culture is called upon to meet the growing requirements of various sections of the population, to provide adequate opportunity for amateur artistic activity, to develop talents, to enrich the socialist way of life, and to mould healthy requirements and fine aesthetic values. For the successful accomplishment of these tasks, the Party considers it absolutely essential to improve the contents and methods of cultural work, strengthen the material base of this work and carry out intensive cultural development programs in the countryside and newly-developed regions.

The Party will promote in every way the role of literature and art, which are called upon to serve the interests of the people and the cause of communism, to be a source of joy and inspiration for millions of people, to express their will, sentiments and thoughts, and actively contribute to their ideological development and moral education.

The main line of development of literature and art consists in strengthening ties with the life of the people, in a truthful and highly artistic representation of socialist reality, in an inspired and vivid portrayal of the new and advanced, and in an impassioned exposure of everything which hampers social progress.

The art of socialist realism is based on the principles of partisanship and kinship with the people. It combines bold innovation in truthful artistic representation of life with the use and development of all the progressive traditions of national and world culture. Workers in literature and art have broad scope for truly free creative endeavour, for the professional mastery and for further development of diverse forms, styles and genres of realism. As the cultural standards of the people rise, the influence of art on the life of society and on its moral and psychological climate is enhanced. This increases the cultural workers' responsibility for ideological orientation of their creative effort and for the artistic impact of their work.

The CPSU takes a careful and respectful attitude to talent and artistic search. At the same time it has always fought and will continue to fight against the lack of ideological commitment, the lack of discrimination in matters relating to a world outlook and artistic dullness, relying in this on the unions of creative workers, public opinion and Marxist-Leninist literary and art criticism.

Soviet culture facilitates mutual understanding and the drawing together of peoples and vigorously participates in the struggle against the forces of imperialism, reaction and war. Embodying the ideological values and diversity of the intellectual life of socialist society and its humanism, it contributes to world culture and manifests itself more and more forcefully as a powerful factor in the cultural progress of mankind and as a prototype of future communist culture.

PART THREE

THE TASKS OF THE CPSU ON THE INTERNATIONAL SCENE, IN THE DRIVE FOR PEACE AND SOCIAL PROGRESS

The international policy of the CPSU is based on the humane nature of socialist society, which is free from exploitation and oppression and has no classes or social groups interested in unleashing war. It is inseparably linked with the basic, strategic tasks of the Party within the country and expresses the common aspiration of the Soviet people to engage in constructive work and to live in peace with all nations.

The main goals and directions of the international policy of the CPSU are:

— provision of international conditions favourable to the perfection of socialist society in the USSR and its advance to communism; removal of the threat of world war and achievement of universal security and disarmament;

— constant strengthening and expansion of cooperation between the USSR and the fraternal socialist countries and the utmost contribution to the consolidation and progress of the world socialist system;

— development of relations of equality and friendship with newly free countries;

— maintenance and development of relations between the USSR and capitalist states on a basis of peaceful coexistence and businesslike, mutually beneficial cooperation;

— internationalist solidarity with Communist and revolutionary-democratic parties, the international working-class movement and the national liberation struggle of the peoples.

The CPSU's approach to foreign-policy matters consists in firm protection of the interests of the Soviet people and resolute opposition to the aggressive policy of imperialism combined with a readiness for dialogue and constructive settlement of international problems through negotiations.

The foreign-policy course for peace elaborated by the Party and consistently pursued by the Soviet state in combination with the strengthening of the defence capability of the country has ensured for the Soviet people and for most of the world's population the longest period of peace in the 20th century. The CPSU will continue to do everything it can to secure peaceful conditions for the constructive work of the Soviet people, to improve international relations, and to stop the arms race that has engulfed the world, in order to avert the danger of nuclear war, which looms over all peoples.

There is no loftier or more responsible mission than that of safeguarding and strengthening peace and curbing the forces of aggression and militarism for the sake of the life of present and future generations. **A world without wars and without weapons is the ideal of socialism.**

I. Cooperation with Socialist Countries

The CPSU attaches primary importance to the further development and strengthening of relations of friendship between the Soviet Union and other socialist countries.

The Party is seeking long-lasting comradely relations and many-sided cooperation between the USSR and all the other states of the world socialist system. The CPSU proceeds from the belief that the cohesion of the countries of socialism meets the interests of each of them and their common interests, and promotes the cause of peace and the triumph of socialist ideals.

The all-round strengthening of relations of friendship and the development and perfection of ties between the Soviet Union and the other countries of the socialist community are a matter of special concern to the Party.

The ruling Communist and Workers' parties are the motive force of these countries' all-round cooperation. To strengthen the cohesion of the Communists of the fraternal countries and to ensure mutual enrichment of the practice of guiding society, the CPSU will continue to help broaden the inter-Party links that embrace Party organisations at all levels, from Central Committees to primary Party organisations; it will promote exchanges of opinions and experience both on a bilateral and multilateral basis.

The CPSU will continue its policy of strengthening inter-state relations between the Soviet Union and other socialist countries, of affirming them in treaties and agreements, of developing contacts between the legislative bodies and between the public organisations of these countries, and of further stepping up their political cooperation in all forms.

Soviet Communists stand for the increasingly efficient interaction of the fraternal countries on the international scene with due regard for the situation and interests of each of them and for the common interests of the community.

As long as the imperialist NATO military bloc exists, the Party considers it necessary to help improve in every way possible the work of the Warsaw Treaty Organisation as an instrument of collective defence against the aggressive ambitions of imperialism and of joint struggle for a lasting peace and broader international cooperation.

In economic relations, the CPSU stands for a further deepening of socialist economic integration as the material foundation for drawing the socialist countries closer together. It attaches special importance to a consistent uniting of efforts by the fraternal countries in key areas of intensification of production and acceleration of scientific and technological progress in order to accomplish jointly a task of historical significance, namely, that of advancing to the forefront of science and technology with the aim of further improving the well-being of their peoples and strengthening their security.

The Party proceeds from the belief that integration is designed to contribute to an ever increasing extent to progress in the sphere of social production and the socialist way of life in the countries of the socialist community, to evening out more rapidly their levels of economic development and to strengthening the positions of socialism in the world.

The CPSU will actively participate in the collective work of the fraternal parties to coordinate their economic policies, to improve the mechanism of their economic cooperation and evolve new forms of cooperation, to deepen specialisation and cooperation in production, to coordinate plans, to exchange advanced experience and to develop direct links between associations and enterprises. It will help enhance the role of the Council for Mutual Economic Assistance and broaden economic, scientific and technical cooperation on the basis of bilateral and multilateral programs.

While considering equal and mutually beneficial economic cooperation between socialist and capitalist states to be natural and useful, the CPSU at the same time believes that the development of socialist integration should enhance the technical and economic invulnerability of the community with regard to hostile actions by imperialism and to the influence of economic crises and other negative phenomena that are intrinsic to capitalism.

In the sphere of ideology, the CPSU stands for pooling the efforts of the fraternal parties aimed at studying and using the experience in building socialism and in the communist education of working people, at developing the theory of Marxism-Leninism while deepening its creative nature and upholding its revolutionary essence. An invigoration of collective thought, a constant widening of exchanges of cultural and intellectual values, and cooperation in science and culture serve further to strengthen friendship between socialist countries.

The Party will continue to enhance awareness of the unity and common historical destinies of the fraternal peoples. Propagation of the truth about socialism, exposure of imperialist policy and propaganda, rebuffing of anti-communism and anti-Sovietism, and struggle against dogmatic and revisionist views—these tasks are more easily accomplished when Communists act in a single front.

The CPSU regards it as its internationalist duty, together with the other fraternal parties, to consolidate the unity and increase the strength and influence of the socialist community. The outcome of the competition between socialism and capitalism and the future of world civilisation depend largely on the strength of the community, on the success of each country in its constructive endeavours, and on the purposefulness and coordination of their actions.

The experience of the development of the world socialist system shows that socialism provides every opportunity both for the society's confident advance and for the maintenance of harmonious mutual relations between countries. But neither comes of its own accord.

The levels of countries' economic and political development, their historical and cultural traditions, and the actual conditions in which they exist are different. The social development of socialist countries does not always proceed in a straightforward manner. Every major stage of this development sets new complex tasks, whose accomplishment involves struggle, search and the overcoming of contradictions and difficulties.

All this, the CPSU is convinced, calls for utmost attention, a constructive comparison of points of view and effective solidarity so as to rule out any possibility for the rise of differences that could harm common interests. Of special importance are the coordination of actions in matters of principle, comradely interest in each other's success, strict carrying out of commitments, and a profound understanding of both national interests and common, international interests in their organic interconnection.

The formation and development of a new society are taking place in a situation of sharp confrontation between the two world systems. Seeking to weaken the positions of socialism and disrupt the mutual ties of socialist states, and primarily ties with the Soviet Union, imperialism is employing a whole range of differentiated measures—political, economic and ideological. It tries to exploit problems that arise and makes use of nationalistic sentiments for subversive purposes. The CPSU proceeds from the belief that strong unity and class solidarity among socialist countries are especially important in these conditions.

The experience of the USSR, of world socialism shows that the most important factors in its successful advance are the loyalty of the ruling Communist and Workers' parties to the doctrine of Marxism-Leninism and a creative application of that doctrine; firm links between the parties and the broad mass of working people, an enhancing of the authority of the parties and their guiding role in society, strict observance of the Leninist norms of Party and state life, and development of government by the people under socialism; a sober consideration of the actual situation, timely and scientifically substantiated solution of problems that arise; and the building of relations with other fraternal countries on the principles of socialist internationalism.

Whatever the characteristic features of each of the socialist countries, its level of economic development, size, and historical and national traditions, all of them have the same class interests. What unites the socialist countries and makes them cohesive is of paramount importance and is immeasurably greater than what may divide them.

The CPSU is convinced that the socialist countries, fully observing the principles of equality and mutual respect for one another's national interests, will continue to follow the road of ever greater mutual understanding and will draw closer together. The Party will contribute to this historically progressive process.

II. Strengthening Relations with Newly Free Countries

Formulating its policy towards former colonial and semi-colonial countries, the CPSU proceeds from the belief that the embarking of the formerly enslaved peoples on the road of independence, the emergence of dozens of new states and their increasing role in world politics and in the world economy are one of the distinctive features of the present epoch.

The newly free peoples, as Lenin foresaw, are to play a great role in the destinies of mankind as a whole. **The CPSU believes that these peoples' increasing influence should promote to an ever greater extent the cause of peace and social progress.**

The Party is consistently pursuing a policy of expanding contacts between the Soviet Union and the newly free countries, and regards with profound sympathy the aspirations of the peoples who had experienced the heavy and humiliating yoke of colonial slavery. The Soviet Union is building its relations with those countries on the basis of strict respect for their independence and equality, and supports the struggle of those countries against the neo-colonialist policy of imperialism, against the survivals of colonialism, and for peace and universal security.

The Party attaches great importance to solidarity and political and economic cooperation with **socialist-oriented countries**. Every people creates, mostly by its own efforts, the material and technical base necessary for the building of a new society, and seeks to improve the well-being and cultural standards of the masses. The Soviet Union has been doing and will continue to do all it can to render the peoples following that road assistance in economic and cultural development, in training national personnel, in strengthening their defences and in other fields.

The CPSU is developing closer relations with the **revolutionary-democratic parties** of newly free countries. Especially close cooperation has been established with those of them that seek to base their activities on scientific socialism. The CPSU stands for the development of contacts with all national progressive parties holding anti-imperialist and patriotic positions.

Relations between the Soviet Union and newly free countries have demonstrated that there also exists a realistic basis for cooperation with those young states that are following the capitalist road of development. This basis consists in a common interest in safeguarding peace, strengthening international security and ending the arms race; in a sharpening contradiction between the interests of the peoples and the imperialist policy of diktat and expansion; and in an understanding by young states of the fact that political and economic ties with the Soviet Union help to strengthen their independence.

However different the newly free countries may be from one another and whatever road they follow, their peoples share a common desire to develop independently and to run their affairs without foreign interference. The Soviet Union is in full solidarity with them. The CPSU does not doubt that it is the sacred right of the newly free countries to decide their own destinies and to choose their own type of social system.

The CPSU supports the just struggle waged by the countries of Asia, Africa, and Latin America against imperialism and the oppression of transnational monopolies, for the assertion of the sovereign right to be master of one's own resources, for a restructuring of international relations on an equal and democratic basis, for the establishment of a new international economic order, and for the deliverance from the burden of debt imposed by the imperialists.

The Soviet Union is on the side of the states and peoples repulsing the attacks of the aggressive forces of imperialism and upholding their freedom, independence and national dignity. Solidarity with them in our time is also an important aspect of the general struggle for peace and international security. The Party regards it as its internationalist duty to support the struggle of the peoples who are still under the yoke of racism and who are victims of the system of apartheid.

The CPSU regards with understanding the goals and activities of the non-aligned movement and stands for an enhancement of its role in world politics. The USSR will continue to be on the side of the non-aligned states in their struggle against the forces of aggression and hegemonism and for settling disputes and conflicts that arise through negotiations, and will be opposed to the involvement of those states in military and political groupings.

The CPSU stands for the equal participation of newly free countries in international affairs and for an increase of their contribution to the solution of the most important problems of our time. The interaction of those countries with socialist states is vastly important for strengthening the independence of the peoples, improving international relations and preserving peace.

The alliance of the forces of social progress and national liberation is a guarantee of a better future for mankind.

III. Relations with Capitalist Countries. The Struggle for a Lasting Peace and Disarmament

The CPSU proceeds from the belief that the historical dispute between the two opposing social systems, into which the world is divided today, can and must be settled by peaceful means. Socialism proves its superiority not by force of arms, but by force of example in every area of the life of society—by the dynamic development of the economy, science and culture, by an improvement in the living standards of working people, and by a deepening of socialist democracy.

Soviet Communists are convinced that the future belongs to socialism. Every people deserves to live in a society that is free from social and national oppression, in a society of genuine equality and genuine democracy. It is the sovereign right of an oppressed and exploited people to free itself from exploitation and injustice. Revolutions are a natural outcome of social development, of class struggle in every given country. The CPSU believed and continues to believe that the "export" of revolution, the imposition of revolution on anyone from the outside, is unacceptable in principle. But the "export" of counterrevolution in any form, too, is a gross encroachment on the free expression of will by the peoples, on their right independently to choose their way of development. The Soviet Union is strongly opposed to attempts forcibly to check and reverse the march of history.

The interests of the peoples demand that inter-state relations be directed onto a path of peaceful competition and equal cooperation.

The Communist Party of the Soviet Union firmly and consistently upholds the Leninist principle of peaceful coexistence of states with different social systems. The policy of peaceful coexistence as understood by the CPSU presupposes: renunciation of war and the use or threat of force as a means of settling disputed issues, and the settlement of such issues through negotiations; non-interference in internal affairs and respect for the legitimate interests of each other; the right of the peoples independently to decide their destinies; strict respect for the sovereignty and territorial integrity of states and the inviolability of their borders; cooperation on the basis of complete equality and mutual benefit; fulfilment in good faith of commitments arising from generally recognised principles and norms of international law and from international treaties concluded.

These are the basic principles on which the Soviet Union builds its relations with capitalist states. They have been affirmed in the Constitution of the USSR.

The CPSU will purposefully help to bring about a universal affirmation in international relations of the principle of peaceful coexistence as a generally recognised norm of inter-state relations that will be observed by everyone. It believes that the extension of ideological differences between the two systems to the sphere of inter-state relations is inadmissible.

The Party will work for the development of the process of international detente, regarding it as a natural and essential stage on the road to the establishment of a comprehensive and reliable security system. The experience of cooperation shows that there is a real prospect for this. The CPSU stands for the creation and use of international mechanisms and institutions that would make it possible to find optimal correlations between national, state interests and the common interests of mankind. It stands for enhancing the role of the United Nations in strengthening peace and developing international cooperation.

The nuclear powers bear a special responsibility for the situation in the world. The states possessing nuclear weapons and other weapons of mass destruction must renounce the use of or threat to use such weapons and refrain from steps that would lead to an aggravation of the international situation.

The CPSU stands for normal and stable relations between the Soviet Union and the United States of America, which presupposes non-interference in internal affairs, respect for each other's legitimate interests, recognition and practical implementation of the principle of equality and equal security, and the building of the greatest possible mutual trust on this basis. Differences between social systems and ideologies should not lead to strained relations. There are objective prerequisites for the development of fruitful and mutually beneficial Soviet-US cooperation in various fields. It is the conviction of the CPSU that the policies of both powers should be oriented to mutual understanding rather than hostility which is fraught with the threat of catastrophic consequences for the Soviet and American people as well as for other nations.

The Party is convinced that all states, big and small, regardless of their potentials, geographic location, and social systems, can and must participate in the search for solutions to acute problems, in the normalisation of conflict situations, and in carrying out measures to ease tensions and curb the arms race.

The CPSU attaches great importance to the further development of peaceful, good-neighbourly relations and cooperation between European states. An indispensable condition for the stability of positive processes in this region, as in other regions, is respect for the territorial and political realities which emerged as a result of the Second World War. The CPSU is strongly opposed to attempts to revise them under any pretext whatsoever and will combat any manifestation of revanchism.

The Party will make consistent efforts to ensure that the process of strengthening security, trust and peaceful cooperation in Europe, which was launched on the initiative and with the active participation of the Soviet Union, develops and deepens, and **comes to embrace the whole world**. The CPSU stands for the pooling of efforts by all interested states for the purpose of ensuring security in Asia and for carrying out a joint search by them for a constructive solution to the problem. Asia, Africa, Latin America, the Pacific and the Indian Oceans can and must become zones of peace and good-neighbourliness.

The CPSU stands for the development of extensive long-term and stable contacts between states in the sphere of the economy, science, and technology on the basis of complete equality and mutual benefit. Foreign economic cooperation is of great political importance, for it helps to strengthen peace and relations of peaceful coexistence between states with different social systems. The Soviet Union rejects all forms of discrimination and the use of trade, economic, scientific and technical contacts as a means of exerting pressure, and will work to ensure the economic security of states.

The CPSU stands for broad mutual exchanges of genuine cultural values between all countries. Such exchanges should serve humanitarian goals, namely, the cultural and intellectual enrichment of the peoples and the consolidation of peace and good-neighbourliness.

The Soviet state will cooperate with other countries in solving the global problems that have become especially acute in the second half of the 20th century and that are of vital significance to the whole of mankind. These include: environmental protection, energy, raw materials, food and demographic problems, peaceful exploration of outer space and the resources of the World Ocean, the overcoming of the economic backwardness of many newly free countries, the eradication of dangerous diseases, and other problems. The solution of these problems calls for joint efforts by all states. It will be much easier to solve these problems if the squandering of efforts and resources on the arms race is stopped.

In the interests of mankind and for the benefit of all nations, **the CPSU and the Soviet state stand for an extensive and constructive program of measures aimed at ending the arms race, achieving disarmament, and ensuring peace and security**.

The CPSU, which considers **general and complete disarmament** under strict and comprehensive international control to be a historic task and is carrying out efforts to achieve it, shall consistently be working for:

— **restriction and narrowing of the sphere of military preparations**, especially those involving weapons of mass destruction. First and foremost, outer space should be totally excluded from that sphere so that it will not become the scene of military rivalry and a source of death and destruction. Exploration and development of outer space should be for peaceful purposes only, for the development of science and production, in accordance with the needs of all nations. The USSR stands for collective efforts in the solution of this problem and will actively participate in international cooperation to this end. The Soviet Union will also call for the adoption of measures promoting the non-proliferation of nuclear weapons and the establishment of zones free from these and other weapons of mass destruction;

— **the complete elimination of nuclear armaments** to be carried out stage by stage till the end of the 20th century by means of discontinuing the testing and production of all types of these armaments, renouncing the first use of nuclear weapons by all the nuclear powers, and freezing, reducing and destroying all their stockpiles:

— **an end to the production of other types of weapons of mass destruction,** including chemical weapons, their elimination, and a ban on the development of new types of such weapons:

—**reductions in the armed forces of states,** first and foremost those which are permanent members of the UN Security Council and countries that have military agreements with them; limitations on conventional armaments; an end to the development of new types of these armaments whose yield approximates that of mass destruction weapons, and reductions in military spending;

— **a freeze on, and reductions in, the number of troops and armaments in the most explosive parts of the world,** the dismantling of military bases on foreign territory, and measures to build up mutual trust and lessen the risk of armed conflicts, including those that might occur by accident.

The CPSU stands for overcoming the division of the world into military-political groupings. The CPSU is for the simultaneous dissolution of NATO and the Warsaw Treaty Organisation, or, as a first step, the disbandment of their military organisations. To lower confrontation between the military blocs, the Soviet Union advocates the conclusion of a treaty between them on the mutual non-use of force and the maintenance of relations of peace, a treaty which would be open to all other states as well.

The Party will make every effort to ensure that questions of arms limitation and averting the threat of war are tackled through honest and strictly observed agreements on the basis of equality and equal security of the sides, in order to preclude any attempt to conduct talks from a "position of strength" and use them to cover up an arms buildup.

The Soviet state and its allies do not seek military superiority, but at the same time they will not permit an upset in the military-strategic equilibrium that has taken shape in the world arena. Furthermore, they are consistenty working to ensure that the level of this equilibrium is steadily lowered, the quantity of armaments on both sides reduced, and the security of all peoples guaranteed.

The CPSU solemnly declares: there are no weapons that the Soviet Union would not be prepared to limit or ban on a reciprocal basis with effective verification.

The USSR does not encroach on the security of any country, West or East. It threatens no one and does not seek confrontation with any state: it wishes to live in peace with all countries. The Soviet socialist state has been bearing high the banner of peace and friendship among peoples since the Great October Revolution. The CPSU shall remain loyal to this Leninist banner.

IV. The CPSU in the International Working-Class and Communist Movement

The CPSU is a component part of the international communist movement. It regards its efforts to perfect socialist society and advance onward to communism as a major internationalist task, the accomplishment of which serves the interests of the world socialist system, the international working class, and mankind as a whole.

Communists, having always been the most consistent fighters against social and national oppression, are today also in the forefront of the struggle for the preservation of peace on earth and for people's right to life. They know well wherein lie the causes of the threat of war, expose those who are responsible for the aggravation of international tension and the arms race, and strive to develop cooperation with all those capable of making a contribution to the anti-war effort.

The CPSU takes into consideration the fact that Communist and Workers' parties in the non-socialist world are functioning in a complex and controversial situation. The range of the circumstances and forms of their struggle is quite broad. However, this expands rather than limits the opportunities available to the movement. The diversity of forms of activity practised by Communists enables them to take better account of specific national conditions and concrete historical circumstances, and of the interests of different social groups and strata of the population.

The CPSU proceeds from the conviction that the Communists in each country independently analyse and evaluate situations and determine their strategic course, policies and means of struggle for the immediate and ultimate goals, for communist ideals. The experience accumulated by the Communist parties is a valuable internationalist asset.

The CPSU thoroughly studies the problems and experience of foreign Communist parties. It regards with understanding their desire to improve their strategy and tactics, to seek broader class alliances on a platform of anti-monopolistic, anti-war activity, and to uphold the economic interests and political rights of working people, proceeding from the conviction that the struggle for democracy is a component part of the struggle for socialism.

The imperialist circles in different countries are closely coordinating their efforts aimed against socialism and all the democratic forces and are trying to set Communist parties against one another. In these conditions proletarian internationalism and comradely solidarity among Communists are assuming ever greater importance.

The CPSU believes that disagreement over individual issues should not interfere with international cooperation among Communist parties and their concerted efforts.

In cases when divergences of views on individual problems arise between fraternal parties, the CPSU considers it useful to hold comradely discussions to achieve better understanding of each other's views and reach mutually acceptable appraisals. But when the issue at hand is the revolutionary essence of Marxism-Leninism, the substance and role of real socialism, the CPSU will continue to uphold positions of principle. This also determines the CPSU's attitude to all attempts to destroy the class essence of the Communists' activity and distort the revolutionary nature of the aims and means of struggle for attaining them. Experience has shown that any departure from the fundamental propositions of the teaching of Marx, Engels, and Lenin weakens the potentials of the communist movement.

In its relations with the fraternal parties, **the CPSU firmly adheres to the principle of proletarian internationalism,** which organically combines revolutionary solidarity with the recognition of the full independence and equality of each party. On the basis of this principle, the CPSU is actively developing its ties with the Communist and Workers' parties, exchanging information, and participating in bilateral and multilateral meetings and regional and broader international conferences held as the need arises.

Soviet Communists always side with their class comrades in the capitalist world. The CPSU will use its international prestige to defend Communists who fall victim to the arbitrary rule of reactionaries. It has a high regard for the solidarity of the fraternal parties and for their struggle against anti-Sovietism. The mutual support of the Communist and Workers' parties in the socialist and non-socialist countries is an important factor for social progress.

The CPSU will continue its policy of developing ties with socialist, social-democratic, and labour parties. Cooperation with them can play a significant role, first and foremost, in the effort to prevent nuclear war. However great the divergences between various trends of the working-class movement might be, they present no obstacle to a fruitful and systematic exchange of views, parallel or joint actions to remove the threat of war, improve the international situation, eliminate the vestiges of colonialism, and uphold the interests and rights of the working people.

The Party attaches great significance to stimulating cooperation among all contingents of the international working-class movement and expanding interaction between trade unions of diverse trends and youth, women's, peasant and other democratic organisations in various countries.

Being fully aware of its historical responsibility to the world's working class and its communist vanguard, the CPSU will continue to work in the following directions:

— to uphold the revolutionary ideals and the fundamentals of Marxism-Leninism in the world communist movement, creatively develop the theory of scientific socialism, consistently fight against dogmatism and revisionism, against all the influences of bourgeois ideology on the working-class movement;

— to do its utmost to promote cohesion and cooperation among fraternal parties and the international solidarity of Communists and to increase the communist movement's contribution to the cause of preventing world war;

— to pursue a consistent policy aimed at achieving unity of action in the international working-class movement, among all working people in the struggle for their common interests, for a lasting peace and the security of peoples, for national independence, democracy, and socialism.

PART FOUR

THE CPSU—THE LEADING FORCE IN SOVIET SOCIETY

The Communist Party of the Soviet Union has traversed a path that is unprecedented in its depth and force of impact on social development. Its ascent has been swift: from the first Marxist circles through three people's revolutions to the leadership of a great socialist power.

The historic achievements of the Soviet people in building a new society, their victory in the Great Patriotic War, the country's confident advance towards ever higher stages of socio-economic and cultural progress, and the growth of the Soviet Union's influence on the course of world development are inseparably linked with the Communist Party's activities. It is the inspirer and organiser of the historical creative activity of the people, our society's leading and guiding force. Equipped with Marxist-Leninist theory, the Party is determining the general prospects for the country's development, ensuring a science-based leadership of the creative activities of the people, and lending an organised, plan-based, and purposeful character to the building of communism.

As a result of the fact that socialism has been built in the USSR, that all sections of the working people have gone over to the positions of the working class, and that the socio-political and ideological unity of Soviet society has been consolidated, the Communist Party, while retaining its class essence and ideology as the party of the working class, has become the party of all the people. This predetermines the revolutionary continuity, the class character of domestic and foreign policy, and the entire activity of the CPSU.

In the new historical conditions, when the country is confronted with important tasks in its internal development and in the international arena, the **Party's leading role** in the life of Soviet society **inevitably grows**, and higher demands are made on the level of its political, organisational and ideological activity. This is predetermined by the following essential factors:

— growth in the scale and complexity of the tasks of perfecting socialism and accelerating the country's socio-economic development; the need to elaborate and implement consistently a policy that ensures the successful fulfilment of these tasks and an organic interconnection between the economic, social, and cultural progress of society;

— development of the political system, strengthening democracy and socialist self-government by the people by enhancing the political and labour enthusiasm of the masses, extensively drawing them into administering production and state and public affairs;

— the need for further creative development of Marxist-Leninist theory, a profound comprehension of the experience of building communism, a search for science-based and timely answers to the questions posed by life, raising the social consciousness of the working people, and the elimination of the manifestations of petty-bourgeois mentality and ethics and all deviations from the norms of the socialist way of life;

— interest in deepening all-round cooperation, strengthening the unity of the socialist countries and the international communist and working-class movement, solidarity with the forces of national liberation, and the struggle against bourgeois ideology, revisionism, dogmatism, reformism, and sectarianism;

— complication of foreign-policy conditions in connection with the growing aggressiveness of imperialism, the need to be more vigilant, to assure the country's security and to make new, increasingly persistent efforts to curb the forces of aggression, stop the arms race, rid mankind of the threat of nuclear catastrophe and strengthen peace on earth.

In carrying out the political leadership of society, the CPSU will continue consistently **to apply the time-tested Leninist principles, assert the Leninist style** in Party work, in all fields of administration of the state and the economy, enhance the science-based nature of its policy; the Party will rely extensively on the collective wisdom and experience of the people and will develop their social initiative. It attaches fundamental significance to the unity of ideological-theoretical, political-educational, organisational and economic activity, to the uncompromising struggle against any stagnation and conservatism, to the creative quest for effective solutions to problems that arise.

The CPSU considers it necessary to take careful account of the specific character of the functions of Party, state and public bodies, to coordinate their work, to avoid duplication of activities, to enhance the role of the Party Committees as bodies of political leadership, to eliminate manifestations of formalism and red tape, bureaucratic and other distortions in the work of the administrative apparatus, to intensify control over the fulfilment of Party decisions and economic plans, to strengthen state and labour discipline and order, and to raise organisational standards.

In the activity of all Party organisations and work collectives, the CPSU will persistently instill a creative attitude, efficiency, high responsibility and adherence to principles, as well as an ability to evaluate the results attained objectively and self-critically, to be attentive and sensitive towards people, their needs and requirements.

The Party inseparably links the higher standards in the guidance of state, economic, and cultural development with further **improvement in working with personnel**. It considers it vital that the Leninist principles of selecting and evaluating personnel on the basis of political, business, and moral qualities be strictly observed everywhere from top to bottom, and that public opinion be given even greater consideration.

By its entire personnel policy the CPSU will facilitate the promotion to leadership positions of Communists and non-Party people who are politically mature, possess high moral standards, are competent and full of initiative; the Party will be more active in advancing women to positions of leadership. The Party attaches fundamental importance to such qualities in a leader as responsiveness to new ideas, closeness to people, readiness to undertake responsibility, a desire to learn to work better, an ability to understand the political meaning of economic management, and high demands on one's self and on others.

The Party sees to it that young, promising workers work side by side with members of the older generation who are more experienced so that they might gain experience and the necessary training. This is a natural process which provides a reliable guarantee against inertia, stagnation, and voluntarism.

Confidence in personnel must be combined with exactingness, with their greater personal responsibility to Party organisations and work collectives for the results of work and maintenance of Party and state discipline, and with stricter control by the people over the activity of managers. Each manager should be fully accountable for the work entrusted to him. He should establish proper relations with people and inspire them by personal example. **No Party organisation, no one should remain outside the sphere of control.**

The development of the Party is characterised by a **further growth and strengthening of Party ranks, and an improvement in inner-Party relations on the principle of democratic centralism.**

Filling its ranks with the foremost representatives of the working class, collective-farm peasantry, and the Soviet intelligentsia, the Party increases its influence in various fields of building communism. The CPSU considers it essential that industrial workers hold a leading place in its social composition. A person's political and business qualities, honesty and decency, readiness to devote all his or her energies to the cause of communism remain the decisive condition for admission to the Party. Attempts to join the Party in order to make a career should be stopped immediately.

Party membership gives no privileges; it implies only an even higher responsibility for all that takes place within the country, for the destiny of building communism and social progress. Every Communist must be exemplary in work and behaviour, in public and personal life. The strength of the Party's links with the masses, its prestige among them depends in large measure on how fully the **vanguard role of the Communists** manifests itself. The Party will steadily raise its demands on each Communist concerning his or her attitude to duty and the honest and pure moral make-up of the Party member; it will appraise each member by his or her work and deeds.

The CPSU believes that a guarantee of the successful activity and of high creative enthusiasm of the Communists lies in further **developing and deepening inner-Party democracy,** in strictly observing the Leninist norms of Party life, in promoting criticism and self-criticism, in ensuring greater openness and publicity.

The Party will continue to base its work on the tested **principle of collectivity.** To ensure its further implementation and development, the CPSU considers it essential to enhance the role and significance of Party meetings, plenary meetings, conferences and congresses, and of Party committees and bureaus as collective bodies of leadership, and to provide favourable conditions for a free and businesslike discussion in the Party of questions relating to its policy and practical activity.

While working for the consistent practical implementation of the democratic principles of inner-Party life, the CPSU simultaneously devotes unremitting attention to **strengthening Party discipline.** Firm, conscious discipline on the part of Party members is a necessary prerequisite for high socialist discipline in all spheres of public life.

Successful Party activity and the growth of enthusiasm of the Communists are inseparably linked with a further improvement in the work of the Party's primary organisations. Since they are the political nucleus of work collectives, they are called upon to contribute in every way possible to bringing about the unity of the Party's policy and the vital creative activity of the people.

The Party will always strengthen the unity and monolithic cohesion of its ranks. It preserves in its arsenal of means the organisational guarantees envisaged in the CPSU Rules against any manifestation of factionalism and cliquishness. **The most important source of the Party's strength and invincibility is the indestructible ideological and organisational cohesion of the Party.**

The CPSU proceeds from the Marxist-Leninist proposition that people are the makers of history, and that the building of communism is the work of their hands, energy, and minds. The vital creative activity of the people is the guarantee of all our achievements.

The Party exists for the people and sees the meaning of its activity in service to the people. The goals and tasks it sets itself are an expression of the aspirations and vital interests of the Soviet people. The Party will continue to work in a spirit of high responsibility to the people, constantly broadening and deepening its links with them and showing understanding for people's needs and concerns. It regards as its duty constantly to consult working people on key issues of domestic and foreign policy, carefully take into account public opinion, and draw non-Party people on an ever broader scale into the work of Party organisations. The more actively the Party is supported by the people, the more it influences the course of social development.

In all of its activity the CPSU is invariably guided by the **time-tested Marxist-Leninist principles of proletarian, socialist internationalism.** It will contribute in every way possible to promoting the cohesion of the international communist movement on the basis of Marxism-Leninism, develop fraternal ties with all the Communist and Workers' parties, actively cooperate with them in the struggle for peace and against the danger of a nuclear catastrophe, and support their struggle in defence of the vital interests of the working people, for national liberation, democracy and socialism.

* * *

This is the Program of the Communist Party of the Soviet Union.

The Party calls upon all the Communists, all working people—workers, collective farmers, and members of the intelligentsia—to take a most vigorous part in the implementation of the historical tasks set forth in the Program. The Party is confident that Soviet people, regarding the Program of the CPSU as their vital cause, will make every effort to implement it.

To achieve a qualitatively new state of society by substantially accelerating socio-economic progress—this is the Party strategy. The all-round perfection of socialism will bring new benefits to every family, to every Soviet citizen. It will lead to a further flourishing of our socialist homeland and, finally, to the triumph of communism.

The onward march of our people to this cherished goal will increase the attractive force of the ideas of Marxism-Leninism, of transforming society on the principles of humanism and social justice. They win the minds and hearts of people by providing an example of better social organisation, a steady growth of productive forces, by ensuring conditions for creative work, for people's happiness and well-being, resolutely rejecting wars of aggression, and affirming the principles of peace and broad cooperation between peoples on the basis of equality and universal security.

Communists, all the working people of our country, are looking optimistically to the future. The Party is firmly convinced that by the selfless labour effort of the Soviet people, a creator and builder, the tasks set will be accomplished and the goals outlined achieved.

Under the leadership of the Party, under the banner of Marxism-Leninism the Soviet people have built socialism.

Under the leadership of the Party, under the banner of Marxism-Leninism the Soviet people will build a communist society.